Screen teen writers

How young screenwriters can find success

Christina Hamlett

MERIWETHER PUBLISHING LTD.
Colorado Springs, Colorado

Meriwether Publishing Ltd., Publisher
PO Box 7710
Colorado Springs, CO 80933-7710

Editor: Arthur L. Zapel
Editorial coordinator: Renée Congdon
Cover design: Janice Melvin

Publisher's Cataloging-in-Publication
(Provided by Quality Books, Inc.)

Hamlett, Christina.
    Screen teen writers : how young screenwriters can
find success / Christina Hamlett. -- 1st ed.
    p. cm.
    Includes bibliographical references.
    Audience: Ages 13-19.
    1-56608-078-9

    1. Motion picture authorship--Vocational guidance--
Juvenile literature. 2. Motion picture authorship--
Vocational guidance. I. Title.

PN1996.H36 2002   808.2'3
                      QBI33-344

     1   2   3   02   03   04

To Mark —
My best critic and best friend —
Who makes every day of our married life a sitcom
I could never have scripted on my own.

Contents

Introduction

If there's a broken heart for every light on Broadway, multiply that number by at least a thousand for every klieg in Tinseltown.

Be warned: Screenwriting is not a career quest for the timid! Nor is it the proper venue for the terminally inflexible or impatient. If writing for the movies is in your blood, you need to be prepared to invest lots of time (i.e., years) and tenacity into the process. Certainly if it were anything otherwise, this book would have been titled, "How to Be Dining with Spielberg by Next Tuesday."

The funny thing is that it all looks really easy from where the audience sits. You may have even thought so yourself when you've gone to the movies with your friends and imagined your own name scrolling up the credits! Writing for the movies, though, isn't just a matter of putting your best story down on paper or even pushing it over the transom of a producer's office. It's a matter of getting it read, getting it funded, and getting it to the screen, all of which call for an understanding of the medium, an appreciation of the available resources, and the courage to keep trying, no matter what obstacles litter your path or how many rejection letters get stuffed in your mailbox.

Unlike careers in math or science in which the answers are black and white, screenwriting is an entirely subjective venue. You may have written what you consider to be the best script in the world and it could still get rejected because: 1. the studio already has plans to release something similar, 2. the tide of popularity has shifted and science fiction flicks are no longer en vogue, or 3. your lead character's name is Dolores, coincidentally the same name as the producer's much loathed ex-wife.

Obviously you have no control over such circumstances. Nor can you second-guess what kind of changes a potential buyer will call for in order to give your script a second chance of review. Whatever you write as an individual is only the ground-floor of a project that will be built to the top by a collaborative team: the director, the actors, the technical crew, the marketing people, and many others. Could a star quarterback win the game without the rest of his team? Of course not! Writing a screenplay and getting it into the theatres works the same way.

In picking up this book, you've already revealed the glimmer of a secret dream to one day sit in a darkened movie house and watch your words come to life. Pretty heady stuff, huh? And all of it simply begins with you, the writer, sitting in a room somewhere and having the unquenchable motivation to type those initial words, "FADE IN ... "

Where you go from there is where I come in.

This book will walk you through the basics of the craft, highlighting those things that separate the amateurs from the pros. Speaking of pros, a number of industry professionals graciously allowed themselves to be interviewed for this book. At the end of each interview, you'll find a series of questions which can either be addressed as a self-evaluation exercise or opened up for discussion in the classroom. The answers that you and your peers come up with may surprise you!

Suffice it to say, even if you've gone to summer film camp, taken classes at school and checked out every text on screenwriting from the local library, there still remains a vast store of insider knowledge that only comes from the experience of trial and error. How do you know, for instance, whether your particular plot is even suited to a movie? What makes a script more salable from the standpoint of a budget? How do you introduce new characters in each scene without making the dialog sound contrived? And what are some of the worst things you can put in a script that will alienate a potential director?

From there, we'll look at the business side of writing for film; i.e., is it necessary to have an agent or can you fly solo? What does an option agreement entail? Should you and your friends collaborate, and if so, how do you divide the fame and fortune? Are independent production companies more or less approachable for freelancers than studios and networks? How is the Internet changing the face of today's movie industry and, accordingly, the accessibility for unknown writers? Most importantly, how do you make yourself known in one of the most competitive arenas in the world when you don't know a single living soul to helpfully hold open the front — or back — door for you?

Daunting as all of this may sound to the first-time screenwriter, the entry requirements and job demands are surprisingly few for a career that can ultimately yield such high rewards and prestige for those who persevere:

1. There is no minimum age requirement to write a feature film or television script, nor is there a mandatory retirement age. As long as you can continue to crank out ideas, filmmakers will want to see them.

2. Although living in or relocating to Los Angeles or New York is helpful in terms of actual face-time with employers, you can reside anywhere in the country.

3. You do not need an undergraduate or graduate degree to write for the movies, nor do you need a license, permit, certification, or insurance to pursue this field of endeavor.

4. It is not necessary to join a select club, association, fraternity or guild in order to pitch your stories to buyers.

5. Unless you are actually working for a studio, the hours you keep are entirely within your own control. There is also no dress code.

6. The only real supplies you need are a reliable computer, an Internet connection, reams of paper, plenty of postage, and the requisite cover stock, brads, and mailing envelopes. Investment in a fancy machine with all the bells and whistles isn't necessary; the yellow pages and the classifieds can lead you to plenty of bargains on used equipment.

7. The level of training in which you engage can be as excessive or as scant as your time and budget dictate. Many writers, in fact, are self-taught; if you have the discipline to stick to a schedule and aggressively apply everything you pick up from books, chat rooms, movie critiques, and watching every kind of film possible, you could easily learn everything you need to know from the comfort of your own house!

8. You don't need to be physically fit or have the nimble grace of a gazelle to break into this business. You do, however, need to know how to type professionally and how to catch errors. (Relying on spell-check alone doesn't count!)

9. You are not confined to writing just one genre of film. (Although if it's successful, they may want another one just like it!)

10. You are also not limited to initiating contact with or writing for only one employer (unless, of course, you've signed a contract which gives them exclusive dibs on your talent).

Can you become rich writing for the movies or TV? Absolutely! Will Matt Damon call you and want to do lunch? A definite maybe. You may, however, have to endure the tedium of a mundane day-job to pay the rent and buy food until that happens. Simply having an idea that would make a really great movie isn't enough; certainly every cab driver and his brother have yearned to win an Academy Award with a story that has yet to be written down, fleshed out, and submitted for critical review.

The reality is that you have to have actually completed a feature-length or teleplay project first before you have anything to sell, much less pitch to someone who might be interested. What's promising, though, is that there have never been more opportunities to place your script in the right hands, as well as garner feedback from peers and mentors on how to make the next one even better. Nor have there ever been more commercial avenues available on a regional level in which to get your feet wet, hone your scripting skills, and start building a portfolio.

By coincidence, all it takes is the one thing that Hollywood itself was built on: Imagination!

What Kind of Movie Should You Write?

The most important question you need to ask yourself is, "Why do I want to be a screenwriter?" The most important — and only — answer is because you have a story inside of you that you really want to share ... and because you've decided that the medium of film is the best way to do that.

Writing What You Know

You've heard it a million times already from your instructors. You're about to hear it all over again from me.

Write what you know.

Whether your objective is to write an article for the school paper, a short story, a stage play, or a film, it's hard to disguise it when you have either a lack of passion or a deficiency of expertise regarding your subject matter. How many times, for instance, have you had to write a term paper on a topic that really bored you out of your mind? Your head may have been telling you that you had to come up with a ten-page report on the politics of Mesopotamia in order to get a passing grade, but your heart was wishing the entire time that you could be writing about last night's basketball game instead.

The bad news is that I can't get you off the hook on your homework. But when it comes to writing something on your own, it needs to not only be a subject that you're excited about but one that you can write accurately enough about to appease others who are just as excited about the same thing.

Why all this need for accuracy? Even in a work of fiction, you will constantly be drawing upon certain non-fiction truths. Whether these take the form of geography, history, science, medicine, or the arts, nothing will turn a fan hostile faster than tossing in a lie — even unintentionally. In order to avoid this, you need to know your subject matter inside out ... and be prepared to go research those elements about it that you don't know.

Your Assignment

Even if you have a pretty good idea of what your first screenplay is going to be about, the following exercise is not only to jump-start your imagination for your next project but to get you to recognize those topics that you're already an expert on.

1. Take a piece of paper and make a list of your ten favorite things.

2. On a scale of one to ten (with ten being the highest), identify your level of knowledge/expertise for each subject you've listed.

3. Highlight the three topics that receive the three highest scores.

4. For each of these three, you'll next list the three best things and the three worst things that are a result or consequence of each one. For instance, let's say that you picked a competitive sport. Under the best things, you might list "popularity with others, building physical strength, and getting to travel out-of-state for tournaments." Under the worst things, you might list "not enough time for homework, a maniac for a coach, and a girlfriend who picks a fight after every game."

5. We're now going to narrow that list down to just one favorite thing. Of the pros and cons you have listed for that topic, select what you think is the most compelling "best" and, correspondingly, the most potent "worst." To use the sports example again, let's say that popularity is the ultimate reward your lead character is reaping from being an athlete; on the flip side, his biggest conflict is with a girlfriend who resents his time with the team.

Therein is your first plot to spin into a full-fledged story.

The Genres

What kind of movie do you want to write? Nine times out of ten, people want to write the same type ("genre") of film that they enjoy going to the movies to see. This makes perfect sense. Someone who is the first in line whenever tickets go on sale for the hottest space-age adventure will want to spin their own versions about intergalactic travelers, borrowing from those elements which kept them on the edge of their theatre seats. Likewise, a romantic-at-heart probably won't be sitting down to pen a violent thriller in which half the cast has been sliced, diced, and fed to wild boars before the final credits!

Although many movies and books contain crossover themes from multiple genres, it's a fact of life that publishers and producers like to see everything neatly boxed into just one category. This is also the way production companies will specify their needs for new scripts. (Wanted: Comedies.) To send them something they're not looking for is a huge taboo. Yet time and again many a new author will preface an inquiry letter with, "I know you said that you're only looking for World War I dramas but I'm positive that once you read my urban dramedy about a street-smart drummer with a side-kick talking cat ... "

The only thing you can be sure of with that kind of approach is that you will be remembered ... for all the wrong reasons!

Your Assignment

Which of the following genres best describes your story?

1. Comedy
2. Drama
3. Action
4. Horror
5. Romantic Comedy
6. Spoof/Satire
7. Science Fiction/Time Travel
8. Thriller/Suspense
9. Western
10. Fantasy/Supernatural

Once you have decided which category best fits your screenplay, identify at least three commercial films that are similar to yours. Compare what elements your story has in common with each of them. Identify those areas in which your particular story is different. As a further brain-stormer, pick two other genres from the list and ask yourself, "Would my plot work in this genre as well?" (i.e., a western theme played out on a different planet).

Location, Location, Location

In any movie worth remembering, the setting of the story is as strong a character as any of the physical beings walking around in it. Where a plot takes place helps define the mood, the pace, and the energy behind how the story is told.

For instance, would *Jurassic Park* (or any of its sequels) be as menacing if it were set in the suburbs of Ohio? Of course not! Why? Because the characters could jump in their cars and drive like crazy to Pennsylvania to escape from those beady-eyed raptors! On a remote island with limited resources, however, it's not quite as easy to get away, thus forcing a scenario of "fight" rather than "flight."

Or take a time travel film such as *Time After Time*: If the villain (Jack the Ripper) transported himself into a relatively small town where everyone knew their neighbors, it wouldn't be as challenging for the protagonist, H.G. Wells, to catch up with him as it was in the crowded streets of downtown San Francisco. In the latter, the concept of "faceless strangers" becomes a metaphor for the Ripper's vicious dispatching of victims whom he feels will not be particularly missed by society at large.

Consider the earlier example I gave of a sports figure who is caught between the satisfaction of being adored by the masses versus the desire to be loved by his or her one special someone. How would the physical environment impact the lead character's choices (i.e., small town versus big city)?

Your Assignment

Take a look at your own plot and where it primarily takes place. If it's in a large metropolitan city, what is it about that city that will most strongly influence the actions your protagonist takes to change his/her life? Now shift the same plot to a country/rural environment. Will your hero/heroine do the same thing as in a big city? Why or why not? Will the pressures/expectations be greater or less? Take the exercise a step further and now move the action out of the country. What country? And how will the culture and social mores of that country drive your lead character's decisions?

Stage, Page, or Cinema?

The first rule of screenwriting is always a hard one for new writers to swallow; specifically, *not every idea makes for a great movie*. While something quite marvelous and imaginative may have been churning in your head for some time now, you need to recognize the difference between good ideas and bad ones.

Granted, cineplexes across the country are replete with examples of the latter. Nonetheless, they share a common denominator beyond the parameters of a flawed plot: Somehow they all got produced. More importantly to you, is that they got produced — in spite of their goofy content — because the writers were able to distinguish the best medium in which to communicate what they ultimately had to say. That medium was film.

A "bad" idea, for our purposes here, will thus be defined as one that is not easily translatable to a movie script and would be better presented in an alternative venue.

Knowing the Limitations

It was Hitchcock who once said that a good movie was one that could be watched without sound. The next time you're on a plane with an in-flight movie, don't rent a headset and you'll see for yourself this is true. Why? Because films are primarily *action-driven*. We don't have to watch one for very long to figure out who's being chased, who's doing the chasing, and who's falling in love in-between.

In contrast, the measure of a good stage play is one that can be enjoyed without visuals. (You've probably heard your grandparents talk about the good ol' days of radio.) Theatre scripts are *dialog-driven*. Even if all three acts take place on the same set (or around the same kitchen table), we are riveted as an audience because we care what the actors have to say and, most especially, how they say it.

Last but not least are books, which are *imagination-driven* and fueled by the individual reader's frame of reference. Why else would they keep us up late at night, peering into the dark corners for evidence of the goblins our minds have crafted from off the printed page? Novels also hold the distinct advantage over film and theatre in that they allow us to look directly into the characters' heads, their hearts, and their souls.

9

Let's see how each of these orientations would work in the following scenario:

EXT/Dusk/The Sahara. Two Horsemen are pursuing a third.

SFX: Single Gunshot.

In just twelve words we're already hooked on a compelling visual. Throw that visual up on a big screen and the audience will be hooked, too, and immediately immersed in a mystery: Who are these guys? Why are they in the desert? Who fired that shot? Is someone now dead as a result?

All right, let's move this same scene to a community theatre. First of all, you're going to need a very large stage to accommodate three fast-galloping horses. Not to mention that the front row might get irritated having all that sand kicked in their faces! OK, let's just scratch the opening chase scene. Instead, we'll have a minor character run into the Casbah and excitedly announce to everyone present, "You'll never guess what I just saw happen out in the dunes!"

Loses something, doesn't it? Every time that you "tell" instead of "show" a critical plot point, it puts the entire story on hold until a jump-start of action can get it rolling again. Trust me. That's not a good habit.

Maybe the best option, then, is to try this as a book. Same desert, same time of day, same trio of horsemen. Can you paint that picture for a reader ... using only twelve words? The point of this, of course, is that it takes more verbiage to spell out the particulars on paper than to simply show them on a screen or stage, depending on how exact an image is desired. For instance, are the horses light or dark? If they're dark, are they brown or black? Are the riders on saddles or bareback? What are the riders wearing?

Time, Space, and Dimension

Books and films have virtually no limits on where they can go, the latter owing much of its freedom to the advent of computer-generated wizardry. A play's parameters, however, are dictated by the physical limitations of the stage on which it will be performed, which accordingly influence the set design, cast size, and feasibility of special effects (i.e., pyrotechnics, prehistoric raptors, and garden variety ghosts).

Transitions from one place to another are also handled differently in live theatre. In a movie or novel, a character can walk out the door of his New York flat and emerge — two frames or paragraphs later — at a trendy cafe in Paris. Furthermore, he may even have aged ten years in the interim. In a script written for the stage, such transitions not only require a change of makeup and wardrobe but a total overhaul of the set and everything in it. While these can be accommodated with intermissions, you can't very well keep sending the audience out in the lobby every time a character has to walk through a door and end up somewhere else.

On the plus side, it should be mentioned that theatre does have a practical way of establishing places and times for viewers who might be slow-witted; they hand out programs before the show that will neatly clarify if it's "Later, the same day" or "Five years later in Amsterdam." (Which is better than having your characters make silly curtain-raiser remarks like, "My goodness! Is it Sunday morning already? Who'd have thought we'd be here in Cousin Midge's guestroom in the Catskills ... ?")

Speaking of time, it passes differently on stage than in the other two, even though all three employ an accelerated pace of storytelling. While books and films can flashback, fast-forward, or hover in multiple zones simultaneously, a play is pretty much relegated to the structured increments of acts and scenes. Audiences can accept these temporal boundaries because they have already accepted the notion that twenty minutes of stage-time does not necessarily equate to twenty minutes of real-time. In fact, it probably more closely equates to dog-years, which means that twenty minutes of theatrical dialog would take up at least an hour and a half anywhere else.

Empathy

Unless you are reading out loud in class, a book is an intensely personal and solitary experience — one in which we can superimpose our own personalities and vicariously "live the plot." With a book in hand, you can skim, you can linger, you can re-read, you can envision anyone you want in the key roles. You can even set the whole thing aside, think about it and come back a month later.

For movies and plays, however, you are being told the story on someone else's clock and with someone else's definition of who the characters are. There is not as much room for your imagination to go wandering off to other things, because at any given time, you are being directed as to what to pay attention to. This is especially true of film, where you are seeing everything from only one angle and point of view — the camera's.

When it comes to arousing empathy, a play shares the novel's capacity to engage an audience in a manner that movies cannot. Can you name a single musical, for instance, that was ever made better by its adaptation to the big screen? There's something electrifying about the presence of real bodies, real voices, real music, and real energy that even the glitziest cast-of-thousands blockbuster can't compete with. Suffice it to say, people on stage are also pretty much the same size as the people sitting in the audience (which always makes for better "bonding" than looking down the tonsils of a thirty-foot-high face).

How well do we get to "know" the characters in a story? In a novel, we get to know them pretty intimately, because we can literally read their thoughts and emotions at every juncture. In a play, we learn about them gradually through the course of their conversations; we only know what they're thinking, though, if they actually express it out loud to someone else or in a monolog. In a film, we tend to get more distracted by "Oh, here's Mike Myers or Cameron Diaz in another role" than we are captivated by the background of whomever they are supposed to be portraying. While flashbacks and voice-overs can reveal what's on their minds, too many of these become confusing for audiences to follow.

Paperwork

A final issue to compare among the three mediums is the length and substance of the physical manuscript(s). A typical screenplay is approximately 120 pages and is comprised of master shots and dialog. A three-act play is a little shorter, with the longest act being first and the balance of the show split between the remaining two (i.e., 40:30:30). An average book runs about 400 pages and, depending on genre, is made up of roughly sixty-five percent narrative and thirty-five percent dialog.

Right away you can see the challenge in adapting a book to a feature film — if that bulk of narrative can't be explained in dialog or conveyed through the lens of a camera, out it goes. Nor can every film smoothly segue to live theatre or a paperback — the first requiring it to substantially contract and the second demanding that it expand with enough intellectual exposition or gratuitous scenes just to fill up space.

Clearly, the easiest transition is from a play to a film, their respective lengths and content being the most similar. Keep in mind though, that in putting a dialog-driven story against a bigger and more colorful backdrop, you run the risk of killing the very charm that made it accessible and unique to begin with.

Your Assignment

1. What is the most recent movie you and your friends have seen?
2. If you haven't seen any movies recently, why not? (You need to know what the competition is doing!) If you don't have a recent movie to use for this assignment, what is your favorite movie?
3. Using your answer in #1 or #2, list all of the reasons that this story "works" as a film.
4. Would this story work as a stage play? Would it work as a novel? Why (or why not)?
5. This same exercise can be applied to favorite books you have read or plays that you have seen. Are they adaptable to the screen? If not, what kinds of changes would need to be made? Who would you cast in the lead roles? How many different locations would you need to convey the story?

Follow Your Dream:
An Interview with Madeline DiMaggio

Former actress and published author Ms. Madeline DiMaggio is a successful author and television screenwriter whose trademark wit and imagination have been stamped on such shows as *Bob Newhart, Kojak and Three's Company*, as well as documentaries, soaps, animation and movies of the week. Her work as a creative consultant and story editor for Paramount Studios and NBC has given her insight on virtually every aspect of writing for the industry. Back when she was in high school, though, her plan for her life was much different.

Q: So what was the dream when you were seventeen?

A: Well, I was a drama major and saw myself as an actress. I was starring in all the school plays, I did summer stock, I went to New York, I got my degree in drama. It was an incredible major for writing because the strength of my writing has always been my dialog. But had I known that I would one day become a writer, I would have learned how to type. And how to spell! I never studied writing but every time I was in a three-act play, I was actually studying structure and character development and how people talked. A lot of actors end up being very good writers just for that reason. It was a good background to come from.

Q: Suppose you attend a rural high school that doesn't offer theatre or film classes for learning the creative side of the craft.

A: Well the first thing I'd do is to take a class at a college or even a weekend workshop where someone such as myself or Michael Hauge will come in and teach a seminar. High school students, by the way, get an incredible break in the cost of these workshops. These kinds of things are really good for an introductory, crash course in the basics. It also doesn't cost them a dime to go on the Internet and download screenplays just to get a sense of structure and dialog and what the formatting looks like.

Q: Speaking of the Internet, do you think it has helped or hurt the newcomers' accessibility to Hollywood?

A: It has helped terrifically! It has changed the face of the industry, which I think really *needs* to be changed. There are young filmmakers, for instance, who are already getting deals as a result of fifteen-minute movies they're making. It's an incredible way to market yourself because people now have access to your work who normally wouldn't.

Q: So what's this going to do long-term to the careers of Hollywood agents? After all, if you can access script sites

and get yourself known electronically, are you going to need a rep?

A: The fact is that if you're recognized on the Internet and you get a movie deal as a result, the first thing you'll *need* is an agent. You may not need an agent to sell but you do need one to have a career. And as far as *getting* an agent, it's just not something that happens overnight. Agents today only want to represent screenplays that they think they can sell very fast. It used to be that they'd take on a new screenwriter because they thought they were very good and that they could build a long relationship together. What they do now is take on a *project* that they can sell.

Q: Do you need a degree in film to have a film career? Or is it better to major in something that will pay the bills?

A: That's a hard one to call. For one thing, film school is incredibly hard to get into, but what's marvelous about film school is that you're meeting all the future filmmakers of Hollywood ... and the world! What you're making is a bunch of incredible contacts, plus part of the curriculum is that they put you at the studios where you can make even more contacts and get a nuts-and-bolts, hands-on internship in the very business you want to work in. If you're absolutely, definitely, passionately certain that you want to do this for a living, then you really do need to make it your focus in college. If you *aren't* 100 percent certain, I think that you should take some classes but also find something that you can make money at while you're pursuing writing as your *second* job. It just depends on how focused you are and how confident you are about what you want to do with your life.

Q: What about books? There's certainly no shortage of them on today's market. How do you decide which ones to add to your bookshelf?

A: That's a very personal thing and as subjective as going to movies themselves. For instance, I can be emotionally struck by a movie that may not be great and may not affect someone else at all. The important thing is that there was something about it that really stayed with me. What you do in the case of looking for a book to teach you about screenwriting is find someone whose tone and style and message you resonate with, the one who says it to you in a way that you can really grasp. Personally, I think the best book and the best self-taught instruction you can get is a screenplay written by a writer who has sold. That's because the greatest teacher a student will ever have comes from reading actual scripts and seeing the writer's vision in its most pure form, minus all the visuals and the Horner score and how good Brad Pitt looks on a horse ...

Q: How about screenwriting contests?

A: Unequivocally, there is not one single thing I know of that gives better access or bigger breaks to new screenwriters than screenwriting competitions and fellowships. The people who are reading the entries are people who are in the industry and will be reviewing your work if you get into the finals. I have an agent, for instance, who once agreed to be a judge in a contest only because it meant a trip to Hawaii and being put up in the Hilton Hawaiian Village for a week. "I'm not going to sign up any new clients," she insisted. On the way back, she told me on the airplane that from the ten scripts she had judged, she was signing one of the writers. She may not have been looking but she certainly knew what she wanted as soon as she found it.

Q: With all the contests to choose from, though, how do you know which ones are legitimate and which ones are just a scam to make money?

A: The first thing is that you need to do your homework. Find out what writers have won the contest before, what the parameters are, how many people usually enter, who the judges are. Don't be afraid to just call up and ask questions. I also don't think any of them should have excessively expensive fees to enter. The Nicholls, for instance, isn't that expensive but attracts a lot of attention. The Monterey Film Competition, the Disney, the Columbus Discovery Awards — these are all very legitimate and provide tremendous exposure.

Q: Well, let's say that someone likes my script and I get invited to a pitch session. Once I get there, though, they seem to have changed their minds. Should I try to convince them that they're wrong?

A: No. If you see them not responding — or responding negatively to what you have to say — what you do is move on to another idea. Trust me — they get really mad if you try to change their minds! You need to remember that the whole point of a pitch session isn't that you're going in to sell *any*thing; it's that you're going in there to get *information*. That's what's absolutely crucial about pitching. It's most likely that they won't take anything that you originally went in with but that you'll come away with a better understanding of what they *are* looking for. You then use that information as an opportunity to come back with an idea that fits in with their agenda.

Q: **What's the best advice anyone ever gave you about writing?**

A: The best advice I think they give anyone in Hollywood is what William Goldman said, and that's "No one knows anything." For me personally, one that stands out in my mind — and because I write a lot of comedy — was that you should never try to be funny. Hearing that from two well-known producers when I was doing "Bob Newhart" took this incredible weight off my shoulders and I've been writing comedy ever since!

Q: **You recently co-wrote a script called *If the Shoe Fits* with Pam Wallace (*Witness*). Any plug you'd like to give for it?**

A: No. It's a terrible movie.

Q: **What?**

A: It's a horrible film but a wonderful script. And that's a good lesson for everyone to learn because it's an amazing lesson about what can happen between a script and a movie. Sometimes it can be improved and other times — like this — it can just be the worst thing you've ever seen! The fact is that Pam and I were paid, we got the money, we got the credit, the movie was made in France on a very low budget, and everything that we spent an incredible amount of time in writing was all taken out. If you read the script and then rent *The Stroke of Midnight,* which they renamed it, you wouldn't recognize it.

Q: So you have no control over it once you sell?

A: That's true. It's the luck of the draw — who gets cast, what's the budget, who directs it, a lot of different factors that can make it better or make it worse. But the end result is that we still got work as a result of that script.

Q: Even if it was a bad film?

A: Exactly. The point is that in Hollywood, when you sell a film, they don't ask to see the video; they ask to read the script. Bottom line is that having a bad movie made is better than having no movie made. It doesn't matter how it turns out as long as the writer gets the money, gets the credit, and can move on to something else. What happens is that you're marketed on the merit that you sold a script, which they all know is no easy feat to begin with.

Q: What if you just go with a pseudonym for the ones that look like they're going south?

A: A lot of people do that.

Q: Was that an option for you and Pam?

A: We actually had the choice of taking our names off of *If the Shoe Fits* and we chose not to do that. The credits were more important to us.

Q: What do you think is the most valuable thing that the next generation of screenwriters needs to know to be successful?

A: You have to detach your ego from your material and recognize that the goal is to make that material better. You may not agree with what people are telling you but you still have to listen to it and try to apply what fits the situation. The other thing is that if you're really passionate, it usually takes about seven scripts before you finally sell something. Consequently, the earlier you start writing, the better. Starting at seventeen or eighteen puts you right in the ballpark, given the emphasis on youth in Hollywood.

Q: If you were seventeen again, what would you do differently, knowing what you know now about this business?

A: I would have paid more attention in school!

18

Madeline's best-selling book, *How to Write for Television*, is a must-buy for anyone who wants to learn the craft of TV script development and market their ideas to the right people.

Topics to Think About and Talk About

1. Identify what steps you are going to take in the next year to advance your career or studies in film, and make sure you "think outside the box" when answering this question!

2. You have written a screenplay about an intensely personal experience. A film company wants to buy the script but wants you to add certain scenes that are entirely fictional. This is your first screenplay. What do you do? (100 words or less)

3. You enter a screenwriting contest. Of the five awards given, you finish third. In fifty words or less, describe your reaction. Would your reaction be different if the contest guaranteed that the top two scripts would be produced?

Where Can You Find New Ideas?

One of the most common questions people ask me when they find out I'm a writer is, "Where do you get your ideas?" My answer — that I get my ideas from real life — always seems to disappoint them. The fact of the matter is, though, that every morning you wake up, there's an entire planet of free material that is waiting to inspire you. You just have to know how to look for it.

Open Your Eyes and Look Around You!

One of my favorite scenes in *Dead Poets Society* was when the teacher played by Robin Williams instructed his students to stand on their desks, thus affording them a different perspective on the same classroom they had been meeting in day after day. Too often, the "sameness" of a situation dulls our senses and we feel compelled to go look elsewhere for creative stimulus.

Yet, look at the genius of novelist Stephen King who can take the most seemingly harmless, everyday subjects — a car, a dog, a lawnmower — and turn them into instruments of terror. How? Because he takes the time to study them from a different perspective.

Right now, I want you to make a short list of things that you: 1. do on a regular basis and 2. do the same way every time. Some ideas to get you started: Do you always take the same route to school or work? At lunch, do you always sit at the same table? Is there a regular study pattern you follow every day? Has the furniture and picture arrangement in your room been the same for more than two years?

What you're going to do next is pick one of the items on your list and do something to significantly change it. Let's say that you're going to start taking an alternative route to school or work. Do this for one week. In a journal, record not only how you are feeling about this switch in routine but all of the things you observe along the way. Would any of them make good stories or character sketches? This is how ideas are born!

Because most of us are pretty resistant to change, our

sensitivities are heightened whenever something new is introduced or a previous pattern is disrupted. We tend to be more observant during these times because we're on foreign turf and not entirely sure what's going to be coming at us from around the next corner.

Even something as simple as sitting at the opposite end of the cafeteria from where you normally sit will yield a wealth of opportunity. For one thing, you'll see different people than you usually see. You'll notice things about the cafeteria interior itself or the buildings and landscapes now visible through the windows from this alternative view. Jot all this down in your journal and ponder the possibilities...

Do you subscribe to a daily newspaper? If you do, go and get it and open it to the want ads. Scan the listings and pick out whatever you think is the most unusual "must-sell" item you can find.

What kind of stories do the following samples conjure:

Wedding gown and veil, never worn. Will sell for $50.

Moosehead, slightly damaged. Best offer.

Shrunken head collection. Will sell individually or as set.

Ask yourself: 1. What type of person is selling the item? 2. Why are they selling it? 3. What type of person would buy it? 4. What will the buyer do with it?

Here's another good exercise which supports the view that ideas are all around you:

Do you have a favorite song you listen to all the time? Imagine that the composer has agreed to let you use his or her song as the soundtrack for your first film. The trouble is, you haven't exactly written the story yet. Play the song and write down all of the feelings that it stirs in your imagination. Is it a song about falling in love? A song about falling out of love? Are the lyrics about being misunderstood or about having a dream to be something better? What kind of scene do you play in your head every time you hear this music? Is it sunny? Is it rainy? Is it daytime or night? Is it in a big city or out in the country? At what point in the movie would this song be heard for the first time — at the beginning, in the middle, or at the end? If this tune were your hero or heroine's signature song, what do the lyrics and tempo say about this person's personality?

All the Best Plots Are Taken

"By the time I get around to writing anything," a friend recently lamented, "all the best plots will already be gone."

Unfortunately, he really believes it. Maybe you've even thought the same thing yourself, that there's only a finite number of storylines that exist in the world and those of us who got a jump-start have pretty much used them up.

Quite a few books have been written on that very subject, each one citing a different number ranging from three to thirty-six. I even had an American Literature professor who trimmed the options list even further: "Everything all gets down to: 1. winning and 2. losing."

No matter what theory or number you ascribe to, the bad news is that every plot *has* been done before. The good news, however, is that it's the "voice" of those plots — specifically, *your* voice — which will set them apart from their predecessors.

My own observation is that the genesis of most stories can be traced to three primary sources: Shakespeare, myth/fairy tales, and the Bible. Whether it's a drama about two lovers whom fate has assigned different rungs of the social ladder, a romance in which a corporate Prince Charming scours Manhattan for his Cinderella, or a thriller in which the seven deadly sins have got faith, hope, and charity in a stranglehold, we haven't seen the last of these popular themes.

Take a film like *Jaws*. Seems pretty modern to have a great white shark and a menacing soundtrack making swimmers afraid to go in the water, doesn't it? Captain Ahab in *Moby Dick* probably felt the same way except that his nemesis was a whale. And speaking of whales, I seem to recall one that had a featured role in a certain biblical tale.

What about *Trading Places* or *The Parent Trap*? The whimsical notion of assuming someone else's identity is a thinly disguised version of Mark Twain's *The Prince and the Pauper*. Shakespeare was fond of employing such themes as well in mix-ups between the sexes, which later emerged in cinema as the crux of the popular *Shakespeare in Love*.

My Fair Lady not only borrowed from George Bernard Shaw's *Pygmalion* but, going further back, also from the Greek myth about

Galatea, a beautiful sculpture which was brought to life by Aphrodite and became the soulmate of her marble-carving creator.

Murder and mayhem in space? No matter what *Alien* menace is running amok in the galaxy and systematically eliminating everyone human, its roots can be found in Agatha Christie's timeless mystery, *Ten Little Indians*.

And don't even get me started on the host of comparisons that have been made between the first *Star Wars* and a girl named Dorothy who took a trip down the yellow brick road ...

Just for Fun

Make a list of your ten favorite films of all time and try to identify their origins.

What If?

What if President Kennedy hadn't been assassinated? What if the first astronauts who landed on the moon discovered that the Russians had gotten there first? What if the captain of the Titanic hadn't ignored those warnings about icebergs?

What if you had taken the initiative and struck up a conversation with the new girl on campus instead of hiding in your locker? Would you be the one she's dancing with now at the prom instead of the geek from science class who spoke up first?

Life is full of options. Whichever road is taken, however, means that all of those other roads will go unexplored. Except, of course, in our imaginations...

Your Assignments

Assignment #1

Grab your history book and open it to any page at random. Whatever historical event is being discussed on the page you've turned to will be your first "what if" subject.

On a separate piece of paper, answer the following questions:

1. What was the event?

2. What year did it take place?

3. Who were the main people involved in this event?

4. What was the outcome?

Just to get you started, let's say that your page fell open to the California Gold Rush of 1849. We all know that Marshall's discovery triggered a mass migration westward in which merchants took leave of their shops, doctors took leave of their patients, and the world at large took leave of its senses for the glittering lure of riches and new beginnings.

But what if Marshall had kept his secret to himself? What would he have done with all that gold? And what might he have done to ensure that no one else found out about it?

Assignment #2

Is there something in your life that you really wish you could do over? Maybe it was an opportunity that you let get away, or perhaps an unkind word to a sibling or best friend that you've wished you could take back.

In this assignment, identify something serious in your life that you either regret took place or that you have daydreamed about making come true. In either instance, examine how your life and the lives of those closest to you would be affected if you had the chance to change the past or control the future.

Assignment #3

In today's newspaper, clip out three articles that especially intrigue you. Perhaps one of them is a story about the discovery of an ancient sailing vessel that ran aground in an unexpected place. Maybe the next one is about a convenience store clerk who went to lunch one day and disappeared. Or let's say that the third one is about an elderly person who lived in a flea-bag hotel; upon his or her death, the authorities found tens of thousands of dollars stuffed in the mattress and in coffee cans in the hall closet.

These three scenarios conjure plenty of possibilities, don't they? And, by the way, periodically clipping such items for your idea folder is a good practice to get into; even if you don't open that folder for weeks or months at a time, they will always be a source of inspiration and ensure that you never suffer from writer's block!

For each story you select, answer the following questions:

1. What was the inciting incident which caused this event to happen?
2. Could something have intervened and prevented the event from happening?
3. What's going to happen next?

Let's use the example of the elderly person living in poverty and yet literally having riches within reach:

1. If this person had been a product of the Great Depression, he or she would have been instilled with a paranoia regarding "going without," and, accordingly, would squirrel away every penny earned or found. 2. If this person had either attained a level of psychological security or had the emotional support of friends and family, he or she might not have become a recluse and died alone. 3. Now that the deceased's financial status has been revealed, how many people will come forward to try to claim it?

Personally, I think the third question is always the most fun to explore — to try to guess how a story will ultimately come out. Unlike the movies, where scripted outcomes are often predicated on either our fondness or on expectations of the star or our preconceived definition of a satisfying resolution, real life is not hemmed in by the same boundaries. Virtually anything can happen ... and often does!

One from Column A, One from Column B

Have you ever looked through the Personals columns in your local newspaper and mentally matched up some of the candidates with each other?

Shy brunette librarian, forty-five, never-married, seeks intellectual equal who enjoys discussing classic literature, art, music and history. Seeks a companion who enjoys the company of animals, especially cats.

Bachelor veterinarian, age fifty, wants to share his time with more than just his beloved family of calico cats and seeks a woman well versed on the classics, Broadway show tunes, and ancient history.

OK, so that's an easy one. These two would probably meet, hit it off on the very first date, and settle down to a life of domestic — and perhaps a smidge boring — bliss. Would you want to go see a movie about their relationship? Probably not.

How about these two:

Big-game huntress seeks financial backer and crew overseer for latest expedition to the Congo. Cowards and wimps need not apply.

Well-educated New Jersey stockbroker seeks immediate overseas opportunity to extricate himself from current romantic entanglement.

Can you picture what these two look like? Who would you cast in these roles? Let's say that you go with Bette Midler and David Hyde-Pierce. What would happen in their first meeting? She's looking for someone with money and brawn who shares her thirst for danger and adventure. He's a guy in an expensive suit who just wants to get out of town for a couple of months but not so far from civilization that he can't have his morning latte. The last thing either one of them is looking for is a new romance.

Your Assignments

1. In a one-page synopsis, figure out how to bring together the two characters I have just described for a happily ever after.

2. Look in tomorrow's paper and randomly select one entry from MEN SEEKING WOMEN and one entry from WOMEN SEEKING MEN. The more opposite their self-appraisals and specific interests, the more challenging it will be. If you really want a tough assignment, make your next stop the classified section and select any ITEM FOR SALE. You can then either set up a scenario in which one of your characters is the buyer and the other the seller *or* the item is the object of controversy which will determine whether they fall in love or fall apart.

3. Yet another idea-starter stems from a game you may recall playing in grade school but which still works in terms of

pushing your imagination to go into overtime. You need at least three people to participate; the bigger the group, the more diversity. At the top of a piece of paper, each person writes down a character type which could be played by either gender. This can either be a one-word tag such as "Astronaut" or a one-sentence set-up such as "An English teacher accepts a job in Appalachia." When you've finished, fold the top of the page down just enough to cover what has been written. (Some people even go so far as to apply a short strip of Scotch tape to prevent peeking.) Hand your paper off to the next person, who will proceed to write down Character Type #2, following the same instructions. Again, fold the paper to hide this second entry and pass it on. In the space remaining on the page, write down an object. It can be an animal, it can be a car, it can be a gold mine. It can be anything you want. After you have written something down, pass it on for the last time. Unfold the one you've just received so that all entries are visible.

Hmmm ... so you're now looking at:

A private-eye

A kleptomaniac salesperson

A package of uncooked spaghetti.

Your challenge? Figure out how to work all three elements into a short story for filming.

Packing Your Bags for Film Camp: An Interview with Shannon Gardner

Would it surprise you to hear that some of the award-winning fare on HBO and Nickelodeon was created by young writers just like you? Mr. Shannon Gardner, President and Executive Director of the Young Filmmakers Academy, is the driving force behind this non-profit corporation in Manhattan Beach, California. Not only does the curriculum give aspiring moviemakers a head-start on the creative tools needed for visual expression, but offers overseas summer programs to Italy and Germany — a forum for cultural exchange with European students pursuing the same dream.

Q: **Let's say that I'm sixteen and have convinced my parents that YFA film camp is a great idea. What can I expect to learn from it?**

A: One of the biggest things we emphasize is the team approach in both production and communications between the students and the mentors and instructors. No matter what kind of job or field the participants eventually go into, the hands-on experiences we provide in the start-to-finish aspects of making a film will give them a better sense of self-awareness, confidence, and how to bring the best out of everybody in the group.

Q: **Do you primarily concentrate on the technical aspects of filmmaking or the creative steps that go into coming up with original ideas?**

A: I think one of the really big differences in what we're doing in our program is that a lot of film camps per se take the approach of putting a camera in someone's hands and simply telling them how to turn it on without first exploring what they want to say with that camera. This is a backwards concept to me, because it puts more emphasis on inanimate objects like the equipment instead of focusing on the interests and insights of the person who's going to be operating it. Although we give everyone a solid grounding in the "mechanicals" of sight and sound and the things that go into post-production such as computer generated imaging and special effects, we want them to know why they want to use film as the medium to express themselves instead of, for instance, writing a poem or short story. We also don't want them to just go out and be mimicking what they saw last week at the movies. Every individual is different and has something inside of them that they want to communicate in story form. Should they shoot in color or black and white? Should it be a bunch of close-ups or do they want to create a mystery through longer shots where a lot of detail isn't seen? These are the kinds of questions that go into the full process of learning what filmmaking can accomplish.

Q: **Do you think it will become easier or harder for tomorrow's young screenwriters to break into the industry?**

A: I think that the Internet and digital TV will be really hungry for new content, some of which young people are already writing for. The market will always be competitive no matter what age you are, but I think America's greatest export and resource has always been its intellectual property. People will always go to movies and want to see new movies, because films are about the human journey and characters who are just like them.

Q: **Let's say that someone is planning on majoring in film in college. What sorts of things should they be doing while still in high school in order to distinguish themselves?**

A: Number one thing: Get involved! Participating in extracurricular activities will not only make you a more well-rounded person in terms of what you know about, but also enable you to meet people who can help introduce you to film-related opportunities. Is there a movie or TV show that's being shot in your hometown? Go see what you can do to volunteer. TV stations often have internships for students who want to learn about broadcast journalism and programming. If you want to be a screenwriter, you also need to write a lot of things and show a variety of range.

Q: **How about shooting a lot of footage with a camcorder?**

A: It's nice practice but no one at college is going to be asking to see your reel. What they want to see is what you've accomplished in terms of activities outside the classroom, that you're a person who's not afraid to step up and get involved. As a matter of fact, YFA has launched a PSA (public service announcement) program nationwide called "Kids Speak Out."

Q: **"Kids Speak Out" on what?**

A: The issues that are affecting them personally in their schools — things like non-violence, drug abuse, alcoholism, teen pregnancy. Teachers enroll in the program and receive guidebooks to use in the classroom and teach students how to develop and script original PSAs on these topics. The best ones are then submitted for competition and, if they win, national broadcast.

Q: **In other words, delivering the message straight from the lips of the audience's own peer group?**

A: Exactly. Hearing it from their own age group can be a lot more effective sometimes than hearing it from a bunch of adults who work at ad agencies.

Q: **I've saved the most fun question for last. Tell us about Germany and Italy!**

A: Well, like our studio programs in L.A., the Germany and Italy workshops are an intensive way to not just learn about movies and how to make your own but totally immerse you in the culture and history of another country. In Germany, we visit castles and museums, take a boat trip down the Rhine, and have even brought in storytellers to talk about the region and the people.

Q: **Sounds like a vacation...**

A: Make that a "working vacation!" The whole time, the students are writing, shooting, and editing their projects. The same with Italy where the workshop is held at a former royal palace near Pisa. If you're a fan of *Gladiator*, you get to see where the story took place, plus have access to gardens and grounds and even a beach to go shoot your story!

Q: **Drat! How come teens have all the fun and we have to stay home?**

A: Oh, but you don't! We also have a crash-course for older students and adults who either want to turn this into a family adventure or who have always dreamt of dabbling in cinema.

Q: **Does that mean we can go enjoy the Roma nightlife?**

A: Not until you finish your homework.

More information on the Young Filmmakers Academy and the KIDS SPEAK OUT program can be found at http://www.youngfilmmakers.org.

Topics to Think About and Talk About

1. Describe in 100 words or less what you view as the obligation of those in the entertainment industry to be to society in general.

2. List five activities in which you are engaged (sports, drama, work, etc.) that you feel would make you a better screenwriter, and explain briefly why.

3. Do you think that film is a "cutthroat" business? What does that mean to you and how will you deal with friends and colleagues who have the same ambitions as you?

What Is Your Movie About?

You should be able to summarize your film in as few words as possible. If you can't, don't expect anyone important to stay around long enough to listen to the pitch. Also, do you know who you're writing this movie for? Yourself? The entire planet? Or that vast majority in between? Screenwriting is as much about the market share as it is about the actual plot. Maybe even more so.

Titles

A common misconception among beginning writers is that whatever brilliant title they give their film will survive, intact, all the way to the movie theatres. Unfortunately, 1. if it's really brilliant, a director will probably appropriate it for some other film he or she is already doing; 2. it may have already been used (although titles are not copyright material); 3. it's a power thing to change the title to something else even if the original title was perfectly fine; or 4. your director/producer is a cement-head who doesn't recognize brilliance when he or she trips over it.

Speaking as one who once had a book editor who fit the profiles of numbers three and four, my advice is not to get too emotionally attached to whatever you have decided to call your project. For obvious purposes of identification, of course, you do need to call it something so that it will know to come when called. Just as parents-to-be excitedly pick out names while their child is still unborn, you too need to start thinking of your film-baby as a specific little being. Unlike parenthood, however, you have the flexibility to change its name to something else as often as you like up until such time as it officially becomes someone else's property and you have been paid a lot of money to go away and leave it alone.

To continue the baby/script analogy, let's look at some practical dos and don'ts:

1. Do not give it a name that sounds exactly like somebody else's. Not only does this cause great confusion but imposes a level of expectation that your fledgling film cannot possibly

live up to (i.e., *Citizen Kane*). Nor do you want to
with a name that, by association or similarity, spells
immediate disaster (i.e., *Ishtar*).

2. The name you give your film should fittingly have some sort
   of viable connection to the plot, thus imbuing it with
   favorable traits and characteristics. Maybe the title will be the
   actual name of one of the characters or perhaps a significant
   location. Twists on popular sayings and phrases from classic
   poems or literature have also frequently found their way into
   screen titles. Do not, however, mislead your public with an
   aristocratic and lofty moniker if the actual plot is--oh, say,
   only about bowling.

3. Last but not least, it's wise to give your project a title that is:
   a. short (six words or less), b. easy to pronounce for regular
   workaday people (which is why — with the exception of
   foreign films — they do not make movies called
   "Ghffellyweedwikin's Fllrppschwig"), and c. sounds good
   when spoken out loud. That last word of caution is a result
   of my experience with a former editor who had a penchant
   for turning brilliant titles into ridiculous ones. The worst of
   these was a romantic suspense which somehow — between
   my keyboard and the bookstore — was released as "Knight
   Dreams." While it looked attractive enough on the cover, few
   of my friends (particularly males) were intrepid enough to
   walk up to a clerk at Barnes and Noble and ask, "Do you
   have ... ?"

Fortunately, this same editor did not find a calling in the science
fiction field. Can you imagine what she would have done with a
novel about Uranus?

OK, So What Are You Going to Call Your Script?

Between now and the next paragraph, write down at least three
titles that would work well for your proposed film. Ready?

1.

2.

3.

Loglines

Even if you've never heard that term before, you've probably encountered plenty of examples of "loglines" every day in your local newspaper. These are the one-sentence plot summaries of episodic television programs or feature length films.

In television show listings, there is an assumption that viewers are not only familiar with the characters but are also up to date on these characters' respective lives at any point during the season. Given this level of familiarity, the following loglines would make perfect sense to a regular fan and compel him or her to program the VCR accordingly:

1. Trivette is forced to choose between his career and a woman from his past.
2. Daphne overhears how Niles feels about her.
3. Andrew reveals to Tess that he wants a different job.
4. Monica catches Chandler with an old girlfriend.
5. Gary discovers his own obituary in the paper.

Movie loglines are more generic in nature (extra points if you can identify the films they're describing):

1. A shipwrecked couple with three sons improvise on a tropical island.
2. An abused wife fakes her own death in order to escape her environment.
3. A losing baseball team is turned around by some divine intervention.
4. An orphaned baby is raised by gorillas.
5. A computer operator inadvertently receives a British agent's SOS.
6. A murdered German Shepherd returns to earth as a human to find his killer.
7. A New York cop plays cat-and-mouse with terrorists in a Los Angeles high-rise.
8. Two western outlaws flee to Bolivia to escape a relentless posse.
9. A sassy lounge-singer witnesses a murder and is hidden by the police in a run-down church.

10. A coma victim's family mistakenly assumes that the woman who saved his life is his fiancée.

What do these loglines all have in common besides posing an intriguing premise? They all beg the question, "So how is it going to turn out?" Will the dog find the killer? Will the shipwrecked family ever get rescued off that island? And what will happen when the coma-guy finally wakes up?

Decide What Your Logline Will Be

Let's say that you have found a potential director who is looking for a plot just like yours. If you only had twenty-five words to explain the entire premise, what would you say?

Synopses

By now, you have no doubt started telling friends and family members that you're reading a screenwriting book and are planning to sell movies for a living. "Oh?" they exclaim in surprise, "What's your movie about?"

"Well, it's sort of this romance-adventure kind of story that ... well, no, it's probably got some mystery in it, too, on account of there are these bad guys who — wait a minute, let me back up a sec. Did I tell you it takes place in Egypt except for this part at the beginning that's in San Francisco but then the lead character, who's on his way to New Mexico for a cousin's wedding, gets this strange letter and ... oh, did I mention there are clowns in it, too? There's this circus that's traveling around the country except that it's really a front for these other guys doing heavy drug-traffic which you don't really find out about until later on when the hero's sister gets a flat tire and this neighbor of hers, who had uncovered a dark plot that extends all the way to the White House, takes her aside and says to her ... "

If your friends have the attention span of gnats, their eyes have probably glazed over by now and they're mumbling excuses about having to be somewhere else — anywhere else — besides listening to you ramble. It's best, of course, that you learn this valuable lesson before you're asked the same question by someone who might actually have the resources to produce it. Hence, the need for a concise synopsis.

If done well, a synopsis should take no more than one typed page (double-spaced) and should be a tidy summary of the film from FADE IN to FADE TO BLACK. Obviously within the confines of that single page, it's not going to be possible to list all of the subplots and intricacies that comprise your story, only those key action-points and characters that keep it moving toward a satisfying conclusion.

In learning to write a synopsis, some students find it easier to write down as much as they can think of, then whittle down the words by at least half, cutting out everything that's unnecessary. Others prefer a bare-bones approach: stating the plot in as few lines as possible and then embellishing outward.

Your Assignment

Write a synopsis of the fairy tale *Snow White*. Now while there's obviously a lot that happens in this story — talking mirrors, murder plots, dwarves in the woods, disguises, glass coffins, etc., the challenge is to reduce all of it to just one page and still convey the plot from start to finish.

Keep in mind that there is a big difference between simply retelling a story in fewer words and relating the story in such a way that the person who hears it will be excited enough to want to read it themselves, *even though you have already told them how it comes out!*

Treatments

Treatments and outlines not only provide a working framework for you, the author, but also show a potential buyer that you do indeed have a fully-fleshed-out story to tell.

Definitions and Purpose

The terms "treatment" and "outline" are often used interchangeably in how-to texts on screenwriting. Basically, their intent is the same: to describe the film in a present-tense, narrative format, much like you would do if you were writing it as a short story for *Reader's Digest*. For the sake of comparison, a treatment is the more intensive of the two and often includes snippets of actual dialog throughout. Outlines are simply one-sentence descriptions of each scene told in sequence and without any lines of conversation.

Don't just take my word for it, though. Our guest definition today comes from indie film director, Jamie Langley:

> Screenplay treatments and outlines play a crucial role in pitching to busy studio execs. Why? Because they save valuable time on having to read entire scripts, especially those written by untried talent. Studios hire readers whose job is to screen out the "bad scripts" and pass on the "good ones." When a studio exec gets one of the selected "good" scripts he/she will then request an outline/treatment (and preferably one which will take no more than five to ten minutes to review). Once an outline/treatment has received a green light, its next stop is the desk of the producer, who will also read the outline/treatment before requesting to read the full screenplay.
>
> For our purposes, outlines and treatments reveal the concept behind the story, whereas a script is the story. Producers very much like thinking that they can change the story, but keep to the original concept. This also accounts for why there are so many rewrites during the filmmaking process! Like a short story, the narrative summary of your film has a beginning, middle, and end and only covers the major aspects of the plot. (Think of it as a buffed-out synopsis!) The first two sentences of this narrative are crucial. Like the first few pages of a script, if something is lacking at the beginning, there's a good chance it's going to wind up on the floor, shelf, or in the shredder.
>
> Treatments can range from as little as three to four pages or as long as fifteen — whatever it takes for you to pitch your story. This is what is going to sell the script so it should be compelling no matter the length. Some of the treatments I've received were only three pages in length, and yet told me everything there was to know about the story as far as setting, plot, conflict and resolution and the happy ending. In fact, I actually liked it when they were only three to four pages long, thus allowing me to get through a bunch of them in one day. Fifteen pages,

however, isn't unreasonable, especially for an action story since there's a lot going on which necessitates a lot of detail to keep the reader engaged.

It's also permissible to incorporate key lines of dialog in this expanded synopsis, although excessive use could backfire and lead a reader to think that you have subliminally snuck the full script under his/her nose!

Checklist

Just like any review sheet you might use for crafting top-notch fiction, there are certain elements your polished treatment should contain in order to be as complete as possible. It's also helpful to keep in mind that a treatment can either be written prior to the script itself (and used as a working framework to lead you scene-by-scene through the story) or written afterwards in the context of a marketing tool to elaborate on the script's high points. As you go through this list, make notes regarding your own script.

The Theme Test

The first of these questions relates to theme. We're going to assume, of course, that the two hours of material that you want to put up on that big screen are cohesive enough to espouse whatever philosophy or message inspired you to come up with this particular plot to begin with; i.e., love conquers all, war is hell, success is the best revenge, etc.

From the very beginnings of literature, all stories hinge on one or more of the following three themes: reward, revenge, or escape. No matter the genre, no matter the circa, no matter the setting, one or more of these underscore all action, all dialog, all decisions to be reached by story's end. Your treatment should reflect such cohesion as well, demonstrating that this is a story about something, not two hours' worth of characters wandering around for no tangible reason.

Just for fun, here are some films to categorize by their themes (and remember they can encompass any combination of the three or primarily be rooted in just one):

38

Casablanca

Star Wars

Shrek

Meet Joe Black

Gone with the Wind

Save the Last Dance

Housesitter

Tomb Raider

Saving Private Ryan

ET

Evita

"Know what your story is about," says screenwriter Eric Heisserer. "Be able to tell your story in three sentences and in three pages. Know what your theme is. Make sure others know it when they read your spec."

The Problem/Solution Test

The next test of a good treatment, which relates directly to the theme issue, is problem/solution. Have you clearly defined in your treatment what the problem is that the characters are going to try to resolve, as well as identified the specific obstacles inherent with that quest? Likewise, have you identified the agents of change who will impact your characters' actions, decisions and growth, and clearly described the solution that was finally reached?

New writers often make the mistake of constructing a lengthy and elaborate "teaser" in the hope that a would-be agent or producer will be so hooked on the initial premise that they will beg to see the rest. Not so. Anyone, after all, can come up with a complex scenario replete with good guys and bad guys and daring exploits in exotic lands or far-off galaxies. The big question, however, hinges on how are they going to wrap all of this up to a satisfying — and even credible — conclusion for the audience. The purpose of this entire display piece is to demonstrate that you know how to tell a complete story, not just an intriguing intro.

It's as true in film as it was back in third-grade English classes: no one, absolutely no one wants to turn to the last page of a pulse-pounding adventure only to discover, "And then Larry woke up and realized it had all been a dream ... "

The Newspaper Test

Let's pretend for a moment that your treatment is destined for the front pages of the newspaper. Has it effectively answered for the reader the questions of Who, What, Where, When, and Why?

Who: We should be able to tell from the treatment: 1. who we should be rooting for and 2. from whose viewpoint this story is being told. Oftentimes, these two are one in the same. An example of one which differs from this pattern is the Nicholas Cage comedy, *It Could Happen to You,* in which the back story about the policeman's life is filled in by an on-screen narrator who is separate and apart from the plot.

What: Remember the problem/solution test? The object of controversy should be readily apparent in your treatment, given that it is the primary conflict around which the entire plot will move. What is it that is standing between the character's present position and where he or she desires to be? What resources, skills or supporting characters are necessary in order for the protagonist to achieve that goal?

Where and When: Although these parameters would be obvious in a reading of the actual script, you still need to address them in the treatment so as to immerse the reader as quickly as possible in the physical environment. As a strictly budgetary concern, it's also important to identify whether the action is spread out over several years and/or locations or primarily confined to one setting. (This is where it's useful to recruit someone who is totally unfamiliar with the storyline to read your treatment.)

Why: This relates back to theme and is the icing on an already delicious cake. Specifically, it is the subtext beneath the characters' words and actions, the layers of personality that are artfully peeled away through the course of two or more hours. What internally motivates them to do what they do is the very same thing that makes us, the audience, care about them as people.

Target Audiences

Back in the days of being a scriptwriter/production assistant for cable television, I'd often sit down with clients and ask them who their target audience was going to be. Invariably, they would exchange confused glances with each other, then look back at me and reply, "Everyone."

Yes, well, although it's nice to think "global" about one's product or service, the truth of the matter is that not everyone on the planet shares the same giddy passion about really obscure subjects such as the mating habits of seahorses. Likewise — and don't take offense at this — not everyone is going to swarm to see your four-hour flick about Sennacherib, especially if they have no clue who he was or why they should care.

Hopefully, you will have given some thought to this issue of commercial value before you ever started writing. While it's not to discourage you from writing what's in your heart, you also need to keep in mind what's going to be in your wallet ... which will be *nothing* if you craft a script that no one will want to see.

Ideally, you should write the kind of films that you yourself enjoy watching. The rationale of this is threefold: 1. you'll be writing something that is fun for you, 2. you'll be familiar enough with the genre to have a sense of what works and what doesn't, and 3. you'll also have an awareness of what kind of audience this type of film attracts. What? You weren't paying attention to all those people seated around you? Well, no harm done. Now that you know, you can pay more attention the next time you go to a film that is similar in tone to the one you're going to write.

Is it a comedy that attracts a broad cross-section of ages or whose humor is slanted toward a particular segment? Is it a romantic, tearjerker chick-flick where the audience is comprised primarily of females or maybe couples on dates? Is it a movie centered on teen angst and viewed by similarly angst-ridden young people? Maybe it's a nostalgia piece, aimed at viewers who want to trip down memory lane ... or perhaps it's a contemporary drama that could have been taken from the front pages of the daily news. On the other hand, don't lose sight of the fact that there are plenty of films in which the solo drawing-power is simply Will Smith whose following will flock in droves to virtually anything just because he's in it.

In addition to observing the composition and reactions of your fellow movie-goers, it's additionally helpful to start reading movie reviews; although totally subjective in scope, they nonetheless provide an overview of a film's plot, as well as hint at the type of audience it was written for. While we're on the subject of reviews, I'm also going to take this opportunity to recommend that you add any or all of film critic Roger Ebert's wonderful compilations to your library. Not only does he provide witty and succinct criticisms of popular and classic films, but supplements them with a host of time-worn cliches that every aspiring screenwriter would be wise to avoid.

Question of the Day

Who are you writing your movie for? And why?

Psst! Wanna Buy a Cheap Script?

Back when I used to run a touring theatre company, there was only one rule regarding the amount of furniture and props for any given performance: If It Doesn't Fit in the Car, It's Not Going. (Fortunately, I was also penning all the plays the troupe performed so I had some control over the situation.)

This sense of economy carried over into my lectures and classes for aspiring scriptwriters, reinforcing the philosophy that if no one is going to mention why there is a moose head above the mantle, maybe that moose head really doesn't need to be there. Little did I know at the time that I was laying the groundwork for my eventual segue into writing for film ... and the necessity to craft a good story that can succeed on the strength of its plot, not the weightiness of its budget.

A case in point was the recent adaptation of my Scottish time travel, *The Spellbox*, to a feature length script for an independent producer. Aside from the challenge of compressing 400-plus pages to 120, there were scenes which I purposely omitted in deference to what it would ultimately cost to execute them (i.e., a banquet in which the Great Hall is set on fire). Anything which involves destruction of sets, utilization of stunt people, or more insurance is going to drive up the price tag of a movie.

For writers who have yet to make their mark in the industry, such items can be a red flag to producers whose coffers are not quite Cameron-esque. While everyone hungers to write a cast-of-thousands epic with a wealth of elaborate sets and technical glitz, the reality is that the lower the author can keep the script's production costs, the higher the chances of a sale.

The bottom line here is that it's easier to add in the glitz later than to have the crux of your plot contingent on its being present in the first draft. If you're wondering how some of these truly lame movies get launched in the first place, sometimes it's just a matter of budget (or lack thereof).

Can your own script pass the following economy test?

1. Contemporary storylines are generally less costly than period pieces.

2. Fires, floods, earthquakes, volcanos, explosions — while many disasters can now be computer-generated, those that can't are going to cost money.

3. Do you really need those swarming crowds? Even though they're paid scale for just taking up space, they're still an expense.

4. Anything with animals — especially trained ones — could be a big-ticket item.

5. Exterior scenes leave the crew at the mercy of time, season and weather, as opposed to interior shots which will look exactly the same whether it's three a.m. in the dead of winter or 7:30 p.m. on a summer night.

6. Night scenes are more expensive to film than scenes in daylight.

7. Are your car chases and crashes necessary or just gratuitous? Vehicular mayhem can put a sizable dent in the budget.

8. Going on location is pricier than staying on a soundstage, especially the travel factor.

9. Specifying that "Mel Gibson has to be in this movie or it simply won't work" probably isn't a compelling pitch.

10. Every time the equipment gets moved, the cash register dings. Try to minimize your locations so multiple scenes can be shot at one time.

It All Adds Up

It's time to analyze your own film in terms of the following elements and give yourself points accordingly:

1. My film is: a. contemporary, b. contemporary with historical flashbacks, or c. historical or futuristic?

2. My film has: a. zero to ten special effects, b. eleven to thirty special effects, or c. over thirty special effects.

3. My film has a total of: a. less than ten actors, b. eleven to fifty actors, or c. over fifty actors.

4. My film has: a. no animals in it, b. animals that are strictly for atmosphere (i.e., grazing cows, sleeping cats, etc.), or c. animals that have a defined role or do special tricks.

5. My film has: a. zero to ten interior scenes, b. eleven to thirty interior scenes, or c. over thirty interior scenes. (Note: If you have three scenes that all take place in the same location [for instance, a kitchen], count it as only one interior no matter how many times it is used.)

6. My film has: a. zero to ten exterior scenes, b. eleven to thirty exterior scenes, or c. over thirty exterior scenes. (Note: If you have three scenes that take place in the same location [such as a park], count it as only one exterior. If, however, you have a scene in a park, a scene at a beach, and a scene at an outdoor cafe, that would be three exteriors.)

7. My film has: a. fewer than ten night scenes, b. eleven to twenty night scenes, or c. over twenty night scenes. (Note: Night scenes are those which take place outdoors and in the dark, not just evening scenes which are all shot inside a house.)

8. My film has: a. no car scenes or simply street scenes where cars are part of the background, b. scenes in which my characters are traveling by car, or c. car chases, crashes, or explosions.

9. My film primarily takes place: a. in a soundstage, b. in an existing house or public building, or c. in a specially constructed set (i.e., a medieval castle built from scratch for the production).

10. My film would be successful with: a. a cast of unknowns,

b. one name star, c. three or more name stars.

11. Physical stunts in my film are: a. non-existent, b. computer-generated, or c. performed by stunt people.

12. For scenes outside a soundstage, the majority of my film takes place: a. in a small town, b. in a major American city, or c. in a foreign country.

To score: For every a. answer, give yourself one point. For every b. answer, give yourself five points. For every c. answer, give yourself ten points. If your total score is less than forty, you have probably crafted a story that comfortably falls into the "low" budget range and would be appealing to a small or independent producer. If your score ranges from forty to eighty, you have hit the mid-ranges, money-wise. This range gives you a lot of latitude since you can adjust up or down, depending on whom you approach with your pitch. If your score is between eighty and 120, your vision may be too "big budget" for someone to take a risk on, especially if you're brand new at this. The fun part of this test, though, is that it's within your power to bring the higher numbers down by looking at your c. answers and determining where appropriate compromises can be made without compromising the intent of your story.

Chapter 4

Movie Terms (and Career Advice) You Need to Know

No matter what occupation you choose to pursue, you'll discover that each one comes with its own specialized language. This chapter includes some of the most common terms that you will be using in your scripts, as well as advice on what you can expect if you want to enter the Hollywood work-force.

Movie Lingo

As a screenwriter, you don't need to be concerned with providing camera directions, save for those instances when it's absolutely necessary to define a special shot. Even then, please use them sparingly.

Among the most familiar are:

Aerial shot — A bird's eye view of the world. Very popular for establishing shots.

Crane Shot — The sort of shot you would get if you were in a cherry picker that was moving up or down.

CU — A close-up shot; for instance, someone's face. An ECU (Extreme Close-Up) would be the person's tonsils.

Dissolve — A transitional effect in which a few seconds of the upcoming scene are superimposed over the current scene.

EXT. — Exterior. Anything that takes place outside.

Fade-in — This is the very first word of your script and literally "opens up" the story.

Fade to Black — This is the final punctuation of your film. The story is over. Time to go home.

INT. — Interior. Anything that takes place inside.

Match Cut — A device in which an element of the second scene is identical to the first. For example, a character is looking at a magazine photograph of a celebrity or a travel brochure featuring the Eiffel Tower. The magazine or brochure is lowered and — voila — we are looking at the real version of the same celebrity or notable landmark.

O.S. — An off-screen voice, which means that the person talking is within the scene, just not seen at that moment. It is written after the person's name, as in MURIEL (O.S.).

PAN — A steady, horizontal sweep of the landscape. In westerns of the 1930s, a fast pan was popular for establishing, "Meanwhile, in another part of town ... "

POV — Point of view. Essentially, the camera is becoming the "eyes" of one of the characters. (This is very popular in murder mysteries in which the victim looks straight at the camera as if it were a real person.)

V.O. — Voice-over. The character is heard but is not actually in the scene being shown. It is written after the person's name, as in HECTOR (V.O.).

ZOOM — an adjustment of the camera's focal length while the shot is in progress (as in ZOOM IN, ZOOM OUT).

What to Use/What to Lose

How many errors can you find in the following set-up?

INT. — BAR — NIGHT

The camera wanders through the bar and discovers that CASSANDRA and BARRY are sitting in a back corner table. It's another cold winter night in Cincinnati but by the hushed heat of their conversation, neither one is feeling it. Cassandra was engaged to Barry back when she was young and foolish. They drifted apart because she thought she could do better by marrying his brother BRETT who owns the garage where her sister ANGIE is the secretary. If Brett finds out where she is tonight, he'll be really mad. Barry is looking deep into her eyes and she knows he's thinking the same thing but doesn't have enough money for them to just run away to the West Coast or maybe Hawaii. Years of rejection as a writer have started to give him doubts about himself. Cassandra gazes fondly at the silver ring Barry gave her back when they were in high school and that she only wears nowadays when she knows she can get away with it. Barry tries to ask her what's on her mind but she's afraid to reply.

Let's see how you did.

1. *The camera wanders through the bar.* I'm conjuring the image here of a droid-like creature on spindly legs. If you want a *Traveling Shot,* that's fine. Just don't imply that the equipment is ambling around of its own volition.

2. *It's another cold winter night in Cincinnati.* How do we know that it's cold, that it's winter, or that we're even in Ohio? Are the characters seated by a window where they can gaze out on a meadow reminiscent of a Currier and Ives Christmas card? Are they wearing winter clothes? Has it already been established that this story takes place in Cincinnati? Could it just as easily be taking place in Fresno, California? You don't have to put this level of detail in the script if: 1. it can be conveyed by some other means or 2. isn't crucial to the plot.

3. *The hushed heat of their conversation.* Oh puh-leeze. Save this for a romance novel.

4. *Cassandra was engaged to Barry back when she was young and foolish. They drifted apart because she thought she could do better by marrying his brother.* If this isn't going to be revealed in actual dialog, leave it out. Granted, it's all a nice backstory about where the characters were before, but spelling it out in the narrative is of no help to the audience since they don't have a copy of the script to follow along.

5. *BRETT who owns the garage where her sister ANGIE is the secretary.* Only capitalize names if these people are actually in the current scene and making their first appearance. Likewise, unless we see Brett and Angie at the garage doing their jobs or this is directly referenced in a conversation, we don't need to read it in the narrative.

6. *If Brett finds out where she is tonight.* Again, this should be in the dialog, not the description.

7. *She knows he's thinking the same thing. She* may know this but how do you get the *audience* to know it? They are not

mind-readers. Same thing for: *Years of rejection as a writer have started to give him doubts about himself.*

8. *The silver ring Barry gave her back when they were in high school.* How do we know Barry gave this to her? How do we know they were in high school? As far as the audience is concerned, it's just a silver ring unless someone talks about its history out loud *or* a flashback shows him giving her the ring.

9. *Barry tries to ask her what's on her mind but she's afraid to reply.* OK, here's something quirky. It's obviously a good *place* for some dialog, but is instead being buried in narrative, suggesting that the actors are just supposed to ad lib. Skilled as they are at the gift of gab, you can't rely on them to simply chat amongst themselves or take up space until you get back to writing actual conversations for them. I once had a student turn in a hospital waiting room scene in which it was instructed: "The doctors explain the procedure they're going to do and the risks involved and everyone decides they should go to the cafeteria in the meantime and maybe get something to eat. Once they get there, they talk about whether Harry is going to pull through."

Your Assignment

After determining which elements of the Cassandra and Barry relationship are the most important in order to convey (via actions and dialog) what they are really like as people, re-write this scene.

Writing on Spec

Up until such time as your screenplays start getting the attention and acclaim they deserve from agents, directors, and producers, the bulk of what you write will be "on spec." "Spec" is short for "speculation" and means exactly that: Maybe you'll sell it, maybe you won't. (Hence, the prudence of having a regular job to keep your creditors at bay in the interim.)

Spec scripts are contrasted to work-for-hire by one word: freedom. When you're writing spec scripts, you are your own boss.

You can navigate the plot and the characters in any direction you wish, as well as take your sweet time from FADE IN to FADE TO BLACK. When you are hired by someone to write a script, however, not only do the ownership rights rest with the employer but so, too, does the integrity of the story. While the guarantee of a paycheck at day's end is certainly nice, both newcomers and veterans agree on the pride factor in calling a work one's own.

If you're typical of a lot of artists, your early works will generally be your favorites — those stories which were crafted with great passion but not necessarily an equitable amount of expertise. Not to worry; the latter will come in time, usually as a battle-weary result of one day realizing that in order to stand out in the crowd, one sometimes needs to join that crowd. Translation: You need to prove that you can write the same kind of thing that is selling.

That's not to say that your pride and joy in a script is relegated to spend its days on a dusty back shelf or propping up the leg of a wobbly desk while you sell out to the lure of commercialism. The present proliferation of independent studios and art-house production companies could even find it a nice home by the time you finish reading this book. How "big" you choose to think in terms of reaching an audience is entirely up to you. Many an author is content with the trade-off of creative control inherent in keeping their projects on a modest level and telling the story exactly the way they want to tell it.

For those who prefer the longer road and larger scale, the spec scripts you've been trying to shop can fulfill a purpose you may not have thought of. They can serve as writing samples to get you in the door of a studio that is either developing new projects or whose material in existing projects needs some serious fix-up.

Let's say that a television producer has done his or her homework on demographics and recent hits and determined that a sitcom involving a pair of Latino twins who marry twin sisters and start a theatre company would be a successful series. The call goes out to agents and into databases. Assuming that you just happen to already have a script that fits these parameters, you're immediately head and shoulders above everyone else who is now scrambling to write one from scratch.

But let's suppose your spec script is a comedy about a Latino actor who works two jobs in between shows and has an on-again, off-again relationship with his high school sweetheart. Should you send a logline and synopsis in response to the quest for scripts? Absolutely! Why? Because there are enough comparable elements between your existing script and their dream project to constitute a possible match. And who knows? They may even like your idea better!

It's also wise to have more than one spec script up your sleeve for opportunities such as this, particularly if each one has something distinctively different to commend it. The more range you can demonstrate in terms of genre, dialog, and budget, the better your chances of being picked up to write or rewrite a film or television show.

"But if I'm good enough to get hired," you lament, "why don't they just take the wonderful script I've already written and pay me for that?" The answer? Risk. Selling your first spec script is a lot like applying for your very first credit card. Everyone would love to say "yes" ... as long as someone else says "yes" first and validates that you're a good risk.

Once you have proven yourself, though, the credit card analogy continues. You could eventually end up with more offers than you know what to do with!

The Bookshelf

One can never have too many books on the craft of writing for movies and television (provided, of course, that you don't spend so much time reading them all cover to cover that you never have time to actually write anything yourself). Each of these references (and listed in no particular order) have respectively wonderful components, including sample scripts, anecdotes, exercises, and cautionary advice on cinematic clichés.

Hollywood 101: The Film Industry (Renaissance Books, 2000) by Frederick Levy

The Complete Book of Scriptwriting (Writers Digest Books 1996) by J. Michael Straczynski

Writing Short Scripts (Syracuse University Press, 1999) by William H. Phillips

Writing Scripts Hollywood Will Love (Allworth Press, 2000) by Katherine Atwell Herbert

How to Make It in Hollywood (Harperperennial Library, 1996) by Linda Buzzell

How to Pitch and Sell Your TV Script (1991) by David Silver (out of print)

The Tools of Screenwriting (St. Martin's Press, 1995) by David Howard and Edward Mabley

The Screenwriters's Bible (Silman-James Press, 1998) by David Trottier

How to Write A Movie in 21 Days (HarperCollins, 1988) by Viki King

Television Writing (1980) By Richard A. Blum (out of print)

Making a Good Writer Great (Silman-James Press, 1999) by Linda Seger

Peterson's Breaking into Film (Petersons Guides, 1998) by Kenna McHugh

Writing Television Comedy (Allworth Press, 2000) by Jerry Rannow

The Insider's Guide to Writing for Screen and Television (Writer's Digest Books 1997) by Ronald B. Tobias

The Business of Screenwriting (Lone Eagle Publishing Co., 1999) by Ron Suppa

The Writer Got Screwed (But Didn't Have To) (HarperCollins 1997) by Brooke Wharton

Writing the Romantic Comedy (Harper Resource, 2000) by Billy Mernit

Development Girl (Doubleday, 1999) By Hadley Davis

Script Magic (Michael Wiese Productions, 2000) by Marisa D'Vari

How Scripts are Made (Southern Illinois University Press, 1990) by Inga Karetnikova

Writing Television Sitcoms (Perigree, 1999) by Evan Smith

Freelance Writing for Hollywood (Michael Wiese Productions, 2000) by Scott Essman

And, for a deliciously humorous look at what *not* to do...

> *Mike Nelson's Movie Megacheese* (Harper Entertainment, 2000) By Michael Nelson
>
> *Bad TV* (Delta, 1995) by Craig Nelson
>
> *I Hated, Hated, Hated This Movie* (Andrews McMeel Publishing, 2000) by Roger Ebert

Your Future in Film:
An Interview with Frederick Levy

Mr. Frederick Levy, Vice President of Marty Katz Productions, was only seventeen when he followed his movie-making dream from his hometown of Stoughton, Massachusetts to the sunny west coast and the halls of USC. In addition to being a pro at development deals, Levy teaches at Emerson College's LA branch, UCLA Extension Writers Program, and USC's prestigious School of Cinema-Television. He has also penned *Hollywood 101: The Film Industry, The Ultimate Boy Band Book,* and *The Hollywood Way,* and can be found at the touch of a keystroke at the popular www.hollywood-101.com.

Q: How old were you and what was the defining incident when you first knew you wanted a career in film?

A: When I was in first grade, we did a project with film strip where we would use markers to draw right on the film for a poor man's version of animation. I was always fascinated by drawing an image on the little piece of film, and then seeing it come to life on the screen. I don't know how defining a moment this was, but it always stuck in my head as my first venture into the filmmaking process.

Q: So how many years passed from that moment until the dream finally became a reality?

A: I think the dream started to become a reality when I was seventeen and moved to Los Angeles to attend school at USC. Even though I wasn't officially in the business, just being close to Hollywood, seeing movie stars at local restaurants, and getting invited to Hollywood parties was close enough to give me the bug! In school, I first got started in journalism writing for the school paper, *The Daily Trojan*. I wrote for the entertainment section and was able to score interviews with several actors from Leonard Nimoy to Rick Schroeder. This was very exciting for a kid from Boston. Then I became one of the first student journalists ever credentialed for the Academy Awards. I covered all the awards shows (MTV, Peoples Choice, Golden Globe, Emmys, etc.) from the red carpet and back stage. Then I got into radio. I produced my own shows that were nationally syndicated on a college radio network. The first show, *Then & Now*, was a talk program where I interviewed some of my favorite stars from classic TV such as Dawn Wells (MaryAnne from *Gilligan's Island*) and Ron Pallillo (Horshack from *Welcome Back Kotter*). The other show was called *The Celebrity DJ Party* which was a music show hosted each week by a different celebrity guest who would play and discuss their favorite songs. Some of my guests included Weird Al Yankovic and River Phoenix. The other thing I did while I was still in school was I got an internship on the TV show *Love Connection*. This led to my first full time job as a guest coordinator on the show. I guess you could say that was my first true Hollywood job.

Q: **What other sorts of opportunities and guidebooks were available to you during that time so you could learn your craft?**

A: Once I moved to Los Angeles, I was surrounded by resources and access. Unfortunately, when I was starting out, there wasn't a guide to help me. That's why I wrote *Hollywood 101: The Film Industry* which is a survey of the film business that examines all the different jobs one could do in the industry and how to get started in each of these careers. It also features advice from many professionals working in the business.

Q: **What if you live in Iowa and it's going to take you a long time to save up the air/train/bus fare to relocate to where the movie-making action is?**

A: Even if you don't live in Hollywood, you can still learn your craft. Get involved helping out on student films at local universities, take screenwriting classes or seminars at nearby colleges, volunteer at your local cable station.

Q: I notice that your degree from USC was in marketing, not film. Was this part of a far-sighted strategy to get into the development aspects of the industry or was it more of a safety-net "have-a-real-job-just-in-case"?

A: It was neither. I didn't know for sure that I wanted to get into film. As I've said, my interests are quite varied. I'm a producer, an author, a college professor. Marketing is one of those useful skills that I use in all three of my careers.

Q: Would you advise seniors who are planning to go into a university curriculum to major specifically in film or, like yourself, pursue a business or other degree instead?

A: Study what interests you. If all you know is film, what will you make films about? There are some great film programs. USC has probably the best film writing program of any university. AFI has wonderful graduate level fellowships in everything from directing to editing. But not studying film in college hasn't prevented me at all from working in this industry. I don't think it's integral. The best thing you'll get out of film school is meeting other people who share your passion.

Q: Whether or not their plans include college, would you encourage aspiring scriptwriters to get any kind of interim job that puts them on a sound stage *or* to take a relatively mindless job which frees them to focus on their writing?

A: I always say, if you want to write, make that your top priority. This means you must not have a job that causes stress, and makes you take work home with you. If so, when will you find the time or energy to write?

Q: "Chutzpah" was the operative word when you bargained your way into an assistant position with Marty Katz. Today, you're vice president of the company. What do you feel set you apart in your work ethic and communication skills which enabled you to move into what sounds like the dream job of influencing what we'll be seeing in tomorrow's movie theatres?

A: For me, this is a lifestyle, not a career. You have to live and breathe this business if you want to move ahead. I work 24/7. Given, my work is very social so it often doesn't feel like work, I'm always doing something that has to do with movies. The other thing is that I never take "no" for an answer. If I want to get a script to someone, I find a way. If I want to get ahold of something, I find it — no matter what!

Q: **Prior to college, what can aspiring filmmakers do to distinguish themselves in high school and extracurricular activities?**

A: Make amateur films with your home video camera. Write screenplays. Volunteer at the local cable station (that's what I did). Read lots of screenplays. Watch lots of movies.

Q: **What would you say are the three most important traits for a beginning screenwriter to have? Likewise, what are the three worst things they can do to make a bad impression on industry professionals?**

A: Present your screenplay in a professional manner (i.e., 120 pages, proper format, etc.) Make sure you have a query letter that is short and to the point and explains what is fresh and different about your script than every other one like it. When you write, know your audience, and know how to market the movie. To make a bad impression, spell my name wrong, send me a script unsolicited, or if I request your screenplay off a query letter, send me a script that is far from finished form.

Q: **The Internet has dramatically increased the film market's accessibility for new writers, as well as increased the chances of the unsavvy being ripped off by fly-by-night producers. In addition to the legal protections of always registering scripts with the U.S. Copyright office and WGA, what are some of the warning signs that a contest or production company may not be legit?**

A: Always check on the companies' credits. If they've been involved with movies you can rent at Blockbuster, they're probably legit. There are a lot of great resources on the web where you can ask questions if you are unsure. I have a web site at www.hollywood-101.com and I also host a discussion forum on breaking into the business at www.creativeplanet.com.

Q: **Suppose you're seventeen and have written a screenplay that everyone (and not just those related to you!) thinks is great. What can you do to keep a prospective producer from telling you to go away and come back when you're old enough to be taken seriously?**

A: How would they even know if you're only seventeen? Most submissions are by query so they wouldn't know in a million years. If you happen to be young and write a screenplay that someone wants to buy, this will only help in the publicity.

Q: **If you could remake any movie from the past: 1. which one would it be, and 2. who would you cast among today's current batch of stars?**

A: I'd remake the old movie *The Four Feathers* and I'd cast Heath Ledger, Wes Bentley, and Kate Hudson. (Actually, my company, Marty Katz Productions, has already produced that film.)

Q: **Last but not least, what is the best thing that being in show business has taught you about yourself?**

A: You can accomplish anything if you set your mind to it!

Topics to Think About and Talk About

1. In fifty words or less, describe what convinced you to want to get involved in film.

2. In 100 words of less, develop a plan that wil:l a. have you in the film industry in five years and b. allow you to pay the rent and buy food.

3. List everything you have done in the past year to further your career in film.

What Should Your Screenplay Look Like on Paper?

This seems like as good a spot as any for a pop quiz on the basics of formatting your first screenplay. Answer "true" or "false" to the following questions, then read on to see how many of them you got right!

1. Character names are always capitalized and centered above the dialog.

2. A synopsis should be included at the front of every script.

3. The only thing that should appear on the title page is the title.

4. Always include a list of characters with each script.

5. Scenes should be numbered and divided by acts.

6. Include as many camera directions as possible.

7. Always right-justify your margins.

8. Sound effects are always capitalized.

9. Page numbers are placed in the center at the bottom of the page.

10. The word "CONTINUED" should appear the top and bottom of each page.

11. It's acceptable to hyphenate lines of dialog in your script.

12. Transitions such as CUT TO and DISSOLVE are placed at the left slug line.

13. The year of copyright or WGA registration number should always appear on the first page of your script.

14. All characters — even minor ones — need to be identified by a name.

15. Scripts should always be printed two-sided for agency or studio submissions.

itself — was typed on a manual typewriter (yes, such exist) which hadn't seen a ribbon-change in eons.

ationalized, perhaps the sender's secretary was laying in a hospital, the latest order for professional letterhead was the printer's, and the sender suddenly found himself in lackout with only an inch-high candle and a rusty by which to craft his plucky note to moi. Could I cast nitial assumptions about the integrity of the business, elieve instead in the sincerity of this amateurish attempt attention for a "once-in-a-lifetime opportunity"? Or was cal side of my personality just looking for a ripe to illustrate a salient point in this chapter regarding the of putting your best foot forward?

ded to the sender's e-mail invitation to "learn more." equently learned was that, "for the start-up fee of only s person would put my book in print and let me keep a n percent of every copy sold. I wrote back and, quite ed why I should fork over $1,000 to someone who together a decent postcard of introduction. How did I nstance, that they wouldn't type up my book on a erwood with a bad ribbon, photocopy the whole thing per, and throw a rubberband around it before stuffing lope to a buyer?

y chosen to respond to my question (which they idn't), I'm sure they would have insisted, "Well, e finished product will be perfect. We were just trying to es a little time and money at the front end and cut to

ty is that you never get a second chance to make a pression, no matter how much time and money you're e.

16. Font type is always Times New Roman.

If you answered false to each of the above, go to the head of the class! If your score wasn't quite as stellar, pay close attention to this chapter.

Formatting

The following is a nifty checklist to refer to as you prepare your script for contests or agency/production submission. You may have the very best story the Western Hemisphere has ever seen, but if the format shouts "amateur," you're not going to get it in the front door.

1. **Character Names** are capitalized in dialog blocks and the first time they appear in the script. They are not capitalized in conversation (i.e., Hi, MARY) or subsequent appearances throughout the story.

2. **A Synopsis** is not included anywhere in the script. It will have been included in your initial cover letter which precipitated your being invited to submit the full screenplay for consideration. You also need to keep in mind that a synopsis increases a studio reader's inclination to pretend he or she read the full script. Don't make it easy for them to reject you.

3. **The Title Page** of the script should always include your name, address, phone number and e-mail address. Should the screenplay become separated from your cover letter, the agent or studio would have no way of reaching you if all they had to go on was just the title.

4. Do *not* include a cast of characters with the script. Allow each one to be introduced with each turn of the page.

5. Do *not* number your scenes or your acts. The difference between a reading script and a shooting script is that the reading script is strictly meant to be *read*. Once the story is in production, a new series of numbers will be added by the director indicating the sequence in which they will actually be shot. And, even though there is considerable emphasis on the three-act structure of screenwriting, do *not* identify your segments as Act I, II and III. Save the "act" differentiations for when you are writing stage plays.

6. Do not include camera directions in your script unless it is absolutely essential. Your job is to write. The director's job is to figure out how to convey all of this visually. You need to trust that he or she will figure out how best to do this.

7. Do not justify the right margins.

8. There are split views on whether every SOUND EFFECT should be capitalized. Personally, I think that CAPITALIZING every SOUND that goes OFF with a BANG or a WHOOSH makes a script ANNOYING to read.

9. **Page Numbers** should be shown in the upper right hand corner of each page.

10. If you read older books on the topic of screenwriting, the use of "CONTINUED" at the bottom and top of each page was pretty common. Eventually, however, someone had the wits to say, "Aren't readers smart enough to know to turn to the next page?" Newer screenwriting books advise against it.

11. Never hyphenate lines of dialog in your script.

12. **Transitions** to new scenes are placed at the right margin, starting specifically at column #55. The words "CUT TO" should only be used if you're going to a completely different scene, not just to a different angle within the same scene.

13. Neither the copyright year nor the WGA registration number should appear anywhere on your script.

14. **Minor Characters** who are only employed for ambiance or who have only one line of dialog do not need to have names. Nor do you need to establish extensive backgrounds for these people. If it's never going to come out in the context of the plot, there's no reason for you to have to spend time fabricating it. If you really like them that much, you can always give them the lead in your next film.

15. Much as I hate to kill trees, the reality nonetheless stands that your script should always be printed on only one side of the paper, not two.

16. The industry standard is Courier 12.

Going by the Numbers

There are a number of scrip[t]
currently on the market. Although the[y]
be aware that your competition is pr[o]
make their manuscripts look as pr[o]
you're saving up to make that kind o[f]
the basic numbers you need to work

At ten character columns per in[ch]
at Column #15. This will give you a
perfect for when the manuscript
Character names start at Column #[3]
the dialog. If you are using parenthe[tical]
line is said, these start at Column #3
parenthetical remarks sparingly!
Columns #25 and #55. Don't right[-justify the]
edge. Transitional directions such a[s]
start at Column #55 but go no f[urther]
leaves you with a right hand mar[gin]
within the dialog paragraphs and
paragraphs themselves.

Neatness Counts!

Not so very long ago, I rec[eived a]
postcard from a fledging publishi[ng]
like to have them publish one of m[y]
as to identify it by its correct title
enthusiastically referred to me by

Knowing this much, of cour[se]
difficult for them to further asce[rtain]
published. Nonetheless, I decided
been living at the bottom of a well
liked the story so much that it tot[ally]
of another publisher liking it first

This in mind, I moved on
approach. Eeek! It was a garden
which the sender had crookedly
delivery addresses. (Did I menti[on]
the second "t"?) The flip-side of

company
things still

OK, I [m]
traction in
delayed at
a rolling
Underwood
aside my
opting to b
to grab my
the whims
opportunity
importance

I respon
What I subs
$1,000," th
whopping t
bluntly, ask
couldn't pu
know, for i
vintage Und
on cheap pa
it in an enve

Had the
ultimately
obviously th
save oursel[v]
the chase."

The real[ly]
good first im
trying to sav

The Cover Letter: Your Calling Card

A cover letter isn't just a piece of paper that goes on the front of your project. It can be the door-opener — or door-slammer — for your script. It all depends on how much you reveal ... and how well you say it. Bottom line: Keep it short and to the point.

Let's take a look at the example below:

1. Bryn Myrddin Studios

   Attn: Susan Blondin, Vice President

   777 Serendipity Drive

   Beverly Hills, CA 90210

Dear Ms. Blondin:

2. Your name was graciously provided to me by Christopher Mitchell, one of your fellow panel members at the recent ASA Directors Forum in Burbank. I have followed your work for several years and have recently completed a new script entitled *Everything But The Groom,* which I believe meets Bryn Myrddin's standards for contemporary romantic comedy. 3. It is adapted from one of my published novels, which is currently available as an e-book through New Concepts Publishing.

4. The premise of the story is that a bridal consultant is contracted to produce the wedding-of-the-century at the private home of a wealthy family in Mill Valley, California. The catch? The too rich/too thin/too snooty bride is marrying Kate's former boyfriend and is taking every opportunity to flaunt her victory and push Kate's buttons. As if matters weren't difficult enough, Kate's regular photographer has an emergency which necessitates him sending an old Army pal, Jack, to cover the nuptials. Jack, however, has his own agenda for being at the Murchie estate that day. 5. The time frame of the story is forty-eight hours, there are no expensive special effects, and everything necessary for the wedding-day scene can easily be rented from — where else — any place in town that caters to real weddings.

6. My publishing credits to date include seventeen books, ninety-eight plays and musicals, and over 250 magazine and newspaper articles. I have also worked in radio and cable television, and am currently teaching an online screenwriting course through WriteRead

University. **7.** Upon request, I would be happy to send you a treatment or the full script, along with a standard industry release.

I look forward to hearing from you at your earliest convenience.

Christina Hamlett
Address
Phone
E-mail

SASE

1. Always address your inquiry to a specific individual ... and spell his or her name correctly! Your stationery should be conservative and professional. This is not the place for neon paper, quirky-sized envelopes, or glittery stars that fall out on their shoes. I even know one writer who swears that "neutral" postage stamps (i.e., the U.S. flag) make a better impression than animals, pop art, or dead celebrities. Return address labels should be neutral as well, no matter how much you may personally favor Snoopy, smiley faces or Psalm snippets. One more reminder: using spell-check on the body of the letter isn't enough. Have at least half a dozen readers proof your correspondence before it goes anywhere.

2. A personal connection is always beneficial, whether it's to comment on a specific work, reference a recent speech or article, or use the name of someone who actually recommended you initiate contact. What you don't want to say is anything that smacks of criticism; i.e., "Given your string of recent flops at the box office, I thought you'd like to read a really *good* script ... "

3. Film companies are always interested in bodies of work which have already been launched in another medium and/or won awards. The fact that you have been able to sell it elsewhere and/or garnered favorable review indicates that you have a commercially viable product to pitch.

4. Provide a brief overview of what your project is about. The operative word here is brief.

5. Why should a studio take on this particular project? Time, cost, and resources are a big factor in what gets picked up and what gets dismissed.

6. Condense your professional background information and yet demonstrate that you've had enough experience for the studio to pay attention to you. Personal tidbits should not be included unless they have some direct bearing on how the script came into being.

7. Never, ever send a script unless you are asked to do so. In fact, many studios won't even open an envelope if it looks like an unsolicited script might be enclosed.

Note: If you just can't resist including your resume, it should be placed directly behind the cover letter and both pages folded as one. The self-addressed, stamped envelope should be folded in thirds behind the correspondence.

Your Assignment

Taking the guidelines above to heart, write three different practice cover letters to "sell" your script to a potential producer. Distribute them to your friends and pay attention to their feedback regarding the strong and weak points of each letter. Revise accordingly.

A Primer on Perfect Packaging

You may have written the best script in the universe, but if it is packaged improperly, it won't get a serious look by a buyer or contest judge. Here are the rules. Follow them.

1. Always submit a freshly printed out copy each time. It is worth the expense.

2. Use white, tan, light blue or light grey cover stock for the front and back. The cover should contain only the title and the author's name. The first page of the submission should contain the title, author's name, WGA or U.S. Copyright registration number, and correct mailing address, phone number, and e-mail.

3. Use #6 brass brads to bind the project. Never use a binder, metal slide fasteners, or Velo plastic strips.

4. Do not write the title on the side binding.

5. Submit the script in an envelope that will be easy for the recipient to open. Layers of heavy-duty tape on the outside or gobs of gray fluffy insulation on the inside are annoying.

6. Always enclose a self-addressed stamped envelope if you want your script returned. It's also a good idea to include a self-addressed, stamped postcard whereby the recipient can confirm that the material has been received.

Age Is a Matter of Mind: An Interview with Thomas Veness

Considering that young people are a primary economic force driving ticket sales for today's films, it's not surprising that many of them are also gravitating toward penning original scripts and stepping behind the cameras. Mr. Thomas Veness is one such entrepreneur who believed in getting an early start on his dream of becoming a filmmaker. Thomas was born in 1981 in London and has lived ever since in a small part of North London called Crouch End. His first foray into film was at seventeen when he directed a music video which won a local competition supported by a neighboring production company. With the first prize of £500, he invested in his film and video training at the London College of Printing where he made three short films: *Life*, *Make Up* and *Room 13*. He was then commissioned by Retina Productions to make *Weekend* which was an adaptation of Jean Luc Godard's film of the same name. Thomas has worked as a continuity editor, cinematographer, first AD and editor. In November 2000, he met producer Aidan Williams and began writing the screenplay for their first feature film. The two also made their first short film together, *Shades of Time*, in addition to running a production company targeted to assisting young writers/directors/producers.

Q: What was the defining moment when you first knew that you wanted a career in film?

A: I became interested in cinema when I was four years old. My grandparents used to show me classic films every Sunday afternoon. The first film I remember seeing and liking was Laurence Olivier's *Hamlet*. My grandfather was a projectionist for many years and he always discusses the aesthetics of film and cinema with me. My mother also has a huge passion for cinema and she always takes me to see a whole range of films. I remember her taking me to see Robert Bresson films when I was very young. This showed me that cinema existed in places apart from America! My mother became my advisor and educated me in cinema. I knew I wanted to make films when I was fifteen and started studying Media at school. I became interested in writing and writers like David Mamet and Woody Allen. I started writing short films. Most importantly, I felt I had a voice, something new to say like Godard or Kiarostami. I knew I wanted to be fresh and diverse.

Q: What resources were available in your community for learning about your chosen career?

A: Near where I live there is a cinema called The Phoenix which has helped me see films from all over the world. Local independent cinemas are important as they show a diverse range of cinema. When I was sixteen, school enabled me to use cameras and make my first films and learn what it's like working within a team.

Q: What about books?

A: Reference books are important but also tricky because invariably they can be someone else's opinion. I always try to buy books containing works or writing from a certain director or writer.

Q: What did you have to teach yourself because there was no one available to ask?

A: I had to learn how to get into the industry and use every possible contact I had to get my first bit of experience. It's very easy to find someone who works in film/TV. By going to film school for a year when I was eighteen, I was introduced to other young people wanting to make films. It also enabled me to use more advanced equipment.

Q: What's your favorite film and why?

A: It is very difficult to say what is my favorite film, but my favorite director is Leos Carax and my favourite film of his is *Les Amants Du Pont Neuf.* I love it because of its beauty and silence. It is also the most realistic film I have seen about people and their lives. Carax is not very well known but he should be! He is one of the most interesting and diverse filmmakers there is. His work is always exciting and uncertain and he is a major influence on my work. French cinema is often discussed in a very complex manner and people are made to feel that they have to be an intellectual to understand it. This is wrong and (is the reason) why commercial cinema dominates and restricts young filmmakers of all backgrounds (from) breaking through. It's important to watch as many different types of cinema as you can. You will see more and learn more.

Q: Tell us about your current production.

A: I have just finished my fifth short film *Shades of Time*, which I wrote, directed and did the cinematography for. The film is in aid of a feature film that I have written and will direct in the near future. I met my producer, who is the same age as me, and we instantly knew we wanted to make films together. The film contains very difficult issues like homelessness and the effects of rape on a young woman. This is surrounded by a thriller plot line to catch the man who committed the attack. The film is in development and we have received the first part of development funds as well as securing copyrights on the film. We are currently looking for the rest of the funding and I am finishing the fourth draft after it has been read by the lead actors. We have received interest from Jeremy Theobald, who starred in Christopher Nolan's *Following*. The other actors in the film will all be fresh new faces.

Q: Is it hard to get a film made in the U.K.?

A: British cinema is struggling, because they are making products to sell to the States. Instead, the industry should help new talent of all backgrounds to make films that are fresh and diverse.

16. Font type is always Times New Roman.

If you answered false to each of the above, go to the head of the class! If your score wasn't quite as stellar, pay close attention to this chapter.

Formatting

The following is a nifty checklist to refer to as you prepare your script for contests or agency/production submission. You may have the very best story the Western Hemisphere has ever seen, but if the format shouts "amateur," you're not going to get it in the front door.

1. **Character Names** are capitalized in dialog blocks and the first time they appear in the script. They are not capitalized in conversation (i.e., Hi, MARY) or subsequent appearances throughout the story.

2. **A Synopsis** is not included anywhere in the script. It will have been included in your initial cover letter which precipitated your being invited to submit the full screenplay for consideration. You also need to keep in mind that a synopsis increases a studio reader's inclination to pretend he or she read the full script. Don't make it easy for them to reject you.

3. **The Title Page** of the script should always include your name, address, phone number and e-mail address. Should the screenplay become separated from your cover letter, the agent or studio would have no way of reaching you if all they had to go on was just the title.

4. Do *not* include a cast of characters with the script. Allow each one to be introduced with each turn of the page.

5. Do *not* number your scenes or your acts. The difference between a reading script and a shooting script is that the reading script is strictly meant to be *read*. Once the story is in production, a new series of numbers will be added by the director indicating the sequence in which they will actually be shot. And, even though there is considerable emphasis on the three-act structure of screenwriting, do *not* identify your segments as Act I, II and III. Save the "act" differentiations for when you are writing stage plays.

6. Do not include camera directions in your script unless it is absolutely essential. Your job is to write. The director's job is to figure out how to convey all of this visually. You need to trust that he or she will figure out how best to do this.

7. Do not justify the right margins.

8. There are split views on whether every SOUND EFFECT should be capitalized. Personally, I think that CAPITALIZING every SOUND that goes OFF with a BANG or a WHOOSH makes a script ANNOYING to read.

9. **Page Numbers** should be shown in the upper right hand corner of each page.

10. If you read older books on the topic of screenwriting, the use of "CONTINUED" at the bottom and top of each page was pretty common. Eventually, however, someone had the wits to say, "Aren't readers smart enough to know to turn to the next page?" Newer screenwriting books advise against it.

11. Never hyphenate lines of dialog in your script.

12. **Transitions** to new scenes are placed at the right margin, starting specifically at column #55. The words "CUT TO" should only be used if you're going to a completely different scene, not just to a different angle within the same scene.

13. Neither the copyright year nor the WGA registration number should appear anywhere on your script.

14. **Minor Characters** who are only employed for ambiance or who have only one line of dialog do not need to have names. Nor do you need to establish extensive backgrounds for these people. If it's never going to come out in the context of the plot, there's no reason for you to have to spend time fabricating it. If you really like them that much, you can always give them the lead in your next film.

15. Much as I hate to kill trees, the reality nonetheless stands that your script should always be printed on only one side of the paper, not two.

16. The industry standard is Courier 12.

Going by the Numbers

There are a number of scriptwriting software programs currently on the market. Although they can be pricey, you need to be aware that your competition is probably already using them to make their manuscripts look as professional as possible. While you're saving up to make that kind of investment yourself, here are the basic numbers you need to work with in the interim:

At ten character columns per inch, your sluglines should start at Column #15. This will give you a 1½-inch left margin, which is perfect for when the manuscript is bound with brass brads. Character names start at Column #35 and are not centered above the dialog. If you are using parenthetical phrases to indicate how a line is said, these start at Column #30 and run to Column #50. (Use parenthetical remarks sparingly!) Dialog is placed between Columns #25 and #55. Don't right-justify, either. Leave a ragged edge. Transitional directions such as DISSOLVE TO and CUT TO start at Column #55 but go no farther than Column #75. This leaves you with a right hand margin of one inch. Single space within the dialog paragraphs and double space to separate the paragraphs themselves.

Neatness Counts!

Not so very long ago, I received in the mail a "personal" postcard from a fledging publishing house, inquiring whether I'd like to have them publish one of my books. They even went so far as to identify it by its correct title and mention that they had been enthusiastically referred to me by someone else.

Knowing this much, of course, it shouldn't have been that difficult for them to further ascertain that the book was already published. Nonetheless, I decided to assume that perhaps they had been living at the bottom of a well for the past two years and simply liked the story so much that it totally blinded them to the possibility of another publisher liking it first.

This in mind, I moved on to assess the quality of their approach. Eeek! It was a garden-variety plain white postcard upon which the sender had crookedly Scotch-taped both the return and delivery addresses. (Did I mention that my last name was missing the second "t"?) The flip-side of the card — the introduction to the company itself — was typed on a manual typewriter (yes, such things still exist) which hadn't seen a ribbon-change in eons.

OK, I rationalized, perhaps the sender's secretary was laying in traction in a hospital, the latest order for professional letterhead was delayed at the printer's, and the sender suddenly found himself in a rolling blackout with only an inch-high candle and a rusty Underwood by which to craft his plucky note to moi. Could I cast aside my initial assumptions about the integrity of the business, opting to believe instead in the sincerity of this amateurish attempt to grab my attention for a "once-in-a-lifetime opportunity"? Or was the whimsical side of my personality just looking for a ripe opportunity to illustrate a salient point in this chapter regarding the importance of putting your best foot forward?

I responded to the sender's e-mail invitation to "learn more." What I subsequently learned was that, "for the start-up fee of only $1,000," this person would put my book in print *and* let me keep a whopping ten percent of every copy sold. I wrote back and, quite bluntly, asked why I should fork over $1,000 to someone who couldn't put together a decent postcard of introduction. How did I know, for instance, that they wouldn't type up my book on a vintage Underwood with a bad ribbon, photocopy the whole thing on cheap paper, and throw a rubberband around it before stuffing it in an envelope to a buyer?

Had they chosen to respond to my question (which they ultimately didn't), I'm sure they would have insisted, "Well, obviously the finished product will be perfect. We were just trying to save ourselves a little time and money at the front end and cut to the chase."

The reality is that you never get a second chance to make a good first impression, no matter *how* much time and money you're trying to save.

The Cover Letter: Your Calling Card

A cover letter isn't just a piece of paper that goes on the front of your project. It can be the door-opener — or door-slammer — for your script. It all depends on how much you reveal ... and how well you say it. Bottom line: Keep it short and to the point.

Let's take a look at the example below:

1. Bryn Myrddin Studios

    Attn: Susan Blondin, Vice President

    777 Serendipity Drive

    Beverly Hills, CA 90210

Dear Ms. Blondin:

2. Your name was graciously provided to me by Christopher Mitchell, one of your fellow panel members at the recent ASA Directors Forum in Burbank. I have followed your work for several years and have recently completed a new script entitled *Everything But The Groom,* which I believe meets Bryn Myrddin's standards for contemporary romantic comedy. 3. It is adapted from one of my published novels, which is currently available as an e-book through New Concepts Publishing.

4. The premise of the story is that a bridal consultant is contracted to produce the wedding-of-the-century at the private home of a wealthy family in Mill Valley, California. The catch? The too rich/too thin/too snooty bride is marrying Kate's former boyfriend and is taking every opportunity to flaunt her victory and push Kate's buttons. As if matters weren't difficult enough, Kate's regular photographer has an emergency which necessitates him sending an old Army pal, Jack, to cover the nuptials. Jack, however, has his own agenda for being at the Murchie estate that day. 5. The time frame of the story is forty-eight hours, there are no expensive special effects, and everything necessary for the wedding-day scene can easily be rented from — where else — any place in town that caters to real weddings.

6. My publishing credits to date include seventeen books, ninety-eight plays and musicals, and over 250 magazine and newspaper articles. I have also worked in radio and cable television, and am currently teaching an online screenwriting course through WriteRead

University. **7.** Upon request, I would be happy to send you a treatment or the full script, along with a standard industry release.

I look forward to hearing from you at your earliest convenience.

Christina Hamlett

Address

Phone

E-mail

SASE

1. Always address your inquiry to a specific individual ... and spell his or her name correctly! Your stationery should be conservative and professional. This is not the place for neon paper, quirky-sized envelopes, or glittery stars that fall out on their shoes. I even know one writer who swears that "neutral" postage stamps (i.e., the U.S. flag) make a better impression than animals, pop art, or dead celebrities. Return address labels should be neutral as well, no matter how much you may personally favor Snoopy, smiley faces or Psalm snippets. One more reminder: using spell-check on the body of the letter isn't enough. Have at least half a dozen readers proof your correspondence before it goes anywhere.

2. A personal connection is always beneficial, whether it's to comment on a specific work, reference a recent speech or article, or use the name of someone who actually recommended you initiate contact. What you don't want to say is anything that smacks of criticism; i.e., "Given your string of recent flops at the box office, I thought you'd like to read a really *good* script ... "

3. Film companies are always interested in bodies of work which have already been launched in another medium and/or won awards. The fact that you have been able to sell it elsewhere and/or garnered favorable review indicates that you have a commercially viable product to pitch.

4. Provide a brief overview of what your project is about. The operative word here is brief.

5. Why should a studio take on this particular project? Time, cost, and resources are a big factor in what gets picked up and what gets dismissed.

6. Condense your professional background information and yet demonstrate that you've had enough experience for the studio to pay attention to you. Personal tidbits should not be included unless they have some direct bearing on how the script came into being.

7. Never, ever send a script unless you are asked to do so. In fact, many studios won't even open an envelope if it looks like an unsolicited script might be enclosed.

Note: If you just can't resist including your resume, it should be placed directly behind the cover letter and both pages folded as one. The self-addressed, stamped envelope should be folded in thirds behind the correspondence.

Your Assignment

Taking the guidelines above to heart, write three different practice cover letters to "sell" your script to a potential producer. Distribute them to your friends and pay attention to their feedback regarding the strong and weak points of each letter. Revise accordingly.

A Primer on Perfect Packaging

You may have written the best script in the universe, but if it is packaged improperly, it won't get a serious look by a buyer or contest judge. Here are the rules. Follow them.

1. Always submit a freshly printed out copy each time. It is worth the expense.

2. Use white, tan, light blue or light grey cover stock for the front and back. The cover should contain only the title and the author's name. The first page of the submission should contain the title, author's name, WGA or U.S. Copyright registration number, and correct mailing address, phone number, and e-mail.

3. Use #6 brass brads to bind the project. Never use a binder, metal slide fasteners, or Velo plastic strips.

4. Do not write the title on the side binding.

5. Submit the script in an envelope that will be easy for the recipient to open. Layers of heavy-duty tape on the outside or gobs of gray fluffy insulation on the inside are annoying.

6. Always enclose a self-addressed stamped envelope if you want your script returned. It's also a good idea to include a self-addressed, stamped postcard whereby the recipient can confirm that the material has been received.

Age Is a Matter of Mind:
An Interview with Thomas Veness

Considering that young people are a primary economic force driving ticket sales for today's films, it's not surprising that many of them are also gravitating toward penning original scripts and stepping behind the cameras. Mr. Thomas Veness is one such entrepreneur who believed in getting an early start on his dream of becoming a filmmaker. Thomas was born in 1981 in London and has lived ever since in a small part of North London called Crouch End. His first foray into film was at seventeen when he directed a music video which won a local competition supported by a neighboring production company. With the first prize of £500, he invested in his film and video training at the London College of Printing where he made three short films: *Life*, *Make Up* and *Room 13*. He was then commissioned by Retina Productions to make *Weekend* which was an adaptation of Jean Luc Godard's film of the same name. Thomas has worked as a continuity editor, cinematographer, first AD and editor. In November 2000, he met producer Aidan Williams and began writing the screenplay for their first feature film. The two also made their first short film together, *Shades of Time*, in addition to running a production company targeted to assisting young writers/directors/producers.

Q: What was the defining moment when you first knew that you wanted a career in film?

A: I became interested in cinema when I was four years old. My grandparents used to show me classic films every Sunday afternoon. The first film I remember seeing and liking was Laurence Olivier's *Hamlet*. My grandfather was a projectionist for many years and he always discusses the aesthetics of film and cinema with me. My mother also has a huge passion for cinema and she always takes me to see a whole range of films. I remember her taking me to see Robert Bresson films when I was very young. This showed me that cinema existed in places apart from America! My mother became my advisor and educated me in cinema. I knew I wanted to make films when I was fifteen and started studying Media at school. I became interested in writing and writers like David Mamet and Woody Allen. I started writing short films. Most importantly, I felt I had a voice, something new to say like Godard or Kiarostami. I knew I wanted to be fresh and diverse.

Q: **What resources were available in your community for learning about your chosen career?**

A: Near where I live there is a cinema called The Phoenix which has helped me see films from all over the world. Local independent cinemas are important as they show a diverse range of cinema. When I was sixteen, school enabled me to use cameras and make my first films and learn what it's like working within a team.

Q: **What about books?**

A: Reference books are important but also tricky because invariably they can be someone else's opinion. I always try to buy books containing works or writing from a certain director or writer.

Q: **What did you have to teach yourself because there was no one available to ask?**

A: I had to learn how to get into the industry and use every possible contact I had to get my first bit of experience. It's very easy to find someone who works in film/TV. By going to film school for a year when I was eighteen, I was introduced to other young people wanting to make films. It also enabled me to use more advanced equipment.

Q: What's your favorite film and why?

A: It is very difficult to say what is my favorite film, but my favorite director is Leos Carax and my favourite film of his is *Les Amants Du Pont Neuf.* I love it because of its beauty and silence. It is also the most realistic film I have seen about people and their lives. Carax is not very well known but he should be! He is one of the most interesting and diverse filmmakers there is. His work is always exciting and uncertain and he is a major influence on my work. French cinema is often discussed in a very complex manner and people are made to feel that they have to be an intellectual to understand it. This is wrong and (is the reason) why commercial cinema dominates and restricts young filmmakers of all backgrounds (from) breaking through. It's important to watch as many different types of cinema as you can. You will see more and learn more.

Q: Tell us about your current production.

A: I have just finished my fifth short film *Shades of Time*, which I wrote, directed and did the cinematography for. The film is in aid of a feature film that I have written and will direct in the near future. I met my producer, who is the same age as me, and we instantly knew we wanted to make films together. The film contains very difficult issues like homelessness and the effects of rape on a young woman. This is surrounded by a thriller plot line to catch the man who committed the attack. The film is in development and we have received the first part of development funds as well as securing copyrights on the film. We are currently looking for the rest of the funding and I am finishing the fourth draft after it has been read by the lead actors. We have received interest from Jeremy Theobald, who starred in Christopher Nolan's *Following*. The other actors in the film will all be fresh new faces.

Q: Is it hard to get a film made in the U.K.?

A: British cinema is struggling, because they are making products to sell to the States. Instead, the industry should help new talent of all backgrounds to make films that are fresh and diverse.

Q: **What was the best advice anyone gave you about breaking into the film business?**

A: The advice that I have been given is probably the same as lots of people:

- It's important to accept rejection and learn from your mistakes. Scripts I read now from when I was fifteen are awful, but they all helped me learn. I'm sure that will be the case when I am fifty and I read things I have done now! It's all a stage of progression.

- When your scripts get rejected, it is difficult, but it is important to know the market that you are trying to sell your films to. I wrote a short film last year which was about young homeless people living in London. I got a very good response to it and many people liked it but felt it was too challenging. This made no sense to me but showed how my work was seen in the marketplace.

- It's important to keep your integrity in what you are trying to create and eventually you will be lucky and someone will pick up on it. Two main things I have learned as a director is to respect and understand your cast and crew. Make everyone feel they are important to the artistic process! Create a good atmosphere on the set. If the environment is enjoyable, then working hard is made easier. The business is very hard especially for young people like myself and you will get disappointments.

- Take in the advice that you feel is important to know. Some people will be very negative as they simply do not want you to succeed.

Q: **Let's say that you're sixteen years old and have just written what you think is a pretty good short. What should you do next?**

A: My suggestion would be to try and raise enough money to pay for stock and food, etc. Borrow a camera or rent one. Find a group of people (either friends or fellow students) and make the film. It's great to start early as you get a head start. It is very difficult to be taken seriously at such a young age, but there are schemes designed to help young people make films. When you are young, make films that are simple and striking. I tried to make films that were way too complex for me and I didn't have the experience or the equipment to make them work. Don't worry about mistakes that you make. Enjoy the experience and learn from it! If you are passionate, you put a huge amount of expectation on your shoulders; don't worry if the film isn't what you expected. You can't be seen as a genius of filmmaking at sixteen or twenty. It takes years to learn how to make films. You will pick up the technical and creative knowledge as you go along.

Topics to Think About and Talk About

1. How often do you watch films? In general, do you watch films more for entertainment or for educating yourself as an aspiring screenwriter? What was the last film you watched and what did you learn from it?

2. List five resources available to you (competitions, job opportunities, educational programs, etc.) to help advance your career as a screenwriter. In 100 words or less, write down what you intend to do in the next six months to take advantage of the opportunities you have listed.

3. What is the first film you remember watching? What did you learn from it? Have you watched it again? If so, have your opinions changed from the first time you saw it? Describe the difference in 100 words or less.

Chapter 6
How Do You Write Good Dialog?

For as many conversations as we engage in every day — and as many more as we can't help but eavesdrop on — it's not always easy to duplicate that kind of energy, flow, and realism in a screenplay. By learning to be a better listener, here are some ways to make your characters better talkers!

He Said, She Said

For new screenwriters, crafting credible conversation is a major challenge. Too often someone who would be better suited to writing novels or short stories tries to put words in the mouths of live actors. It's a dead giveaway that you don't know what you're doing. Why? Because: 1. the characters all talk exactly the same way, 2. they talk more eloquently than normal people ever do, or 3. they talk way too much!

The Critical Dos and Don'ts of Dialog

Don't have your characters waste time talking about nothing. You only have 120 pages to tell this story, remember? Make every bit of dialog count. If a conversation or reminiscence does not advance the plot, leave it out!

Try to avoid long monologs unless it's pertinent to the character or plot. If a character has something particularly lengthy to say, break it up with interruptions from his or her listeners or bits of business/action for variety.

A pet peeve of mine is when characters explain things to each other that, presumably, they already know. For example:

"Well! If it isn't my cousin Bob from Dubuque! How have you been, Bob? And are you still involved in that telemarketing campaign to sell crawdads to the Asian market which my ex-wife, Maris, told you would be a good investment?"

Such a contrived device attempts to fill in the blanks for the audience but in no way represents realistic banter.

71

Speaking of realism, enlist your friends and fellow students to read your scenes out loud for you after you have written them. Are your sentences so long that the actors could not conceivably take a big enough breath to deliver them? Have you used too many "s's" or combinations that make for outrageous tongue-twisters? Have you accounted for the fact that a lot of people speak in fragments, use slang, and get interrupted?

You also need to remember in film that much can be conveyed without words, and take every advantage to let your characters' body language and facial expressions reveal something beyond the convenience of dialog.

Are your characters doing something visually compelling while they are talking/not talking? Do not, and I repeat, do not just put your characters at a table and have them yak back and forth. Make them move!

Learning by Example

One of the best places to learn about writing scripts is to read scripts ... and as many of them as you can! Some good resources to check out on the Internet are:

www.script-o-rama.com

www.scriptdude.com

or outlets such as:

Hollywood Collectibles

308 West Verdugo Ave., #103

Burbank, CA 91502

(818) 845-5450

(For $2, they'll send a comprehensive catalog of
movie and television scripts.)

In addition, you'll find everything from classics to hot new releases at: www.scriptshack.com, And, for those harder-to-find screenplays, Harvest Moon Publishing located at www.harvestmoon.com/default.asp. Writers Digest Books has also expanded their offering of film hits such as *Life Is Beautiful* and *Shakespeare in Love*. If you're on their mailing list, it's well worth looking into!

Your Assignment

Locate the screenplay of your favorite film and, while playing the film on a VCR, compare how what is written on the page translates to what you are actually seeing on the screen.

First Appearances

When it comes to introducing characters in a scene for the first time, my beginning screenwriting students usually fall into one of two categories:

1. Those who explain too much.

2. Those who leave us clueless.

Contrivance is the biggest sin among those who strive to impart the entire backstory through doofy dialog. Example:

JACK: Why, if it isn't my older brother Cecil who just returned from Monaco with his wife Sophie and stepson Arnold! And this must be your longtime girlfriend, Melanie, from Michigan.

CECIL: Yes, it is, Jack. And are you still working at the same job as a piano tuner here in Poughkeepsie with your best friend Al?

JACK: Yes, I am, Cecil.

CECIL: That's great, Jack. And how is your wife, Ann?

Arghghgh! Real people don't talk this way. Nor do they feel compelled to keep repeating each other's names.

On the flip side are writers who imbed reams of background in the narrative. Example:

FIONA enters. She is Larry's thrice-divorced cousin and is currently getting over her affair with Martin, whose wife Alice has cancer and has gone to Cleveland to care for her daughter from a previous marriage to Larry's boss, Sam.

You need to remember that the audience doesn't have a printed program to follow all this scintillating intrigue. Cardinal rule: if the camera can't film it and the dialog doesn't reveal it, leave it out!

How then, do you introduce your players and their histories without making it sound like a Weight Watchers meeting?

Try these for some variety:

1. Office phone calls (either outgoing or incoming)
2. Name tags (for those in service professions)
3. Office titles on doors
4. Parties/business scenarios whereby introductions are natural
5. Third-party references prior to appearance
6. CU's (close-up's) of correspondence opened byaddressee
7. Soliloquies where characters talk to themselves
8. VO's (voice over's) which book-end the film or run continuously throughout
9. Paging (effective in hospital scenes)
10. Newspaper/magazine matchcuts

Finally, don't forget the power of body language and facial expressions to convey relationship hints and stir viewer interest before your characters ever utter a word.

Your Assignment

How have you introduced the protagonist into your story? Would a different "entrance" be more effective? Come up with three new ways to bring him or her on the scene. Repeat the same process with your story's villain.

Not Without Purpose

Film dialog serves four main functions:

1. To reveal character,
2. To advance the plot,
3. To explain the past, and
4. To articulate feelings that can't be conveyed visually.

If your characters' conversations aren't accomplishing one or more of the above, cut them out!! Unlike the rambling chatter we engage in every day with family and friends, "screen talk" needs to have a good reason to be there. Ideally, it should also serve more than just one purpose at a time.

For instance, let's say you have a protagonist who admits, "I've been terrified of the water — even wading pools — ever since I saw my cousin drown in the Hudson when I was a kid."

This line:

1. Reveals that he or she is vulnerable,

2. Suggests that water will make an unbidden appearance somewhere in this story and force the protagonist to confront his or her fears,

3. Explains the source of the fear, in addition to establishing familial and geographical connections, and

4. Expresses what could otherwise only be shown in a flashback.

Your Assignment

The following scenarios will hone your dialog-writing skills. For each scene, write one page of dialog. You can have as many or as few characters as you want, but every line spoken should be assessed in terms of what purpose(s) it fills:

- A chance encounter with an ex-roommate with whom things ended badly.

- A winning lottery ticket sparks controversy on how to spend the prize.

- Mistaken identity at a hospital.

- A wedding where one of the principal players hasn't shown up yet.

- A blind date in which both sides discover they have more in common than they expected.

The Danger of Dialects

I'm going to make a confession about *Gone with the Wind*. The fact of the matter is that, voracious reader as I am, there were quite a few pages I opted to skip when it first fell into my hands in high school. No, it wasn't because I was impatient to see what Scarlett and Rhett would do next (oh, all right, maybe it was *partly* because of that). Nor was it because I pretty much knew how the Civil War came out and thought all of the expositional battle scenes were tedious.

The real reason is that I got vexed with the phonetically illustrative Southern dialect because it slowed down the momentum, forcing me to concentrate on the pronunciation of individual words instead of the flow of emotions being evoked. That same vexation surfaced years later when I encountered Diana Gabaldon's Scottish time-travel novels about the star-crossed lovers, Jamie and Claire. Passionate as I am about Highland history (I got married in a Scottish castle), the author's good intentions to capture the full texture of a good brogue became cumbersome when spread over the course of too many pages.

This may seem like an odd remark coming from someone who not only spent almost two decades in theatre but learned to master a number of useful and/or exotic dialects in the process. Wouldn't I want to know how to convincingly mimic a foreign tongue? As an actress, yes. As a reader, no. And readers, more than likely, are the personages who will initially be reading your script.

Rather than slog down the pace by trying to phonetically capture the meter and pronunciation of foreign and regional characters in your script, concentrate on their colloquial expressions and speech patterns instead. For instance, an Englishman can easily be conveyed with phrases such as, "Oh I say we'd best queue up for the lift post-haste," *queue, lift,* and *post-haste* being easily recognizable as the U.K. versions of *line up, elevator,* and *quickly.* If in doubt, go find someone who is actually *from* the region whose speech patterns you are trying to capture and use them as a resource.

Above all, be *consistent* if you are attempting to do this type of dialog. Among the most common mistakes I find with new students is when they to try to imitate black, urban lingo (difficult to do when you are white and live in the middle-class suburbs of Iowa) and go from, "Yo, Theo, whassup, bro?" to the same character suddenly becoming articulate on the next page and saying, "I don't believe that we've been introduced."

Where the Actors Are

Actors, like sharks, need to keep moving forward in order to survive. No sooner does their current film wrap than they are already in production or on the precipice of production for their next one.

So what kind of scripts are they looking for? Some actors like to stick to tried-and-true roles or those genres in which they have already won recognition and acclaim. Others like to explore new ground, which will not only stretch their boundaries as performers but also maximize their options for future employment.

Most of the new scripts come to them through their agents, who also need to keep moving forward. They accomplish this by: 1. screening and forwarding those scripts which best meet the actor's interests and parameters and 2. aggressively pursuing specific roles which they know have not yet been cast.

Actors additionally create opportunities for themselves via mediums outside of film; i.e., falling in love with a book and deeming that the lead character is one whom he or she would be perfect to recreate on the big screen. In cases such as these, the next step is to seek out the author, option the novel, and either engage the author to adapt the actual screenplay or turn the project over to an existing screenwriter for development.

If, like me, you have a published novel that you think would be right for a particular star, don't hesitate to send it out yourself, or if you have an agent, request that your agent make the appropriate inquiries to the star's representative. You may or may not be asked to adapt the script. That's not what's important. What's important is that you still get credit on the screen ("Based on the novel by_____") and have put your storytelling abilities under the nose of an actor who, if the film is successfull, just might ask you to write something new!

It should also be kept in mind that actors — like everyone else — have passions, pet projects, and worthy causes that they endorse (i.e., animals rights, research funding for diseases, environmental issues, etc.). Not only do these provide a ready-made forum for initiating communication with them, apart from their glamorous day-jobs, but also create an opportunity to deliver a script with a unique set of merits.

Fellow screenwriter Jenna Glatzer is the webmistress of the popular Absolute Write (http://www.absolutewrite.com), a lively website with articles, interviews, and links to publishing, playwriting, and screenwriting. She has used her initiative to pitch a contemporary script on a subject dear to one actor's heart:

Never overlook any possible source for publicity. If your script is ready to roll, tell the world about it. I wrote a TV movie called *Seeing the Light* about a young man with Down Syndrome, and my father suggested that I send the script to the National Down Syndrome Society. He said, "You never know. They may have contacts in the film industry."

I thought it was a long shot, but I did it, mostly to appease him. A few weeks later, I got a phone call from Chris Burke, the actor who played "Corky" on the TV series *Life Goes On*. He introduced himself and told me that he wanted to play the lead role. We met a few weeks later, and he is now attached to the script.

The funny part of that story? I had already contacted Chris' agent. He wouldn't even look at the script. The Down Syndrome association had saved my script, so when Chris walked in their door for a presentation, they handed it to him personally.

I've learned my lesson. Explore every possible avenue. Don't wait for Hollywood to come to you. Think hard about any special interest groups, communities, or organizations that might have an interest in your story, and ask for their help in promoting your script.

Star Gazing

Stymied on how to reach the stars? The following sites on your computer are an excellent jumping-off place.

Eagle i. Website launched by Lone Eagle Publishing
www.loneeagle.com

Updated on a weekly basis and at the current $20 per month subscription cost, this is a site which allows you to search a database of more than 6,000 working actors.

Screen Actors Guild

www.sag.com

This is generally the organization which first springs to mind when one is seeking information on specific actors. Suffice it to say, it is not as user-friendly to authors as one might assume. There is, however, an Actor Locator hotline at (323) 549-6737 which enables screenwriters to make three requests at a time regarding those agents amenable to reviewing new scripts for their clients. Given the number of other resources available on the Internet, I'd personally save this route (and save the long distance charge) as a last resort.

Film Partners

www.filmpartners.com/index.cfm?action=starsagent

There is no charge at this film site, which allows you to do a star search and find out who is representing whom. Even better, if the star you are looking for isn't in the listing, there is a feature which enables you to query the Film Partners staff; they can generally get back to you with a name and contact information in less than forty-eight hours.

ScriptSales

www.scriptsales.com

One of the best links found at this site is an extensive listing of film and television production companies. What's pertinent about this list is the fact that many of them are owned by actors and actresses who, in addition to using them as tax write-offs, wanted to establish companies which could produce films consistent with their individualized tastes and interests. Jodie Foster, Antonio Banderas, Jason Alexander, and Sigourney Weaver are just a few of the names you'll find there.

And Speaking of Actors ...

Don't overlook that wealth of talent playing in your own school and neighborhood theatres while your script is still a work-in-progress. Certainly one of the biggest advantages I had when I first tried my hand at playwriting was that I already had my own touring acting company. What better way to test new dialog and dynamics than by hearing the words spoken by real performers and gauging the reactions of real audiences.

Using local actors to read for you in the screenwriting process is particularly valuable, as whimsically illustrated by Liverpool writer/actor Tommy Donbavand (http://www.wobblebottom.com):

I'm presuming you don't work in a theatre, or at the very least, a rest home for retired thespians — although if you do, simply provide some light refreshments or a solid defibrillation unit (depending on which category you fall into).

If professional actors are hard to come by, then your next stop should be your local amateur dramatic group. Keep an eye on the What's On section of your local newspaper to discover their whereabouts. You should find anyone interested in acting more than willing to take part — even if only because they're hoping the film will get made, and they'll have the upper hand on Johnny Depp when it comes to casting. ("He doesn't understand the motivation of the cyborg captain the way I do. I've played him, darling.") This is the only time that you, as a screenwriter, will feel any sense of power in this business.

One other option is the drama club or theatre class at your local school or college. If you can convince the teacher that your project will be of great educational value to the students, you should be home free (and of course, there's always the chance you'll get the class with Spielberg's niece in it).

Once you have your cast, you'll need to provide everyone with a copy of the script (no, they can't look over one another's shoulders). If you have plenty of minor characters in your screenplay, consider assigning them all to just one or two of your cast. Not only will this keep your printing costs down, but will also avoid an enthusiastic thespian waiting all afternoon, just to yell "Look out!" as PASSER BY on page 94. Make sure you deliver the scripts well in advance of the reading. Your actors need plenty of time to get inside your characters' heads. I also find it very useful to record the session on cassette, so that I can listen back later on and make notes.

Here's what I discovered from my own reading: I was describing things that didn't need describing. I had a scene early on in the script set in a bank. I'd described the layout, the décor, and the customers — albeit briefly, but it took up a couple of lines. Not necessary. Most people know what the interior of a bank looks like, and if the layout isn't vital to the script, don't mention it. It might only be a line or two, but multiply that by every scene, and you can lose a couple of pages by taking it all out.

My protagonist wasn't active enough. I hadn't realized it before, but a good deal of my protagonist's decisions were being made for him by his sidekick. This only came to light when the guy playing the sidekick was getting all the laughs, and the main character dutifully followed along with his suggestions. Never forget that your protagonist (or antagonist) must drive the story forward.

My third act sucked. As written, the entire climax of the script took place in a rapidly collapsing hotel. My bad guys got their just rewards, and my good guys clinched victory from the jaws of defeat. Except it all sounded incredibly dull. In the rewrite, the scene still takes place in the same crumbling hotel, but I've opened it out around the building, and been more inventive with the ways my bad guys bow out. Aside from those major points there were lines that were impossible to say, characters that disappeared for pages on end, and much, much more. But hey, you'll find this all out for yourself.

Arranging a reading will bring out the very worst in your script. In places, you'll be truly horrified at what you hear — and yes, you did write that. However, you will emerge armed with a set of rewrite notes like no other. Follow them, and your script will be several steps closer to the world-beater you always knew it was.

What Theatre Can Teach You About Film:
An Interview with Professor Jerry Abbitt

One of the most interesting common denominators I've discovered in the course of interviewing experts for this book is how each of them actually began their careers as drama students. Is there just something magical about the performing arts that helps pave the way to Hollywood? Professor Jerry Abbitt, Chair of the Department of Theater at California State University, Northridge, has taught his share of theatrical courses from freshman to graduate level for over twenty years. He has also spent many years overseeing the production program — ensuring that CSUN's mainstage plays get the production support they need from faculty and students. His insights on the educational value of "treading the boards" are shared below.

Q: **Why don't we start out with some background on who you are and what you've accomplished as department chair.**

A: I grew up in Kentucky, where I was the first person in my family to finish college. I actually started out in art and then switched to theatre as an undergraduate. I have worked in theatre from coffee houses to carnivals, from Shakespeare to saloon shows. In the summer of 1971 I was the youngest theme park general manager in America. I received my MA and MFA in scenography at Purdue, studying with professors whose training had a direct line of descent from my own personal hero, Robert Edmond Jones — a design visionary in the early to mid-twentieth century. As chair, I have presided over five very exciting years — we have expanded our community links (we're known as one of the best sources for Latino theatre, for example), have undertaken a second exchange to China, strengthened our graduate program and had undergraduates granted fellowships in graduate programs in Harvard and Yale.

Q: **What sort of theatre curriculum can be found at the Northridge campus?**

A: At CSUN, we offer undergraduates a liberal arts program. We're not a tightly focused, pre-professional program and this is by choice. This means that our aim is not to create actors, designers, directors or playwrights, but to provide a comprehensive education, through theatre, for a full range of students. In this sense, we follow Stanislavsky's advice, who once said that the best training for the theatre practitioner is life. We support our program with an extensive main-stage theatre season as an integral part of the curriculum. There is also a student-run experimental Theatre Guild season.

Q: It sounds as if you not only pack audiences into the shows but plenty of students into the classroom!

A: At the moment, we have approximately 200 theatre majors, and a small covey (fifteen to twenty) of graduate students. We also serve the entire undergraduate community at CSUN with General Education courses, such as Acting for Non-Majors, World Drama, and Creative Dramatics. We normally offer about twelve sections of Acting for Non-Majors each semester: at thirty students per class, this represents a sizable number of students!

Q: Just as a rough estimate, how many of your students who major in theatre arts actually go on to *have* a job in the performing arts or film?

A: Well, it's interesting to note that, despite the humanities-based nature of our program, I would say over half of our undergraduates go on to graduate programs in theatre or find jobs within the profession. By "within the profession" I include the film and television industry. A large number of our graduates work their way into these fields as well as live theatre.

Q: What can the live theatre experience teach you about writing for today's film industry?

A; How to tell a story! After all, that's the essence of both theatre and film. Both tell a story which helps people understand their place in the universe. In theatre, we find this in a through-line of activity with the audience being an active participant. In film, the through-line only becomes fully realized through the editing process. Aristotle listed this ordering of events (I believe his word for it was *praxis*) as the most important of his six elements.

83

Q: Although live theatre has existed far longer than the medium of film, its evolution in terms of production techniques hasn't been nearly as great.

A: It may seem that way but that's because many people don't realize that the illusionary aspect of theatre keeps going in and out of favor. In the sixteenth century, for instance, the technology and production techniques for the court masques were pretty advanced for the time. The same can be said for ancient Rome. Some of the technology utilized in staging the theatrical events in the Coliseum were very much "state of the art!" We are now at a period where the illusionary aspect is playing second fiddle to the metaphorical, but the pendulum will swing back at some point.

Q: So what do you think accounts for the longevity of live performances over electronic ones?

A: The reason for the continued life of live theatre is very simple. It's the same reason that in spite of the high quality of CD recordings there is something special about a live concert. The live performance, be it music or theatre, is a dynamic form of the art. It is every moment alive and every moment being born. The audience members are not there to just observe; they are constantly providing the performers with feedback and this guides the performers in the creation of the performance. A "frozen recording" (film or CD) doesn't have this feedback loop of "performer to audience to performer" and therein lies the essential difference. The audience is observer, not active participant.

Q: Let's say that a student asked you whether they'd be better off writing for the stage or writing for the screen, what would your answer be?

A: I'm not sure what "better off" means. There's probably more total money paid to screenwriters, but it really depends on what provides the most satisfaction on an individual basis.

Q: I think it would also depend on what you see as the future of the American stage. Is it really dead or just undergoing an undefined rebirth?

A: It is, and has always been, in the process of being reborn. In a sense, theatre is a reaction to _____ (Each artist must fill in their own blank). As long as we have human beings being conceived, born, and dying, someone will fill in the blank and theatre will be created.

Q: **Last but not least, students often cite the space and "special effects" limitations of a physical stage as a good reason not to write for the theatre. What would be your counter-argument to that?**

A: The "limitations" of a physical stage — the fact that it involves a sharing of time and space — are actually theatre's greatest assets! Everyone in theatre, whether acting, writing, providing tech support, directing or watching, takes part in a *live* dynamic process. It's active. It's involved. At its best, it's kinetic, participatory ... a community experience. Performers, designers, crew, audience — these are *live* bodies and minds connecting. The laughter, the tears, the sweat, the "aha!" moment shared in the dark — this is what theatre is all about. What writers wouldn't want to be part of this?

Topics to Think About and Talk About

1. Do you think it is important to experience acting in order to be a successful screenwriter? Please explain your answer in fifty words or less.

2. How would you distinguish the importance of plot between stage plays and film? If you think there is a difference, how does that affect your ability to be a successful screenwriter?

3. Describe whether it is easier to listen to a play or to a movie with your eyes closed, *and* whether it is easier to watch a play or a movie with no sound.

Chapter 7

What Do Each of Your Characters Want to Achieve?

Everything has a price. What is it that the characters in your story desire more than anything ... and what are they willing to sacrifice in order to get it?

Reward, Revenge, and Escape

What was it that made the evil queen in *Snow White* disguise herself in order to deliver a poisoned apple?

What was the inciting incident which thrust *Braveheart's* William Wallace into the role of a Scottish rebel?

What was Indy's father seeking in the third Indiana Jones movie?

What prompted *Butch Cassidy and the Sundance Kid* to go to Bolivia?

Why did Eliza Doolittle agree to participate in the professor's plan to turn her into *My Fair Lady*?

Why did Doc Brown modify the DeLorean for time travel in *Back to the Future*?

What did *Gone with the Wind's* Scarlett O'Hara really want?

What is the result of a *Fatal Attraction*?

Why did guests sign up for a weekend at *Fantasy Island*?

What was *The Gladiator* thinking about when he was in the Coliseum?

No matter how expansive the storyline or exotic the setting, the seeds of conflict are always rooted in three distinct human needs— the quest for reward, the passion for revenge, and the dream of escape. Sometimes a story will contain elements of all three linked by the common denominator that the primary focus is on getting the protagonist from where he or she is (or was) to where he or she ultimately wants to be at the end.

"Reward" can take several forms. There is the obvious, materialistic goal of tangible wealth: money, jewelry, land, a hidden treasure, a scientific discovery. There is also the reward of accomplishment: recognition/acceptance by one's peers, a coveted title or job, winning an important competition, reconciling with a lost friend or relation. And, of course, there is the immeasurable prize of every great romance: finding someone to love and to be loved in return.

"Revenge" is predicated on events in the past: a death, a deception, a disappointment, a dalliance. Whatever the triggering event, it is what sets the lead character on an obsessive course to see justice done, the guilty parties punished, and the soul restored to peace. Jealousy is also a common theme behind tales of revenge, wherein no expense is spared to make another character's life miserable and, accordingly, cause that person to forfeit what the opposition wants to have.

"Escape" falls into one of three categories. The first is based on the lead character's personal assessment that his or her immediate environment truly sucks and that there has to be something better "out there" if they can just muster the courage and wits to go find it; this is a voluntary and self-directed exit. The second form relates to any form of physical enslavement, confinement, mental cruelty or oppression; someone else is holding all the cards of a character's fate and preventing them — by whatever means possible — from running away to more favorable circumstances. The third variation on an escape-based theme is the "flight of fancy." The characters in this type of story yearn to either trade places with someone else or participate in an adventure that will free them from the day-to-day monotony of their lives. More often than not, the resolution is their discovery that whatever they thought they wanted to escape from wasn't really that bad after all and they can't wait to return to it.

Your Assignment

1. Name three films (besides any of the ones listed at the start of this section) in which *reward* was the primary motivation.
2. Name three films in which *revenge* took center stage.
3. Name three films in which *escape* was the main objective.

Extra Credit

1. Name three films which melded two of the primary themes. (i.e., reward and revenge). Were they equally balanced or was one of them a sub-theme of the main story?

2. Name three films which successfully utilized all three themes.

The Character Arc

When you were five years old, what was the most important thing you wanted out of life? Was it a toy? A cookie? A nap with your favorite stuffed animal?

OK, let's move the clock forward five years. What was important to you at age ten? A new bike? Getting together after school with friends? A science class that really excited you?

Where are you now? Chances are that your life these days doesn't revolve around getting a cookie. Likewise, you may not even remember your science teacher's name or exactly why the class was so much fun. Why? Because you're older and you have moved on to something else.

I like to use this analogy in explaining what is called The Character Arc — the emotional currency of the character between the time you type FADE IN until you close with FADE TO BLACK. Although your hero or heroine may not physically age during the course of the story, the events which occur during that two-hour block of cinema will impact your character's ultimate "worth" as a human being.

Let's use *My Best Friend's Wedding* as an example. At the start of the film, the Julia Roberts character is recalling the pact she had made with her best friend that the two of them would marry each other if no one else had grabbed them up in the meantime. When she learns that he is going to marry someone else, she embarks on the single-minded purpose of making his fiancée look bad so that he will call off the wedding and run away with her instead. When each of her machinations fails, she comes to realize that: 1. maybe this really is true love and 2. she needs to put the needs of her best friend's heart ahead of her own.

Bottom line: She is not the same person by the final scene that she was at the beginning. She has learned from her mistakes, and with this new awareness she will achieve a contentment with herself and her bachelorette status that was not present when we were first introduced to her character.

Your Assignment

Rent the film *Sabrina* (either the original version or the 1990s remake with Harrison Ford).

1. Who was Sabrina in love with when she was a teenager?
2. What was the primary attraction to this person?
3. What were her feelings toward his brother when she was a teenager?
4. What were the brothers' respective feelings toward her at the beginning of the film?
5. How did her experiences in Paris influence her heart and psyche?
6. How did the brothers respectively act toward Sabrina when she returned home?
7. At what point did her feelings of romance start to shift gears? Why?
8. How did Sabrina's change of heart ultimately impact the lives of everyone around her?

Analyzing Your Own Screenplay

1. Describe what your protagonist is like as a person when we first meet him or her. What does he or she want the very most when the story begins?
2. Will your character stay true to this objective all the way through the story? Why or why not?
3. Will he or she achieve the desired outcome? Will it be less? Will it be more?

How will the characters who are closest to the protagonist be affected by his or her success or failure at the story's end?

The Importance of Foreshadowing

I still cringe whenever I recall a mystery I read way back in junior high. The premise was that someone was methodically bumping off members of a graduating class who all had the misfortune of returning to the hometown for the big reunion. Having grown up on a reading diet of Nancy Drew and Agatha Christie, I fancied myself pretty good at picking out clues and solving the crime du jour.

You can, thus, imagine my annoyance when the killer turned out to be a cab driver who: 1. had absolutely no connection to any of the victims, 2. was never introduced by name, and 3. didn't even have a whole paragraph to himself until the final pages when he got caught and confessed.

What was this plot missing? The crucial element of foreshadowing at the start in order to support the "discovery" at the end.

Although audiences enjoy being surprised, what they don't like is being led astray and tricked into a lame ending. In the case of a mystery story, the assumption is in place at the beginning of the book that one of the characters is not what he or she seems to be and that it's our job as readers to pay attention to all the clues. Through the process of elimination, the suspect list grows smaller. As we near the end of the book, we're pretty confident that we know who the murderer is.

And then ...

What? Where did *this* guy come from?!

Don't you just hate it when that happens?

To paraphrase a theatrical observation made by Anton Chekhov, if a gun is shown to the audience in the first act, it better be fired by someone in the third act. Likewise, if a gunshot rings out in the third act, we better have known it was in the room or on a particular person's body in the first act.

I've always felt that the sign of a good movie or book was one that you could go back and watch or read a second time and delight in how cleverly you were manipulated into missing prominent clues which were laying right out there on the living room table. Obviously the best time to "hide" clues in any sort of story is at the very beginning ... when the audience is still trying to learn all the characters' names and concerns and acclimate themselves to the fictional environment being depicted on the screen. In an upcoming chapter on structure, you'll see how the element of foreshadowing fits into a convenient template that you can use for all of your scriptwriting projects.

The Powers That Be

In my experience of mentoring students in a wide range of genres, the second most common instance (after mysteries) in which a plot can be "foreshadowing-deficient" is in the realm of science fiction. If your own script takes place in this venue, pay special attention to what I'm about to say:

> Even in a realm that is pure fantasy and peopled with beings who have powers beyond human comprehension, that realm and its inhabitants are nonetheless governed by strict parameters that have to have been established for the audience from the very beginning.

To illustrate how these "boundaries" operate, let's say that you have a Kevin Sorbo type protagonist whose special powers have been delineated as: 1. can function without any sleep, 2. has the strength of twenty warriors, and 3. can jump to heights of 100 feet. Pretty cool, huh? Unfortunately the villain has orchestrated a cunning trap, which not only renders the protagonist a prisoner but is also about to render him dead via the release of poisonous intergalactic fumes into the chamber.

Yikes! Our dashing hero is doomed for sure!

But wait. What's happening now? "I can hold my breath for 72 hours," he conveniently remembers. "Certainly those poisonous intergalactic fumes will have dissipated by then and I can overpower the enemy's henchmen when they come to retrieve my body ... "

I don't know about you guys, but frankly I'd be pretty annoyed with that solution. Why? Because the movie is nearly over and it's the first time we've ever heard about this nifty breath-holding trick.

91

Where did *that* come from? Granted, it's a talent that will ultimately save his life, but it will also cheat the audience out of their expectation that he will somehow utilize those other three talents which were already spelled out at the beginning.

If you're going to imbue your characters with super powers, think of those powers as being the various tools in a toolbox. You allow the audience to look inside that box before the project (the plot) really gets underway and familiarize themselves with the contents. Yep, there's a pair of pliers and a wrench and a screwdriver and a lot of different sizes of nuts and bolts and nails. Looks pretty complete on the surface. As the plot starts to develop, it's clear that your protagonist is building something important. He or she is suddenly confronted with a dilemma which the rest of us recognize could probably be easily remedied with a hammer.

But wait a minute.

Was there a hammer in that toolbox? We're pretty sure that there wasn't. Consequently, you can't have your protagonist rummage around in the box and magically "find" one to solve the problem. He or she must creatively make do with what's already there, affirming the adage that necessity really is the mother of invention in both real life and the cinema.

The flip side of foreshadowing, of course, is giving your audience information which they *assume* is vital to the plot but then turns out to have just been fluff.

I'm going to stay with the science fiction analogy here just because it works really well. Imagine that your Kevin Sorbo hero has revealed early on in the story that whenever he eats strawberries he can become invisible. Wow! That's something we'd really like to see. And wouldn't we be disappointed if we *didn't* see it after that nice set-up? Certainly he didn't just drop it casually into the conversation and not have it mean something?!

No matter how intriguing the premise or compelling the characters you come up with, all it takes is one little loose end to aggravate an audience and send them out of the theatre shaking their heads in mystification. They want to see promises kept, emotional turmoil resolved, accounts settled, lost baggage claimed, and yes — if someone says they have the power to turn invisible after one strawberry — they want to see every word of it proven.

Your Assignment

Using the toolbox analogy, make a complete list of your lead character's special talents and abilities.

1. How do you plan to convey these talents to the audience early in the story?
2. What is the one thing that your character is missing?
3. How can he or she improvise with his or her existing "tools" when the moment of truth, decision, or action finally arrives?

When your script is finished:

1. Have all the outstanding issues in it been resolved?
2. Have your characters delivered on everything they promised?

Extra Credit

Think back to recent movies you and your friends have seen. If there were loose ends or if the ending wasn't satisfactory, discuss what the writer could have done differently in terms of foreshadowing and resolution.

Silent Observer

When was the last time you went somewhere and simply "people-watched"? Chances are that you frequent any number of places where there's a regular turnover of interesting strangers engaged in conversations that you can't overhear. For example, coffee houses, airports, community parks, restaurants.

I want you to start thinking of these situations as free material for your imagination. One of the best ways to hone your skills at creating believable characters on screen is to pay more attention to all the real ones that are walking around you every day!

There are only three rules to the exercises I'm going to share. The first one, of course, is that you can't have any personal knowledge of the people you're observing. The reason is that you would then be ascribing known traits which, in turn, could influence the direction of the stories you come up with.

The second is that you need to position yourself so that you can't hear any part of the conversation going on. What you will rely on will be strictly their physical appearance and their body language.

Third, the subjects you choose to observe must not know they're being observed. No staring, no binoculars, no following them around. Even in public — and I think the dangerous times we live in are a reflection of this — people have become especially wary of strangers paying more than a passing notice of them. Although this exercise is strictly for fun, the moment that they notice you, you have to stop. Agreed?

The silent observer game is one that you can either do by yourself or with friends. Likewise, you can observe one person or an entire table full of people. The objective is to come up with a background for each person you observe, and from that, translate your observations into a short script.

Here are some questions to get you started:

1. How are your subjects dressed? What does their style of clothing suggest about their financial status? Their comfort level with their physical appearance? Is their attire appropriate to the surroundings or the event in which they're participating?

2. What do these people do for a living? Are they subordinates or managers? Do you think they like their jobs?

3. What kind of dwelling do you think they live in? How would it be furnished? Do they have pets?

4. If you are at an airport or train station, who are they waiting for? Where are they going?

5. If you are in a restaurant or cafe, what kind of meal have they ordered? Do they eat it quickly or slowly? Do they seem to be in this restaurant more for the food, the ambiance, or the company they are keeping?

6. What is their relationship to whomever is with them? Give them fictional names which seem to suit their personalities. If they are by themselves right now, why?

7. Do these people have any repetitive mannerisms or interesting quirks?

8. What might they have been doing yesterday at this same time?

9. If they are engaged in a conversation with someone else, what do you think they are talking about? Are they in agreement with each other? Are they angry? Is one of them lying? What makes you think so?

10. Where are they going to go after they leave?

Of Glass Slippers and Glass Ceilings: An Interview with Carolyn Miller

What Cinderella among us wouldn't want to dress to the nines and go to the castle ball? Though the land knows no shortage of aspiring female screenwriters who long to crash the gates of Hollywood and become overnight successes, only about seven percent will see their names in the credits on feature films. Award-winning screenwriter, Emmy nominee, and new media specialist Ms. Carolyn Miller shares her views on where the film industry is going and where the hottest break-in opportunities will be in the twenty-first century.

Q: Having written for virtually every medium that exists — and, most recently, CD-ROMs and the Web — what would you say has contributed the most to your current success in new media?

A: In terms of education, I'd have to say my Masters Degree in Journalism (from the Medill School of Journalism at Northwestern) was really helpful. Unexpectedly, actually. My Bachelor's in English Literature (from Cornell University) was pretty unhelpful except that I love to read and it certainly gave me a solid foundation of what good writing was all about. When it comes to writing things yourself, though, the kind of writing you do as an undergraduate in English literature is mostly academic writing and when you go to journalism school, you learn to write more cleanly, effectively, and to the point. When I got my first interactive job, which was as a writer on a CD-ROM project, I really relied a lot on my journalism background because, in those

95

days, most CD-ROMs were text-based. The same thing happened when I went to work on one of my first Internet projects, which was also text-based. Journalism school is a good foundation in that it also teaches you courage.

Q: Courage? In what way?

A: Well, in the program I was in, they'd try to figure out what you were most leery of or most uncomfortable with and then they'd send you to cover it. You'd learn very quickly that you could do it and you'd learn that you could tackle stories that were very complicated and that you had the power to do the research and gain the understanding of just about anything.

Q: Hmmm ... I would have said "I'm terrified of chocolate. Eeek! Keep me away from the stuff! Especially Godiva!"

A: Unfortunately, we didn't have a chance to make that part of our strategy!

Q: So when you were seventeen, was the course you were mapping for yourself primarily targeted to being a reporter?

A: I didn't even think about going to journalism school or being a reporter when I was in my teens. I always wanted to be a writer, but I didn't really know what kind of writer, though I was more interested in writing stories — fiction — than non-fiction. I also used to write little plays, and force my cousins and my friends to be in them. But when I finished my undergraduate college program and tried to find a job, what do you do with a degree in English literature? How do you make a living as a writer? I looked at advertising agencies and newspapers but no one would hire me because I didn't have any background in those fields! Also, at the time, if you were female, all they cared about was how fast you could type — not how well you could write — and I absolutely refused to start out as a secretary. If guys who write don't have to be secretaries, why should a woman?

Q: Were there any screenwriting programs available?

A: Well, there were some film schools but they weren't really focusing on scriptwriting, more on production. By then, I knew that's what I really wanted to do, to write scripts, but I thought that if I went to journalism school maybe I could study something related to script writing and get a job doing television reporting. What happened after journalism school is that I was able to work for a newspaper for a couple of years and also worked for a magazine. While still at the newspaper, I got a freelance job doing a documentary about old-fashioned circus parades that turned into one of those fairy-tale stories, because even though it was a fairly modest project, somehow a high-level executive at CBS saw it and was impressed by my work. Ultimately, he hired me to do live specials for CBS. Eventually, it led me to a staff job on the *Captain Kangaroo* show, which was a CBS show, and then, indirectly, to writing Afterschool Specials, which are one-hour dramas for teenagers. And those shows led to movie of the week projects and some feature film re-write opportunities. That documentary opened a very important door for me! It let me do what I really wanted to do!

Q: **So is there anything you know now that you wish you had known — or paid more attention to — when you were in high school or college?**

A: I wish I had started writing scripts a lot sooner! I also wish there had been some kind of course to teach me. Everything I've learned, I've had to learn the hard way and on my own. In high school, of course, there were always a lot of opportunities to write short stories or poems, but nothing in terms of playwriting or film writing. Certainly if someone today doesn't have access to courses, they should just start writing something anyway.

Q: **Even if they don't have a clue what they're doing?**

A: Absolutely! You learn as you go. I think the most important thing to know if you really want to be a scriptwriter is that you need to have good writing samples. The more you write — and the more polished you get — the more samples you'll then have to show people. Likewise, the more variety and different genres you can demonstrate, the better. A cross section, like comedy, a love story, a crime drama, a mystery, a science fiction story — so people can see you are capable of more than one thing. It's also good to have a sense of the realities of the industry and figure out what part you want to play in it. I was very naive and started my career in New York, for instance, which is quite different from Hollywood even though there was an active entertainment industry going on there. In New York, you don't really have any idea of how things operate in L.A., particularly the differences between writing for television and writing feature films. If you want to be a professional screenwriter, I think you really do need to be in Hollywood. Once you're established, you can always live outside of the city, but at the beginning, it's very hard to get anywhere without starting here first.

Q: Let's talk about Hollywood's glass ceiling. What advances or setbacks have you seen regarding women in the industry since you first began?

A: Well, I became chair of the Women's Committee of the Writers Guild back in the mid-eighties and we were tracking statistics about female writers. The figures were pretty dismal in both television and feature film. Women were very much in the minority: in the overall Writers Guild, it was about twenty percent female and eighty percent male. Women writers also made a lot less money than the men.

Q: How about today?

A: The ratio of males to females in the Guild hasn't changed a whole lot; maybe it is up to twenty-five percent female now. And while the number of women in TV has gone up a fair amount, especially in the sitcom arena, the number of women who write feature films and get screen credit for them is unspeakably low: about seven percent.

Q: That *is* dismal. What do you think accounts for it?

A: My feeling is that where you have a lot of money and a lot of glamour and a lot of power and you have an "ol' boys system," the old boys want to keep it all to themselves. It's hard for women to break through all of that. In fact, when I was chair of the committee, we had statisticians — professors from the University of Santa Barbara — whom we hired to calculate the numbers and then figure out what exactly it was that was keeping women from breaking in. I should also add that it's not just women having a hard time; it's also ethnic minorities, people with disabilities, older people.

Q: Speaking of "older people" ...

A: There's a terrible ageism problem in Hollywood. The reality is that the professional life of a writer can be fairly short, sort of like an athlete's. People planning to make screenwriting their career need to be prepared for that and have a Plan B.

Q: This sounds like *Logan's Run*; when you hit thirty, you're terminated?

A: It's true. People are really having trouble getting work after a certain age — it starts getting tough when you are in your forties.

Q: Yes, but unlike an athlete who will eventually have to step down because of physical limitations, it would seem that a writer with brilliant mental capacities could keep going forever.

A: There's certainly the argument that your expertise and fluidity and your knowledge will increase with age. I think it is true.

Q: So?

A: So it's just *stupidity*. There's no other word for it. The network executives and the people at studios tend to be very young and they just feel more comfortable around people who are just like them.

Q: As someone well past the perceived "prime," I'm finding this all very alarming.

A: So do others. In fact, it's so bad now that there's a major discrimination lawsuit going on among older writers to try to make this public and change this attitude. They are suing the major studios and talent agencies in Hollywood. I know a lot of very good writers who are getting desperate about where their next job is coming from ...

Q: But back to the statisticians. Did they come to any conclusions about female screenwriters?

A: Well, it's primarily because, as I mentioned, there's this ol' boys network and because of the studio execs wanting to hire people who are just like them. And the ol' boys don't want to let go of any of the jobs. There was also a strong perception that women couldn't write action-adventure material and they couldn't write "funny" either. Women have managed to change the attitude that they couldn't write comedy and many have become very successful in the sitcom field, but a lot of the old perceptions about other genres still haven't changed. You'll mostly find women writers in certain "ghettos" — like soap operas, children's programming, documentaries, and programming for public television. These are all areas with less money and less prestige. And you will find very few women who can successfully get a feature film script made.

Q: So can the next generation of female writers change that?

A: I think they might if they're just persistent and want it badly enough and do their homework to get their script samples out there. Also, a lot of success in Hollywood is built on the concept of networking. If you move here and make a group of friends and move along with each other, you can all help each other get jobs. There's a great organization called Women in Film which I'd really encourage female screenwriters to look into. There are also some churches that have groups in the film industry and would be a positive resource. And certainly once you've qualified for membership in the Writers Guild, that's a great group to be part of and stay connected with; you can become involved in committees and make friends in the industry, and this will help you learn where the jobs are.

Q: So what's the forecast for new writers getting their foot in the door? Will there be more or fewer opportunities?

A: The number of prime-time programs with story-based content, such as dramas, comedies and movies of the week, is going down. There are more of those reality-based shows all the time and that means that there are less opportunities for writers. Networks like the reality shows because they're so cheap to produce and they pretend they don't need writers for them ... although in fact the producers on them often perform writing tasks.

Q: Do you think these reality programs are here to stay or just a current, scary trend?

A: Hopefully, they're just a trend. We need to get back to good storytelling. But unfortunately, there are signs that they might be here to stay.

Q: How about the outlook for feature films?

A: The number of feature films being produced is pretty much the same as it always has been; it's not exactly a growth market. It's also not the most sensible profession to get into, because of the ageism problem. While it's true that there can be tremendous financial rewards and personal recognition and creative satisfaction, you do need to be aware of the downside.

Q: As wedded as today's young people are to their computers, what's the projected promise for the sort of interactive scripting you do and how would you recommend they go about breaking into this genre of writing?

A: I think there's going to be a huge amount of opportunity in this field and not that far into the future. There'll be a great need for people doing interactive TV. The video game business is also huge. And there are a great number of multi-player online games on the Web. All of these use story content. The trick, though, is that not all these companies that do video games and other forms of interactive entertainment use writers to write them. Sometimes they'll just use the person who sweeps the floor! OK, I'm exaggerating, but often someone like a programmer ends up writing them; they don't necessarily think of using professional writers. A lot of young people, however, have gotten jobs in this field because they're so good at computers and are already writing their own programs and games. A lot of classes are now being offered in the technology side — for instance, in Flash Animation or HTML — both of which are helpful to know if you are putting together websites. If you can combine that with the writing skills you already have, you can really have something special to offer. In terms of selling original material to a buyer, it can be pretty hard. Staff writing jobs or freelance jobs are easier to get than selling your own material. But one thing you can do is to start your own website and get it up and running with your friends who also have creative talents. Maybe one's good at cartoons and another is good at music and you can put it all together and create something unique which will be a great calling-card to show off your work. It's the old "let's put on a show" idea.

Q: Any other advice you'd like to impart to someone whose dream is to write for the movies or television?

A: Be an original! A tendency of a lot of new writers is to copy things they've already seen and liked, whether it's a movie or a book they've read. I think they're afraid sometimes to express their own voice. It's one of the hardest things as a writer to find that voice and figure out what you want to tell and how you want to tell it. Aspiring writers really need to look inside themselves and pick something which is close to them, something they want to write about which is based on real life and real feelings. I also want to repeat that it's important to have many *different* kinds of writing samples to show people what you can do. You can't be afraid of criticism, either. You have to be able to hear it and to learn how to take notes from people on what works and what doesn't. Last of all, you have to stay open to opportunities. Lots of the breaks I've had in my life came about in really strange ways. Someone you just meet casually at a party could mention that they heard someone is starting a new TV show, and you can't be afraid to speak up and say, "Oh? Who's over there? Do you know that person? Can you get me an introduction?"

Q: Bottom line?

A: You've gotta be gutsy! And you've got to be persistent, too. And it doesn't hurt to be a little bit lucky, too.

Further information on Carolyn and New Media can be found at her website at www.CarolynMiller.com.

Topics to Think About and Talk About

1. Would you consider using a pseudonym to hide your gender or race if you thought it would enhance your ability to sell a script? Please explain your answer in fifty words or less.

2. Films such as *Roots* and *Schindler's List* have increased social awareness of how we relate to our fellow human beings. How do you reconcile the power of film to bring people of different cultures together with the business of film that seems to perpetuate bias? Please explain in 100 words or less.

3. How do you intend to promote opportunities for others when you become a successful screenwriter?

Chapter 8
Who Are These Guys, Really?

How dull indeed the movies would be if the only characters in them were doers of good deeds for whom everything always went right! In this chapter, you'll learn the importance of giving your heroes and heroines a quest to pursue, a weakness to overcome, and an enemy who — by being the worst — will bring out your lead characters' best. You'll also learn how to define your characters from the inside out and not only leap from the printed page onto the screen but straight into a viewer's heart.

Love Me, Love My Flaws

No one is perfect. Not even those larger-than-life characters we see on the screen. The irony is that it is because of their imperfections that we are so strongly drawn to them, silently rooting for them in the darkened movie house that they will somehow overcome their fears and inhibitions and get ahead, get the girl, and get the gold. We want for them the same thing we want for ourselves: acceptance, love, and success.

Movies — and real life — are all about two things: ordinary people in extraordinary dilemmas *or* extraordinary people who are forced — often through events and circumstances not of their making — to endure ordinary times. In both cases, the people around them — whether supporters or detractors — are impacted by the strengths and weaknesses of the protagonists.

How often have you heard it said that the heroes who emerge from a crisis such as wartime or a natural disaster are simply workaday people who happened to be in the right place at the right time to step up and make a difference? Or that people who were once looked upon as different, peculiar, or strange because of their talents or physical appearance came to be embraced by their peers as the salvation to a problem no one else could solve?

Your Assignments

Think of three movies in which a common person was thrust into an uncommon environment. What skills and/or knowledge did this person need to solve the problem? Which of these special talents did the person already possess before the problem began? Why were these talents either not appreciated or acknowledged by his or her peers before?

Now think of three movies in which someone who was considered "different" by the standards of society was forced to function in an everyday world. How did this person's actions and/or feelings impact those around him or her? How, in turn, did society's prejudices influence this character's level of self-esteem and confidence?

Sending Your Character on an Interview

One of the questions that frequently arises on a job interview is "Tell us about your strengths." Humility aside, that's one of the easy ones to answer, right? You really want that job and so you already will have made a mental list of all the good reasons they should hire you instead of any of those other guys sitting in the waiting room. "I'm dependable," "I'm punctual," "I'm easy to get along with," "I saved my last employer X amount of money by inventing a new product."

If they ask you what your strengths are, however, it's a pretty sure bet that the very next question will relate to what you perceive as your weaknesses. Obviously, you're not going to reply, "Well, I like to take naps under my desk" or "I pilfer computer supplies to support my drug habit." What savvy job-seekers resort to instead is the "acceptable flaw" — an answer which the prospective employer will view as more of an asset to the company than a debit against the candidate (i.e., "I'm a workaholic; I just can't call it a day until the job is done.").

It works the same way with your protagonist. If he or she is afraid of something, it needs to be — in the eyes of the audience — for a valid and forgivable reason. Let's say your hero has a prominent physical scar. A scar acquired in the line of duty by doing something brave is more acceptable than having been stabbed by an angry homeowner for breaking and entering. A woman who is fearful about romantic trust will be more sympathetic to the viewers if we learn that she lost her first love tragically than if she's simply painted as a noncommittal flake.

Your Assignment

A big-name producer is interviewing candidates for a new movie. Your hero/heroine is next on the list. That fateful question about weaknesses comes up in the conversation. What does your protagonist confess? (Note: this assignment can either be done in writing or acted out in group role-play exercises.)

Extra Credit

Pretend that your character has just come home from his or her interview and is telling you all about it. Will it be a truthful recitation of what just happened or will it be embellished to put your character in a more favorable light?

Heroes and Villains: Making It a Fair Fight

Movie audiences have always loved a good showdown. Even more importantly, they love the kind of competition where — if only for a dire instant — it looks as if the champion they've been rooting for might actually lose. For a story to work convincingly on screen (or anywhere else!), your antagonists must always be as powerful — and enticingly charming — as the characters you have cast as hero material. If it's an easy win, there's just no challenge in watching it through to the finish.

I liken this to my stint in high school when I belonged to the junior varsity chess club. Yes, there really *was* such a group, comprised of kids who were brainy enough to make the honor roll on a regular basis but not socially savvy enough to ever get a date on Saturday night. Twice a week — and usually during the lunch hour — we'd get together in the designated nerds corner of the cafeteria to play chess.

I'll never forget the satisfaction I felt on those rare occasions when I managed to trounce the likes of Terry, David, or Arthur. They were the best of the best, a trio of chess strategists who had probably devoured every book that had ever been written on the game and who would routinely make observations about one's opening moves such as, "Oh, I see you're going with the 1922 Gerschenval advance this time." Having no clue what this meant, I'd blithely proceed to scoot my pieces around the board if for no other reason than to just maneuver them out of harm's way. My opponents perceived it to be part of an elaborate, calculated plan. I knew the truth. It was just luck.

I remember equally well the complete lack of joy I felt in beating the pants off of lesser challengers. Granted, I was winning. But winning what? These were, after all, the kids who: 1. had just barely learned the rules (i.e., yesterday), 2. were easily distracted (i.e., "Isn't that Joel Carter talking to your girlfriend?"), or 3. were playing the game for the wrong reasons (i.e., to look really intellectual).

Apply these same principles to how easily villain subordinates get dispatched by the hero throughout the majority of today's movies. Be they medieval henchmen, Nazis, or intergalactic ghouls, they don't have the vested interest in the evil outcome that the star antagonist ascribes to, thus, their lack of attention to critical details and susceptibility to stooge-like diversions. This, of course, also accounts for the scatter-effect once the cruel leader has mortally fallen; with no one to oversee the payroll, anyone left standing may as well hightail it back to Thugs-R-Us for their next assignment. We have no respect for these flunkies, largely because their only perceptible quality at any given time is quantity — assemble enough of them together in one room and they look pretty darned intimidating.

In contrast, the hero (or heroine) always wages a lone battle, or at least a hugely outnumbered and grossly under-financed one. He or she is also encumbered with the burden of vulnerability, possessed of a single personal flaw which concurrently proves to be as endearing to us as it is anxiety-inducing. Will the protagonists we cheer for be able to summon enough inner courage in the final showdown to overcome the obstacles that have previously inhibited them? Will they emerge battered but better? Weary but wiser? Sadder but stronger for having stretched themselves to the absolute limits of cunning and endurance? As a screenwriter, you have a responsibility to make your heroes aggressively push the envelope, for only in doing so will audiences feel gratified that their faith was well placed.

The biggest difference to keep at the forefront of any confrontation between heroes and villains is that the designated good guys in the plot still have something significant they need to learn about themselves in order to emotionally, physically, or spiritually grow. Villains, on the other hand, sport a self-satisfied gloat from the very first frame which reveals they are completely content with their badness; the world is their personal oyster, ripe for the seizing. Charismatic rogues such as these are much too caught up with marinating in their own testosterone to ever entertain the notion of self-improvement courses or a trip to the confessional.

"What if I should fail in my mission?" the hero constantly agonizes to those who have elected/volunteered/ordered him to lead. "What if I'm not man enough to do what must be done in order to right the world's wrongs?"

The villain, of course, has no such worries. In fact, the villain probably spends a lot more restful nights than his counterpart, secure in the knowledge that all of his machinations up to this point will yield nothing less than success and world domination. Nor can this evil-doer be criticized for surrounding himself with minions who have the collective IQ of paste. It's all part of the plan, you see. Minions are not only expendable to the ultimate cause but serve to tax the resources of the opposition. And certainly no self-respecting villain would ever recruit anyone smart enough to one day become a contender to the throne.

Just as you craft a credible and compelling background to account for your protagonist's actions, so, too, must you have a solid understanding of what drives your villain to be so villainous. He cannot simply be rotten for the sake of being rotten. Even the Sheriff of Nottingham in *Robin Hood, Prince of Thieves* offered up the excuse that a sad childhood can forgive a multitude of dysfunctional sins as an adult.

If you have truly captured the villain's soul and made him a worthy adversary of your hero, audiences won't be able to wait for each new dastardly scene in which he appears. They also won't be able to wait for the definitive moment of victory, confident that you as the author have equitably equipped both sides with the wits, will and weaponry to make it a fight well worth watching.

The Hero vs. Villain Checklist

1. In the movie you plan to write, list your hero's ten strongest qualities on the left-hand side of a piece of paper. On the right-hand side, list his or her ten weaknesses.

2. Start the same kind of list for the villain in your story.

3. For both the hero and villain, take a look at your ten/ten lists and narrow them down to the three most predominant traits in each column.

4. You're now going to take a close look at those three strengths and three weaknesses for your hero and your villain and narrow them down to just one each. For instance, it may come out that your hero is fiercely loyal to his friends but his Achilles' heel is that he has a fear of snakes. Correspondingly, your villain is a world-class genius when it comes to computers but was born with hemophilia.

5. Assuming that the hero and villain have knowledge of each other's strengths and weaknesses, how are they going to use them to draw each other into a trap from which only one will emerge? In the above example, the villain will use the hero's loyalty to bait him into taking a risk, then turn loose the cobras! At the same time, the hero not only knows that his adversary can sabotage anything he tries to do electronically but that he lives in fear of bleeding to death from a wound that would be superficial to anyone else.

The Backstory: Motive, Means, and Opportunity

Every mystery you'll ever read essentially boils down to three questions: What was the motive? Did he or she have the means to commit the crime? Did he or she have the opportunity to carry it out?

Even if the screenplay you plan to write doesn't fall into the mystery genre, these same questions still need to be addressed with your primary characters. Otherwise, they will simply be wandering around the screen taking up space.

What is it that your protagonist most wants to accomplish in this story? Is it to find the lost treasure? Is it to win the heart of the girl? Is it to gain acceptance from his or her peer group?

Whatever reply you give to the above is only the *what*. The *why* is your character's motive. Maybe she wants to locate the treasure in order to validate all of the years her recently deceased father spent looking for it. Maybe he wants to get the girl, because he knows that together they would have the happiest life imaginable. Maybe he just wants to be acknowledged as "normal" because of a lonely childhood without any close friends.

Take a moment now to identify: 1. *what* your lead character wants and 2. *why*.

Next, we'll move on to the means of *accomplishing* this objective. Let's say that our female adventurer wants to take up where her father's archaeology work left off. To launch an expedition, however, takes more money than she currently has in her bank account. Until she has the necessary money to pay for equipment, supplies, and plenty of big brawny men to carry it into the Amazon for her — the *means* — her quest is pretty much dead in the water. Where is she going to get those kind of sums? Can she sell off the ancestral home? Can she go to the bank for a loan? Should she take on a wealthy partner and agree to split whatever fabulous treasure they find?

How is your character going to accomplish his or her own goal?

On the same sheet of paper where you just identified the motive, list what talents or resources your character needs in order to make the dream a reality. If they are not readily available (i.e., the car, the money, the high-security job that will get him or her into the facility), what steps does the protagonist need to take in order to procure them?

Suffice it to say, all of the good intentions and resources in the world won't be of much help if the right opportunity simply doesn't present itself. To put it on a parallel with meeting the love of one's life, the chances of finding someone are probably much better in a large city than if one is stationed at an outpost in Antarctica with only penguins for company. Likewise, a thief who was planning a heist at an art gallery would be more savvy regarding the security system if he or she actually worked in the gallery as opposed to planning the whole caper from the outside.

Now that your character has the requisite means to accomplish the goal, identify how you intend to create the opportunity. To keep the audience guessing, it's especially effective to employ the "ticking-clock" element. Translated: the protagonist only has one chance to get the whole thing right!

As an example, I'm going to illustrate with an *actual* ticking-clock: In order to send Marty McFly *Back to the Future* where he belongs, Doc Brown needs to make sure that everything is properly connected in order to send the powerful surge of electricity into the DeLoreon when lightning strikes the old clock tower. If he fails, Marty will be permanently trapped in the fifties. If he succeeds, the road will be clear for two sequels ...

Extra Credit

Once you have finished identifying the motive, means, and opportunity for the protagonist, do the same thing for your villain. Keep in mind that the antagonist in your plot shouldn't just be bad for the sake of being bad. Something in this person's past *compelled* him or her to gravitate toward the dark side. Had circumstances been different, the villain and the hero might even have been friends. The more you know about your characters' backstory, the more plausible their actions and reactions will be in the current storyline you are trying to tell.

Reading Between the Lines:
An Interview with Kathie Fong Yoneda

What is Hollywood looking for? Ms. Kathie Fong Yoneda has seen it all in twenty plus years of story analysis and development at Paramount, MGM, Columbia, Walt Disney, 20th Century Fox, Filmways, Inc., and Universal Pictures. An accomplished speaker, author, and international teacher, she shares her views on today's entertainment industry and what makes a winning script.

> **Q: Being a script development consultant has to rank as one of life's "dream jobs"! How did you get from the halls of C.K. McClatchy High to the bright lights of Paramount Studios?**
>
> A: Well, back in high school I worked on the school paper so I was basically in journalism and art. Although I majored in English in college, my original plan was to go to California Fashion Institute. It didn't take too long to flounder around and discover that fashion design wasn't exactly what I wanted to do, but I still knew I wanted to do something very

creative. I know my parents, especially my mother, really preferred that I pursue something more stable and conservative like being a teacher or a pharmacist or a secretary. I actually granted their wish by becoming a secretary but as a secretary in the motion picture industry. As a matter of fact, I was the first Asian female hired on a full-time basis at Universal back in 1969; that was when less than one tenth of one percent of the people who were in the industry were minorities.

Q: Was it even more of an ol' boys club than it is now?

A: Oh yes. Very, very traditionally ol' boys. One of the people who really helped me out, though, was my boss, Dick Shepherd, who was the head of production at MGM. He was a production executive at Warner Brothers when we met and I became his assistant. In between that, he became a producer and when he was away on location, the scripts would really start to pile up. I was just so hungry for knowledge about things and I was also very organized, both of which led to my reading all of these scripts. When he came back, he'd start looking over the mail and I'd say, "Oh, you don't have to read that one. It's really not very good."

Q: Never underestimate the power of a good assistant ...

A: Anyway, I'd proceed to tell him what it was about and why I didn't like it, and he said, "Well, can you do me a favor? Can you write up a couple paragraphs about the story?" To his surprise — and mine, too, I was very good at it. After all, book reports were one of my favorite things in school, and reading scripts is essentially the same thing.

Q: It's not just about commenting on the story, though, is it?

A: It's a lot of different factors, actually. It's the characters and the structure, it's the production value, the dialog — it's the whole picture, literally. I tell people that structure is merely a beginning, a middle, and an end and trying to make the whole thing interesting. If you go back to our common ancestors — cave people sitting around a campfire telling stories — what those stories have in common with what's being written today is that they all had to have an intriguing set-up. They had to have complications and challenges, and you had to have a satisfying ending that entertained everyone and wrapped up all the loose ends.

Q: So how did you transition from secretary to studio reader?

A: Well, by the time my boss went to MGM and became head of production, I was really hooked on doing script coverage and he made me a deal. Basically he said that if I set up the office and trained a new secretary — my replacement — he'd do whatever he could to get me into the Story Analysts Guild.

Q: And what's that?

A: It's a very closed union shop and all the studios have to hire union story analysts. The main distinction is that story analysts read material only for the studios. Then there's a group of freelance readers who read and do coverages for agencies and independent production companies. The freelancers don't belong to the union and make considerably less money.

Q: But back to your career path ...

A: Well, I made it into the Guild on my first try and started to move around, building on what I had already learned. One of those moves, in fact, led me to become a development executive for Disney for eight years during the time when Eisner and Katzenberg first moved over there and wanted to get a lot of new movies going.

Q: What are you doing now?

A: I've worked for nine years now for Paramount in their longform division and evaluate books and scripts for TV, cable movies and occasionally mini-series. A lot of the movies you see on Showtime, for instance, are things that Paramount may have done. I've also been doing a number of speaking engagements and workshops around the world and even have a book coming out in the summer of 2002 (Michael Wiese, Publisher).

Q: There's a lot to be said about how technology is shrinking the globe. Is it inversely expanding the opportunities for new writers?

A: Absolutely! What I find really encouraging is that because there *is* so much technology, there are so many different ways to pursue storytelling. Unlike some of my associates, I don't view technology as a foe or feel as if it will spell the end of motion pictures because kids are glued to the Internet. What I see is that there are a lot more websites available for people to express themselves and to get critiques of their work. A lot of the studios now, for instance, have people who are assigned to surf the Net and to take a look at some of the projects that are out there. Aspiring filmmakers can get very industrious with their digital camcorders and are producing "mini-trailers" that are getting the attention of these studio execs. Thanks to the Internet, no longer is Hollywood like that big black monolith that no one could figure out in *2001: A Space Odyssey*.

Q: **Based on your experience as a reader and a movie-goer, are films today getting better or worse?**

A: Well, I do think that movies which have a lot of special effects or action or sci-fi/fantasy are a lot more eye-catching. And, of course, the largest movie-going audiences today are the young adult males. That's probably not going to change. In fact, it's been that way for at least the thirty years I've been in the industry! Remember how every other movie in the eighties and early nineties was some kind of an action film? Well, it seems as if the public — and even all those male adults — finally got a little tired of it and then came the trend of doing *scary* movies. Horror movies in a way, but still sort of campy. Finally, the trend in the late nineties and into 2001 are movies along the order of *Something About Mary* and *American Pie*. What you notice, though, about scary movies *and* the latest crop of teen movies is that there aren't a lot of special effects; in both cases, they're mostly about the *anticipation* of something big happening. That's the irony of these films which coincidentally is what one of my favorite directors, Alfred Hitchcock, used to do; it was the anticipation that you *knew* what was happening or what the danger or risk was, and yet you still couldn't keep your eyes off the screen! But back to the question, I think that audiences have gotten a lot smarter and they're expecting more than just special effects. They watch things because they're *different*.

Q: What about the copycat syndrome, that insatiable quest for writers to imitate what is currently "hot"?

A: I think what happens is that people see a film that's different and that they really like and their reaction is, "Wow! I can write something just like that!" What doesn't sink in their heads, though, is that by the time they write this thing and give it to someone — even if gets snatched up right away — it's going to take at least another eighteen months before it gets made and comes out. By the time that happens, you're going to be the third or fourth or eighth person to use that theme and it's already old news! By the way, the top grossing movies of all time — the top ten — are almost always family movies. And the one thing that sets them apart is the fact that they all have in common a look at the human condition as told through characters that audiences instantly related to and could believe in. It's something that writers tend to forget, because they're concentrating on the high-tech aspects of telling the best possible story, instead of looking at how to simply touch the audience in some way and make them say, "Oh my God, I've been there, too!" Whether it's getting them to realize that they have the same fears or the same phobia or the same dream, a movie needs to say something to you and you need to respond to it in such a way — through the heart or through the soul — that you just don't want to leave your theatre seat even when the usher says, "OK, bud, move along. The next group is coming through."

Q: As a studio reader, what are some of the major turn-offs when a new script falls into your lap?

A: What overall is really bad is when people try to cram too much into a story ... or too little. It's about not having a clear-cut view of what your story is and changing back and forth as far as what the goal is going to be. The second thing is not fully developing the characters. Some people know how a story should start and how it should end, but they just don't know how to have the characters carry the story all the way through. Character and dialog are actually the two most important things for me, probably even more important than the story. Most of the stories that readers at studios read are actually variations of things we've all heard before ... but with a twist. What *makes* those twists unique always has something to do with the characters and how they look at life and, accordingly, react to it.

Q: **So what kinds of things really make you sit up and take notice?**

A: I'd have to say that it's what I just mentioned, only put them in reverse! I also have to add that I like it when I can tell that there's a real sense of passion behind the writing. Sometimes when I feel that level of passion coming through in the words — a story that's personal and really means everything to the person who wrote it — this is something that comes from such an honest place, I can't help but be attracted to it and be interested in how it's going to turn out!

Topics to Think About and Talk About

1. List three ideas you have for a film project. After each, name a film whose theme is essentially similar to your idea. In fifty words or less, explain why each of your ideas is different.

2. What activities are you currently engaged in where you assist or review the work of other people? Do you find collaborating or critiquing to be a satisfying activity? Please explain your answer.

3. How much time do you spend reading other screenplays or literature on screenwriting? What general lessons are you learning from reading these materials and how does that affect your ideas for your own screenplay?

Chapter 9

Does Every Story Need a Happy Ending?

Define "happy."

Audience Satisfaction

In *Love Story*, Jenny dies.

In *Titanic*, Jack dies.

In *Romeo and Juliet*, both Romeo and Juliet die.

In *Witness*, John and Rachel return to their respective worlds.

In *My Best Friend's Wedding*, the best friend marries someone else.

In *Casablanca*, Ilsa leaves Rick.

In *Shakespeare in Love*, young Will loses the love of his life.

In *Braveheart*, William Wallace loses everything, including most of his body parts.

In *Castaway*, the Fed Ex guy doesn't marry his beloved.

In *Bicentennial Man*, Andrew learns what it's like to be human.

Do any of these endings make us feel sad? Probably. Are they each the *right* endings for the stories that have just unfolded? Yes. For even though they may fail the happily-ever-after finale of a traditional fairy tale, they have nonetheless touched a powerful chord of emotion and made us feel *something*. Truth be told, we will probably remember longer those films that leave us with a keen sense of yearning or heightened introspection than those which wrap up nicely like a Christmas present and send all the characters home with a smile of contentment.

"Apathy," a theatre friend of mine once opined, "is worse than just feeling hatred." At the time, he was referring to his future mother-in-law, a woman who was going out of her way to let him know that she really felt her daughter could have made a better choice. It struck me as curious that he didn't harbor absolute contempt toward her for all of her attempts to chase him off. "At least with hatred," he candidly replied, "I'd feel *something*. With her, I feel nothing at all."

As a screenwriter, apathy is the kiss of death to you and your characters. If in two hours you haven't moved them to some sort of definitive emotion, they may as well have been made of cardboard (your characters, not the audience). Second to that in terms of disappointment is giving viewers a gratuitous ride-into-the-sunset just because you feel that you're supposed to.

Such was the trademark of many of this country's earlier films. Even if the characters seemed totally mismatched or the villain was significantly smarter than any of the good guys trying to catch him, audiences in the past were accustomed to expecting nothing less than a boy-gets-girl, good-triumphs-over-evil, peace-will-reign-again-in-the-valley conclusion by the final credits. Movies, after all, are supposed to be everything that real life isn't, an affirmation that if we all just hang in there long enough, something good will eventually come of it.

A "happy ending," however, isn't always synonymous with a "plausible closure." Unless you feel competent enough to have written a multi-sequel epic that audiences will hunger for, each script needs to be a stand-alone product and resolve within itself whatever issues or crises were brought to the table at the beginning. Like the mythical phoenix, the loss that your characters may experience in terms of love, fame, or fortune is equitably balanced by the emotional and spiritual growth they gain in the process to become better people.

There are two rules in writing endings to your stories. The first is to give the audience what it wants to see but not in exactly the way it was expecting. The second is to give them something completely unforeseen but have it logically supported by all the actions and reactions leading up to it.

Your Assignment

For each of the films listed on page 117, identify what it was that the character acquired as a result of not getting what he or she really wanted.

Three Different Endings

What would have happened if Romeo lived but Juliet died? Would he have been charged with her murder, convicted by a jury of his peers, and sent to the nearest gallows?

What if Juliet had lived but Romeo died? Would she have joined a convent? Would she have met some other lad a few years down the road, fallen madly in love, and dismissed her earlier teen romance as just one of life's little tragic infatuations?

What if Shakespeare had allowed both of them to live? Would true romance have been enough to sustain them in the aftermath of having their respective inheritances cut off, forcing them to dwell in a drafty hovel and eat gruel? What if they had produced a brood of children? Would the feuding Montagues and Capulets have mellowed and welcomed the grandkids into their homes at Christmas? Would Juliet have turned into an incessant whiner, eventually compelling Romeo to seek solace in the arms of their new blonde neighbor, Desdemona? What if Juliet had decided to better herself by going to night school classes? What if Romeo couldn't keep up with his new-and-improved beloved and tried to turn her back into the wispy, moonstruck little thing she had once been?

Perhaps such scenarios danced through Shakespeare's head as he sat at his desk with quill in hand, carefully contemplating the star-crossed lovers' final moments.

"Methinks a death most bittersweet be best for all," he may even have murmured, satisfied that he had neither agents nor critics to pressure him into penning a more appealing ending.

How does your own story come out? How do you know it's the best possible outcome, given everything that has happened in the preceding two hours? Sometimes we can get so fixated on how we think things should resolve that we limit ourselves in exploring potential alternatives that could, in fact, make for a more compelling, memorable, and perhaps even less predictable story.

The best way to test this is to purposely construct three different endings for the lives of your primary characters. Even if you should decide to still stick with the first one you came up with, the value of this exercise is in yielding new insights about your characters. Would they still survive if they didn't get exactly what they wanted? If they get what they want, will they be completely happy or still yearn for the chance to have done something different?

For practice before you examine your own script, construct three alternative finales for the lead characters in some of the following movies:

Billy Elliot

Titanic

The Princess Diaries

Indiana Jones and The Last Crusade

Sweet November

Pay It Forward

The Talented Mr.Ripley

Save the Last Dance

Just Visiting

Big

Bicentennial Man

The Mexican

Love and Basketball

The Blair Witch Project

Using Proverbs as a Moral Roadmap

We've all heard that "crime doesn't pay," "love is blind," and "the early bird catches the worm." Countless books, plays, and films have been spun from these oft-used expressions which, in turn, are the unifying "glue" that keeps your characters from wandering too far afield of the plot.

Proverbs have also found their way into loglines, often tweaked with spelling or word puns or enhanced by conditional twists; for instance, "Crime doesn't pay ... unless you own the bank."

Your Assignment

Listed below are some multi-cultural philosophies that may be new to you. Pick the one that most appeals to you and develop an original storyline in which that proverb is the central theme.

1. "Death will come, always out of season." (Big Elk, Omaha Chief)
2. "A boy is easier cheated than an old lady." (Welsh)
3. "He who serves two masters has to lie to one." (Dutch)
4. "It does not require many words to speak the truth." (Chief Joseph, Nez Perce)
5. "All are not cooks that walk with long knives." (Russian)
6. "If my warriors are to fight, they are too few; if they are to die, they are too many." (Hendrick, Mohawk)
7. "There is no good accord where every man would be lord." (Romanian)
8. "The seeking for one thing will find another." (Irish)
9. "There is no death, only a change of worlds." (Chief Seattle, Suqwamish and Duwamish)
10. "A man without a smile should not open a shop." (Chinese)
11. "An egg today is better than a chicken tomorrow." (Italian)
12. "Why should you take by force that which you can obtain by love?" (King Wahunsonacook, Powhatan)
13. "Rain beats a leopard's skin, but it does not wash out the spots." (Ashanti)
14. "If you are in hiding, don't light a fire." (Ashanti)
15. "He who cannot dance will say the drum is bad." (Ashanti)
16. "Don't estimate the value of a badger's skin before catching the badger." (Japanese)
17. "He who hunts two rats catches none." (Buganda)
18. "What is said over the dead lion's body could not be said to him alive." (Zaire)
19. "Don't throw the fireworks before the party." (Portuguese)
20. "The day on which one starts out is not the time to start one's preparations." (Nigeria)
21. "A borrowed fiddle does not finish a tune." (Zimbabwe)
22. "When you know who his friend is, you know who he is." (Senegal)

23. "One sure thing is better than two maybes." (French)

24. "Beautiful is not what is beautiful but what one likes." (Yiddish)

Extra Credit

Find a proverb which best exemplifies your own screenplay. Experiment with different ways to weave it into your logline.

The Envelope Please:
An Interview with Pamela Wallace

When a young Amish boy named Samuel witnesses a murder in the restroom of a city train station, he and his widowed mother, Rachel, are suddenly plunged into a modern world where frequent violence contrasts sharply to the old-fashioned, peaceable lifestyle they're accustomed to. Enter policeman John Book, whose objective to protect the crime's only witness carries with it the potential to put the entire community of Amish farmers in harm's way. The Academy Award-winning *Witness* is a must-rent film if you want a good example of story structure and conflict. Its author, Ms. Pamela Wallace, tells how the plot came to be.

Q: Did you always know that you wanted to be a screenwriter?

A: I knew that I wanted to be a writer but I think my heart was set on being a novelist. Being a screenwriter was something so completely distant and foreign that I never even thought about what that might be as a career. It wasn't until I had actually become established as a novelist that I began to think about writing for the movies.

Q: What kind of novels were you writing?

A: Popular women's fiction, romance, that sort of thing.

Q: So what was the inciting incident that pushed you from novels into films?

A: Well, I had written a proposal for my next book and my publisher turned it down. That book was the basis for *Witness*.

Q: Which leads to the question of how you came up with the plot.

A: I had read an article in the L.A. Times about the Amish and it really intrigued me. I had never heard of them before and I wasn't aware that there were still people in this country, in this day and age, who were living such an old-fashioned lifestyle. I started to do a lot of research because I thought it would make a good story. At that time, I was married to a screenwriter and when my publisher turned down the proposal, he felt that it was very filmic and would make a good movie. What we decided to do from there was a spec script. Three years and many rejections later...

Q: So the first person you took it to wasn't excited about it?

A: (*Laugh*) They didn't exactly leap at the chance to buy.

Q: What happened to the novel? Did it ever get published?

A: It was published but as what they call a novelization of the script. I, however, wasn't the one to do it.

Q: How long did it take you to write the script for *Witness*?

A: Well, if you consider how long it took from the moment I first got the idea, through all of the research, through several drafts of the outline and then doing the script, the whole process took about a year. That one actually came together pretty quickly.

Q: How many rewrites did it go through from what you originally set down to what the rest of us saw on the screen?

A: Probably about half a dozen.

Q: Did you feel that you knew everything about your main characters, John and Rachel, when you first started writing or did they reveal themselves to you as the plot developed?

A: You never know your characters truly until you've written their story several times, because every draft you do you get deeper and deeper into their personalities and how the story impacts them.

Q: Do you rely on a lot of feedback from others during the creative process or do you wait until the whole thing is finished before showing it to anyone?

123

A: If it's a spec project, I personally like to get feedback from friends and other writers I respect. If it's a project I'm doing because it's an assignment, whether I want feedback or not, I get it from everybody involved!

Q: **What — or who — has been the biggest influence on your writing?**

A: There have been so many, I couldn't possibly name just one! Almost everyone I have ever worked with has influenced my work — directors, producers, TV executives, other writers I've read. You really learn a lot from reading the work of other writers. No matter what kind of writer you plan to be, whether it's novels or scripts or poetry, you need to see what others have done before you and try to learn from them. I also think one of the big mistakes that aspiring screenwriters make is that they only read screenplays instead of a well-rounded balance that includes fiction and non-fiction. You need to be well read in general to be successful.

Q: **Let's say you're a high school student on a limited budget and you want to add three really good screenwriting how-to books to your home library. What would you recommend?**

A: The most thorough academic approach is Robert McKee's book, *Story*. It's a very big, very dense, very intellectual book. It takes a lot to wade through it, but it really is a very in-depth study of screenwriting and, like the name implies, it focuses on the story, which is the most important element of the whole process. There's another book which is very good by Dona Cooper, who teaches at the American Film Institute, and is called *Writing Great Screenplays for Film and TV*. Just about anything by Linda Seger is also great and full of helpful information.

Q: **You've also written a book yourself, haven't you?**

A: Yes. It's called *You Can Write a Movie*, and it's published by Writer's Digest. I like to think it's helpful to people because almost no screenwriting books are written by working screenwriters. Consequently, no matter how good they are, they lack the perspective of what it's really like in practice as opposed to theory. In my book, I talk about what it's really like from the writer's viewpoint in establishing yourself in a very difficult business.

Q: What's your favorite movie?

A: I think it depends on the genre. It's hard to narrow it down to just one! For comedy, for instance, I love the original *Ghostbusters*. As a comedy, it just did everything right. If you want to go back to classic movies, I'd pick *It Happened One Night*. Again, everything worked on all levels in that film. I'm mentioning movies that I think would be good for new screenwriters to study and learn from. *Field of Dreams* I think, is the quintessential movie, because it's about myth and touches people on a very deep level. After all, the essence of movies is all about myth and fantasy and magic.

Q: From a technical standpoint, movies have gotten better. What about the storylines — are they getting better or worse?

A: Well, I think that up until about ten years ago, the quality of movies overall was infinitely better than it is now. Most people who really know movies tend to agree with that. What happened is that about ten years ago, movie studios started focusing on blockbusters. Generally speaking, blockbusters aren't the most high quality, best written movies because they're very much about special effects. Even in terms of TV movies, they started worrying more about getting good ratings than putting out good stories. There was a dumbing-down of plots and characters to reach a broader range of viewers. These days, if you want to see something that isn't just a fun roller-coaster ride, it's really hard to find.

Q: With that in mind, what advice would you give someone who says, "I know I'm supposed to write solid, character-driven material but all the big, commercial films are about glitz. What should I do?"

A: I get asked that all the time! There isn't a simple answer to that question, either. The one thing I always say, though, is that you're going to do your best writing if you're writing a story that you personally feel passionate about. Even if it's not commercial and the kind of thing that probably isn't going to sell, you should still write it anyway, because your talent will always shine through when you're involved in something you really like. People will read your work and *see* that talent and commitment and maybe give you a chance to write something else. In this business, you need to impress people with your ability and write the kind of story *you* want, not just the kind of story you *think* they're looking for. It never works to say, "OK, today I'm going to write a blockbuster," because if it were possible to define exactly what a blockbuster is and to craft a story to *be* that, then everyone would be writing them all the time. In fact, oftentimes movies that are *supposed* to be the big summer blockbusters turn out just the opposite and fall flat. *Pearl Harbor,* for example. Everything about it was supposed to be a big picture and it was a total failure. On the other hand, if you genuinely enjoy a certain kind of movie like a high-concept comedy or an action movie that tends to be very commercially successful and you have what you think is a great idea for that genre, then you should go ahead and do it and hope for the best. In my own experience, every time I've done the kind of stories that I didn't think would be particularly commercial but were very heartfelt, those were always the most successful movies I did.

Q: What's the best advice anyone ever gave you about writing for the movies?

A: Some of it was that the best critical element in every scene you write should be conflict. You have to look at the scene and ask yourself what the conflict is and is it strong enough to hold the audience's attention. A lot of times the reason a new script fails is because it just isn't compelling enough. I was also told — and by an Oscar-winning screenwriter — that it's important to put your characters through hell, that you really let them suffer, because in doing that you will make the audience really care about them and relate to them on a personal level. Since your main character has to undergo a profound transformation, the more they have to struggle, the more profound that ultimate transformation is going to be.

Q: So what's on your plate now?

A: Well, Madeline DiMaggio and I just did a script based on the Newbery award-winning book, *Catherine Called Birdie*. It's a very popular story that's like a teenage *Shakespeare in Love* and we're waiting to see if that's going to get made. I have some other projects in the works, too. One thing about this business is that you're never just working on one script!

Q: Any last words of advice to the next generation of writers?

A: I just want to encourage people that no matter who they are or where they're from or what their ethnic or socioeconomic background may be, Hollywood truly is open to anybody now. If you're talented enough and persevere, anybody can make it!

Topics to Think About and Talk About

1. In 100 words or less, define what will make you a successful screenwriter.

2. Do you think it is more important that a movie be commercially successful or that it be well written and compelling? Are these two objectives mutually exclusive? Of the top-ten grossing movies right now, which have screenplays that you would consider to be excellent?

3. What are the benefits of reading books on screenwriting? Based on your own experience, have you read books or articles on screenwriting that you feel gave you bad instruction or advice? Explain in fifty words or less.

Chapter 10
How Should You Pace Your Scenes?

Have you ever sat through a television show that dragged so interminably you ended up changing channels or leaving the room to make a sandwich? On the other hand, have you ever felt that two hours at a movie theatre absolutely flew by because it was one exciting moment right after another? The secret is in the pacing.

A Template for Timing

Television writing is formulaic. You probably already knew that even without knowing exactly what the formula is. Let's look any prime-time half-hour sitcom as an example:

It begins with a one-minute prologue or teaser, which either introduces what the episode will be about or is a slice-of-life vignette involving the regular characters (i.e., the gang from *Friends* sitting in the coffeehouse and lamenting their respective love lives). Following commercials is the first ten-minute act. This is followed by another set of commercials and then the second act, also ten minutes. The entire thing is capped off by a one-minute epilogue, which is either a postscript to the preceding story or a series of blooper outtakes from the same episode.

Hour-long programs follow the same scheme of things, the only variation being how the commercials are distributed during the forty-four minutes of actual story-time. I like to use *Murder, She Wrote* as a prime example of formulaic writing, largely because a friend of mine once wrote a paper for her master's program based on an entire season of JB Fletcher solving crimes and was enthusiastic to share the results. Her findings: 1. the most significant clue — usually something innocuous like a loose earring or a missing piece of lemon meringue pie — was always introduced into the plot at exactly the same time every episode; 2. the wrong person was always arrested at exactly the same time every episode; 3. Jessica would always blink her eyes in startlement and proclaim, "Lemon meringue pie — that's it! I know who the murderer is" at — you guessed it — exactly the same time every episode. (For those of you who remember the old *Perry Mason* series, the wrongdoer's identity was always revealed like clockwork there as well.)

"But I want to write something original!" I can hear all of you protest. "Who needs a formula?"

The answer is: *you* do. And so does anyone else who wants to write a film script that works. While the very word implies a degree of predictability, there is nonetheless an expositional hierarchy that movie-goers and television-watchers have come to expect and that you, as the writer, are required to deliver. Once you come to recognize the formula as friend not foe, it will make your outline — and the actual writing — much easier.

A number of books have been written on the subject of structure, my favorite of which makes the "sheet and clothesline" analogy; specifically, your plot is a giant white bedsheet that needs to be secured to the line with a succession of clothespins so as not to allow any of the sheet/story to dangerously sag. I'm going to use a similar model for this exercise but one that you can actually construct as a working template on your computer and which conveniently breaks a full script down into manageable parts. This will be very useful to you in a later discussion when we get into the arena of treatments and outlines.

To begin with, the layout of your template is going to be landscape rather than portrait (horizontal as opposed to vertical). You will want to define a table of six columns for this page. (I suggest you allow a half-inch left/right margin so as to maximize the amount of space you will have to fill things in.) The middle four columns should all be the same width; the first and sixth columns which bookend the middle four should be roughly one third the size of the others.

Short Column #1 will be labeled Foreshadowing.

Column #2 will be labeled Act I.

Column #3 will be labeled Act II.

Column #4 will be labeled Act III.

Column #5 will be labeled Act IV.

Short Column #6 will be labeled Conclusion.

Last but not least, and after you have printed this out, I want you to hand-draw an arrow at the mid-point of Column #5 and write in "Uh-Oh." Preferably in red.

While you're busy doing that, I'm going to go make myself a snack.

Filling in the Blanks

Well, how did it turn out? You'll need to add a couple more labels before we proceed. These new additions will help you to understand time frames, as well as how many pages should be allotted to each "act" in your film. Speaking of acts, this exercise represents a departure from what you may have previously learned about screenplay structure, specifically, that everything is executed in three segments, not four. While this will soon be addressed, the template you're about to work with is a valuable tool in terms of keeping a realistic handle not only on how much time has elapsed but ensuring that there is an equitable distribution of action, conflict, and character development. Remember when I mentioned that an average movie was 120 pages? This conveniently equals two hours of on-screen time (one typed page of script equals one minute of film). This nifty number works well for our purposes, as you'll soon see.

At the far left border of your table, I want you to write "0." This is where the movie begins. At the far right border, you'll now write "120," which is where the movie ends. You're now going to label the columns in thirty-minute increments. Columns #1 and #2 *together* comprise "thirty minutes." Column #3 by itself should be labeled "sixty minutes." Column #4 by itself is "ninety minutes." Columns #5 and #6 *together* comprise "120 minutes." What all of this is telling you is that by the end of Act II (Column #3), your movie has run sixty minutes and is at the half-way point.

I'm sure you've all heard the expression, "Chase your character up a tree, throw rocks in the tree, help your character get down from the tree." It's a classic formula of building conflict and emotional tension: Make your character's life miserable and then help him resolve his problems. Although you don't have to write this down, consider Act I as "chasing your character up a tree." In Act II, you want to start throwing rocks — big, sharp ones. By the time you get to Act III, I want you to set that tree on fire. That leaves Act IV to be helpful and offer your poor protagonist a ladder.

Or do you?

Take a look at the short bookend columns on your table, respectively dubbed Column #1 (Foreshadowing) and Column #6 (Conclusion). The two roughly represent the first and last ten minutes of the story. They are probably the most important minutes of your entire film because of the purpose they serve in: 1. hooking the audience and 2. tying up the loose ends satisfactorily.

Within the first ten minutes of the movie, you not only need to hook your viewers on the plot but also plant what will inevitably turn out to be the most vital "clue" on which either: 1. the main character's ultimate fate will hang and/or 2. the mystery will be solved.

Let's apply this to our character in the tree. Suppose he's setting off for a walk in the woods to try and figure out how to deal with the villain who has just threatened to foreclose on his house/fire him from his job/steal his girlfriend/all of the above. An aggressive but well-meaning little salesman comes up and tries to sell our hero some new-fangled, high-tech alligator-repellent. Our character thinks this is rather bizarre, given that alligators are not even indigenous to his state. He feels sorry for the salesman, though, and ends up purchasing a small can of the stuff just to be polite.

Fast-forward now to the end of Act III. Our protagonist is really in a bad spot — he's trapped in the tree, he's bruised from all those sharp rocks, and — oh good grief — the tree is starting to burn. But what's this?! Someone is coming down the road with a ladder. Hurrah! With half an hour to spare, we know his life will be saved and that all will be well. What our hero hasn't realized yet, of course, is that the person offering the ladder is, in fact, the same meanie who set up all this mayhem in the first place and has simply thought of a new and torturous way to dispatch him.

The hero starts down the ladder and what should he encounter at the bottom rung? No less than the world's biggest, angriest, hungriest alligator on the planet. Uh-Oh! Was he better off being burned in the tree? Sometime during the next agonizing twenty minutes of indecision and high drama, he suddenly sees his nemesis, laughing from a distance. "You'll never escape now!" the villain chortles in glee, and indeed it seems as if everything is lost.

But wait! What about that can of high-tech alligator repellent? Will it really work as well as the salesman insisted? With time running out, there is only way to see if the claims are true. Our hero pulls it out of his hip pocket, fumbles, and nearly drops it. He nearly drops it again as he snaps the cap off. He knows he needs to get closer in order to squirt it in the alligator's snapping face. He nearly loses his balance as he leans out as far and as low as he can. Squirt! The alligator recoils, thrashes around, starts snapping even more viciously, biting off the ladder's bottom rung Oh no! Has our hero been sold a worthless product? He knows that if he doesn't get close enough the second time, he's toast. The branch directly above him has now burned almost all the way through and is about to fall. Squirt! Right between the eyes! The alligator shakes his head, momentarily blinded by the foul-smelling spray. During this brief period of disorientation, the hero jumps to the ground ... and safety. Only a split second later, the tree branch crashes to earth. The villain — who is stupid enough to be intrigued by all of this confusion — makes the mistake of coming closer to investigate ... and is promptly eaten by the alligator who has by now conveniently regained his sight. FADE TO BLACK.

Timing Is Everything

OK, silly as the above story is, it illustrates several valuable points about structure and development:

1. The Big Uh-Oh always relates back in some way to the foreshadowing from the first ten minutes. In this case, the very thing that the hero was not going to purchase becomes the only tool that can save his life. It's also a common device to establish early on that the hero or heroine has some deep-seated phobia (snakes, flying, heights, etc.) which, of course, will be the very test they are forced to confront in order to survive and/or save the life of someone they love.

2. The necessary characters are all introduced at the right time. It would not do, for instance, to have the nerdy little salesman come ambling along three-fourths of the way through the film, look up in the tree, and remark, "Say, would you like to buy this new product I'm selling just in case any alligators come along?" It's important as well that the person who offers the ladder at the start of Act IV is someone we already know from earlier in the story; specifically, the villain. A popular variation on this theme, of

course, is to have someone who has presumably been an ally of the hero up until now turn out to be deadly. Although you can add as many subsidiary characters as you want to the mix, try to make sure that your main players have either been seen or substantially talked about by the end of the first thirty minutes.

3. There's a lot of room for a liberal sprinkling of red herrings in a plot such as this. The deeper an audience gets into the story, the more attuned they become to trying to ferret out evidence, thus overlooking any real clues that are right under their noses. A word of warning about red herrings, though: They must be things that can stand the test of multiple interpretation. Just to keep things dynamic, they should be in at least a two to one ratio against the hints that are genuine.

4. It has become almost a trendy phenomenon in films these days to have "anti-heroes" — brooding, troubled loners who triumph over all manner of horrible complications but still emerge brooding and just as aloof at the story's end as they were to start out. Concurrently, there have been a number of films with villains who are actually more engaging (and smarter) than any of the people we're supposed to be rooting for. Personally, I prefer a plot in which some sort of universal balance or justice wins out, affirming that whatever values a person embraces will either prove their salvation or destruction. In the above scenario, the hero's kindness toward the salesman results in his being saved; the villain's ultimate-destructo-man-eating-accomplice ends up eating him instead.

What all of this adds up to is a wide latitude of creativity within the parameters of an equitably-paced outline. While certain things need to happen at given intervals, the essence of "movie magic" is that anything can. It's also imperative that the tension build progressively. You wouldn't, for instance, start out with the hero in the burning tree and an alligator chomping at his ankles. While it would certainly get the audience's attention right away, you've left yourself with nowhere to go, nothing to build on.

The Three-Act Structure

The difference between the template you have just designed and the expectation of agents and producers once you start submitting your ideas to them is that the latter is accustomed to operating on a traditional three-act structure. In fact, most of the books you'll ever read on the craft of screenwriting address the formula of every story in terms of the Conflict, the Confrontation, and the Solution.

Fortunately, the four-act method you have just learned translates very easily to what Hollywood likes to see: Act 1 (the Conflict) is the same, Acts 2 and 3 (the Confrontation) become Act 2, and Act 4 (the Solution) becomes Act 3. The four-act model is also more workable for beginning screenwriters in terms of the ability it gives them to equitably allocate the action. Without the template, beginners run the risk of too much exposition at the beginning; before they realize it, they've just spent seventy-five minutes introducing all their characters and the story hasn't even gotten underway yet!

All right, so you've just done the math and discovered that Act 2 is now an hour's worth of action, with half an hour of conflict and resolution on either side. That's OK. The reason is that the most likely place for any story to sag is in the middle. There needs to be plenty going on to keep the audience's attention. By merging the elements of your former Act 2 and three into the new Act 2 paragraph of your synopsis, you're demonstrating the awareness that Confrontation brings together every possible obstacle to prevent your protagonist from reaching his or her end-game objective.

Your Assignments

1. Select a fairy tale, myth, or biblical story and write a three-paragraph synopsis which reflects the Conflict, Confrontation, and Solution structure. For extra credit, "pitch" the idea to your peers as if they are Hollywood producers.

2. Brush up on your Shakespeare! Select any of the Bard's plays and use the plot as the basis for a contemporary storyline set in your hometown. Describe the modernized version in terms of a three-act structure.

3. From the list below, select three different films and reduce their respective storylines to just three sentences, each sentence representing one act. (For example, "Girl meets boy. Boy is abducted by aliens. Girl rescues boy.")

Shakespeare in Love

A.I.

The Green Mile

She's All That

The Road to El Dorado

Steel Magnolias

Mission Impossible

Dave

Field of Dreams

The Talented Mr. Ripley

Don't Break the One-Minute Rule

Remember that one-page little test that teachers were so fond of handing out in elementary school — the one which began, *"Read all of the directions before you start,"* then proceeded to list a long series of silly behaviors such as quacking like a duck, running around your desk, and putting your shoes on opposite feet? Not until you got to the last entry did you discover, *"Now that you have read all the directions, please print your name at the top of the page and sit quietly until the rest of the class is done."*

The screenwriting world is not much different from this childhood lesson in paying attention and following the rules. The standardization of fonts, margins, and pages in the script market, for instance, is necessary for prospective directors to know whether they are dealing with a teleplay, a two-hour feature, or the next *Titanic*. Even the cover stock and brads used to assemble a finished screenplay are an industry standard; many a wannabe screenwriter has discovered that the only thing a glitzy presentation binder with bells and whistles accomplishes is in drawing glaring attention to the owner's amateur status.

In a nutshell, breaking the rules when it comes to formatting your script and keeping it within the required time parameters will get you sent to the end of the line.

Certainly as an instructor, one of the most frequent rule-breakers I see in student scripts is the disregard for the "one page equals one-minute" concept. When instructed to turn in the first ten pages (ten minutes) of their screenplay for review, I can always count on at least half of them to either submit a scant two and a half pages with the explanatory margin note that "the rodeo scene takes up a whole lot of time" or seventeen pages with directions that "everyone talks really fast."

I think one of the faults in this probably lies in the fact that it's hard to visualize exactly what a minute *is*. It doesn't seem like you could accomplish very much in that short a time, does it? And yet if I asked you to sit perfectly still and do absolutely nothing for sixty seconds, it might seem to drag on forever!

It's also apparent when new writers haven't "walked through the scene in their heads" and actually timed it after they committed it to paper.

Can you guess what the two most difficult kinds of scenes are when it comes to conforming to the one-page equals one-minute rule?

If you answered "fight scenes and food scenes," you'd be right.

In fight scenes, there's a tendency for beginning writers to want to describe every left punch, right jab, high kick, staggering fall and so forth. What they don't realize is that in the amount of space it takes to describe every bit of footwork, positioning, and bloodied reaction to blows, the fight itself would probably long be over! It's also pretty likely that a director will have his or her own ideas on how this violent choreography should go and will be annoyed at the level of "right-fist-to-left-jaw" detail being provided. Think brevity when it comes to describing fight scenes, battle scenes, chase scenes, etc.

The same thing should be applied to any scenes in which your characters are eating a meal. Unless the plot is *about* the food, you're not going to be writing direction that includes:

Martha picks up her fork and spears a couple of carrots.

She brings the fork to her mouth.

She chews.

She swallows.

She sets the fork down and picks up her glass of water.

She takes a sip.

She sets the glass down and picks up her fork again.

This time she takes a bit of mashed potatoes.

Nor do you want to fall into the trap of what I call "accelerated dining." Many a time I've read a single page of dialog in which the characters: 1. arrive at the restaurant, 2. are shown to their table, 3. hear the list of specials, 4. peruse their menus, 5. make their selections, and 6. are now halfway through their meal by the bottom of that very same page!

Again, the practice of mentally walking through the action, as well as saying the lines of dialog out loud, will help you hone your skills in having the pace of the story accurately reflected in the content of the pages.

Your Assignments

1. Write a fight scene in proper screenplay format.
2. Write a food scene in proper screenplay format.

How Do I Handle Transitions?

Motion pictures were still a new-fangled phenomenon in 1934 when John Wayne made a series of cookie-cutter Westerns with Gabby Hayes. Now available on video, these grainy black-and-whites speak to a cinematography dilemma that still plagues aspiring scriptwriters; specifically, how to move characters from one time/place to another.

The vintage westerns addressed this problem in what now seems a comic fashion: a rapid left/right pan of the camera. Logistically, this maneuver made sense, as the "old timer's cabin" and "the nearest town" co-existed about 100 feet apart on the same back lot. The intent of the fast blur, of course, was to trick audiences into believing that the distance was at least half a day's hard ride.

While modern technology has elevated the art of flawless film segues, the burden still rests on the writer to craft a credible transition.

Food for thought: Classroom and hospital waiting room scenes seem to have all purchased their big ominous wall clocks from the same store. Modus operandi? Speeding up of their own volition or magically "melting" from 3:00 to 8:15. They share a kinship with prominent wall calendars, in which an invisible force rips off the days to illustrate time's passage. And let's not forget digital "subtitles" (de rigueur for espionage films), which concurrently reveal what exotic city we're in (very helpful in night shots if we couldn't figure it out).

Dialog is another popular method of establishing transition; i.e., "Raida will be here at six," "Can this wait? I'm leaving for Phoenix," or "Three days from now is the coronation." These verbal clues help bookmark and advance the action like a computer hyperlink, minus the tedium of scrolling through everything in-between. Speaking of tedium, many new writers make the mistake of assuming that if two characters are going to lunch, it's necessary to show them leaving the office, catching an elevator, crossing the street, entering the café, etc. Wrong! Unless something significant is slated to happen during their trek from Point A to Point B, simply cut from the office straight to the meal.

Sunrise, sunset ... it's easy to show day/night transitions in exterior shots. But what about interior? If the curtains are closed, how will your audience distinguish morning from evening? Some quick hints: character clothing, visible food, an opened door, a television/radio/answering machine whereby the hour is referenced.

If it's Tuesday, this must be Amsterdam. Why do you suppose directors are so fond of opening a movie with recognizable cityscapes or landmarks? Because if they didn't, we'd wrongly assume that every story ever written took place in a Hollywood soundstage. Stock shots instantly establish where we are — and where we're headed — without anyone having to say it out loud.

Last but not least are plots which should come with their own frequent flyer miles. While the sky's the limit in relocating your fantasy and sci-fi characters, you can always rely on good ol' eerie dissolves, warp-speed, dry ice, dizzying spins, or a simple "cut-and-paste."

Beam us up, Scottie. We're outta here!

Your Assignments

1. What transitional devices have you used in your own script to move the action from one location or time frame to another? Would a different transition be more effective?

2. Sitcoms usually limit their locations to three primary sets, plus exterior establishing shots. The action of *Friends*, for instance, is primarily set in the two apartments and Central Perk, the group's coffeehouse hang-out. In any given episode, what types of transitions have the writers used to shift the action and/or reflect that time has passed?

3. Apply what you have just observed from watching a sitcom to watching a feature-length film which has a wider range of locations and is told over a longer period of time. Were there transitions which you thought were especially clever? How can you use this new insight in your own work?

Spotlight on Youth:
An Interview with Laurel Bosque

You may not have heard of Ms. Laurel Bosque before today, but chances are good that she could emerge very soon as one of Tinseltown's brightest new talents. If you're planning to give her some competition, though, it's only fair to warn you that she already has a head start: as of this writing, Laurel is fourteen years old.

Q: When did you first get interested in writing and what kind of stories do you like to create?

A: I think I got interested in writing when I was in second grade because that was when I first started learning about creative writing. I do not limit myself to one particular style, but my protagonists are often mentally unstable or villainous.

Q: Is anyone else in your family a writer?

A: My father has had about a dozen poems and several articles published, but as far as I know he is the only other person in the family interested in writing.

Q: What sort of classes have you taken in school that either excited you about the craft of writing or enhanced what you already knew?

A: The school I've gone to for the last nine years does not offer many classes that are not necessary for the entire student body, so I guess that I learned most of what I know about writing from reading.

Q: **What are your three favorite movies so far and why did you like each one?**

A: My favorite films change with my moods, but currently my three favorites are *Citizen Kane, Rashomon*, and *Dr. Strangelove*. I was in a film class where we watched *Citizen Kane* frame by frame as our mentor, Ronald Chase, pointed out what was beautiful about each shot. It really made me appreciate the cinematography! I also liked *Rashomon* because of the cinematography. I have never seen forests, rain, and mist done so well. I enjoyed *Dr. Strangelove* because the screenplay was ingenious in portraying how distrust and coincidence can lead to extremely messy situations. I thought it was witty and the acting was inspired.

Q: **What kind of movie would you like to write someday?**

A: Right now I am more interested in independent and underground films than mainstream movies, but that could change in time.

Q: **What sort of themes/topics do you think are the most important to other young people who are your age?**

A: I think that it is difficult to generalize about what kind of movie people my age enjoy. I know that romance and action are both very popular among teenagers, but many of my friends and I prefer more serious films.

Q: **Do you plan to major in film in college or in something else? Why?**

A: I would like to major in film in college, but it might be more practical to major in English. On the other hand, I am also interested in art history which is extremely *impractical!*

Q: **I understand you've already shot some short videos of your own. What are the titles and what are they about?**

A: The titles of the films are *Mission* and *Tres Sheik*. *Mission* was shot in the Mission Dolores graveyard and had no actors. It illustrated some of the conflict between the Native Americans and the Franciscans. I used two statues as symbols for each side and combined Gregorian chant and a traditional Inuit song for the music. *Tres Sheik* was about the secret life of a couch potato. When alone in his house, the protagonist would dress up in a sheet and pretend to be Lawrence of Arabia. I was lucky enough to find an actor that looked like Valentino. *Mission* only showed at one film festival, but *Tres Sheik* made it to five, including one in Philadelphia.

Q: What are your favorite television shows and why?

A: I do not watch TV too often, but I do enjoy *The Simpsons.* Even though it is often mindless comedy, it sometimes is a political satire and has made references to some great movies such as *Citizen Kane.*

Q: Would you rather write for the movies or for TV? Why?

A: I would rather write for movies than for television because the writer has more freedom with films. Plus, I think that scripts are often better for films than for TV.

Q: What is the most important thing you have learned so far about being a writer?

A: I think that the most important part of writing is revising. I have also learned to recognize how much procrastination is possible before it starts affecting your work.

Topics to Think About and Talk About

1. Have you ever watched classic films, and if so, which films made the greatest impression on you? If not, then why not?

2. As a young person wanting to make a career in film, what do you think it takes to be taken seriously by film producers and investors?

3. What role do you see your closest friends playing as you focus your energies on a career in the film industry?

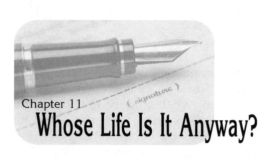

Chapter 11

Whose Life Is It Anyway?

Anyone who has grown up with siblings can attest to the fact that there are multiple sides to every story. No matter what the inciting incident is, every spectator and participant — just like a crime scene — has a different rendition of what happened. Which version is right? It all depends on who's doing the telling ... and the listening. The same can be said of film. Once you've decided what your plot's going to be, the next big challenge is identifying whose voice gets to deliver the message ... and how.

Point of View

I recently finished reading the manuscript of what would make an excellent book. You'll note that I said "book" and not "film," even though the latter was clearly the author's ultimate goal. It was one of those stories that not only spanned continents but spanned the course of sixty years, exploring the twisted relationships of a dysfunctional family that made the cast of *Dallas* look like *The Brady Bunch*.

While I enjoy the quirkiness and comic fodder generated by dysfunctional families just as much as the next person, my problem with the story kept coming back to one thing: I never really knew who I was supposed to root for. Just when one character started to get interesting and emerge as the one whose hopes, fears, and dilemmas I thought I was supposed to follow, another character jumped to centerstage and began to project her hopes, fears, and dilemmas.

Whose story was this anyway?

By the time the entire family and their social circle had all been introduced, I was completely confused, especially since there was no unifying objective on which they — and a potential audience — could collectively focus. There were no perceptible cause-and-effect relationships amidst all of this intercutting and mini-plots, which resulted in a complete lack of continuity and momentum.

What were they all doing here besides just taking up space?

Because film is a vicarious medium, it's important to establish as early as possible in the script whose story is being told. More often than not, the events which unfold will be from the viewpoint of the protagonist or, in the case of a romance, the dual viewpoints of the leading man and leading lady in their quest to achieve the same goal. The moment you start giving more lines and more screen-time to the antagonist and/or subordinate characters, the more you've diluted the protagonist's point of view.

A good example of this is Kevin Costner's *Robin Hood, Prince of Thieves*. We know from the star billing and English history that the story is supposed to be from Robin's perspective. Yet how often did you find yourself waiting in anticipation for his arch enemy, the Sheriff of Nottingham, to reappear?

While there are some films which *have* successfully juggled multiple viewpoints (*Reversal of Fortune*, for example), it's probably not a good idea to attempt "ensemble narration" on your very first script. Decide whose primary story it's going to be ... and stick with it!

Your Assignment

The tale of *Little Red Riding Hood* is generally told from the omnipotent, third person point of view. Although it is primarily Red's story, we're nevertheless aware of the wolf lurking in the woods and the sweet-faced grandmother waiting for her favorite relative to deliver a basket of fresh fruit and scones. Your job as a screenwriter is to pitch three different versions of this tale to a producer: one from Ms. Hood's point of view, one from the viewpoint of the wolf, and the third from the viewpoint of the grandmother.

For each one-page synopsis that you write reflecting these three different views, examine what the goals and objectives are of each party, their state of mind during the events leading up to the woodsman's fortuitous arrival, and what each of them did with their lives after "fade to black ... " (assuming they were still alive to tell about it). When you have completed all three synopses, assess which of these three characters has the most compelling point of view and, thus, should drive the action.

Agents for Change

At the start of the story, the protagonist's point of view stems from where he or she is at that particular moment in time. Maybe they are content with the status quo and abhor the idea of any revision to it. On the other hand, maybe they're desperate to be somewhere else or to acquire something they're presently lacking. What will it take to light a fire under them and ultimately force a decision about their future?

In order to chart a new course and alter his or her current perspective, what your lead character needs most is to be introduced to a catalyst, an agent for change.

The agent for change is an individual whose own point of view (or personal circumstances) is often in contrast to the protagonist. While agents for change have well defined goals and objectives of their own, they generally don't have to undergo any character transformations themselves in order to achieve those quests. Instead the agent for change is responsible, either by design or accident, for setting up the requisite strategies and events which will impact the hero/heroine's emotional growth.

The classic *Casablanca* is a nice demonstration of how this works. Although there is a strong undercurrent of romance between Rick and Ilsa, the story is related to us through Rick's viewpoint. Here is a man who has basically declared himself neutral while the world around him is gripped in the grim reality of war. Enter Ilsa, the agent for change. Ilsa is as determined to be proactive in securing the letters of transit to save her husband, Laszlo, as Rick is steadfast to stay passive, cynical, and not to stick his neck out for anybody. By the final credits, Ilsa has not only achieved her objective of getting safe passage but influenced Rick to rejoin humanity and take up a cause that is higher than his own self-interests or the feelings they have for each other.

Your Assignment

Identify the agent for change in each of the following films and discuss how he or she specifically impacted the protagonist's change of heart or purpose:

While You Were Sleeping

Star Wars

Witness

Groundhog Day

The Piano

True Lies

Jerry Maguire

Seven

Tootsie

Shakespeare in Love

Lethal Weapon

Moonstruck

How Do We Know What They Know?

If you were a director and encountered the following staging:

LAURIE notices JACK across the room and thinks to herself that he reminds her of someone who once broke her heart in Nebraska.

How would you film it?

The "noticing" part is easy because it is a physical action/reaction. What's impossible for the camera, though, is getting inside a character's head and showing us exactly what's going on there. Unlike a short story or novel which can be liberally sprinkled with internal segues such as, "she thought," "he wondered," "he worried," "she mused," "he reflected," and "she hoped," the only way we can know these things on a big screen is if the character in question can find a verbal or visual way to communicate it to us.

How do we know, for instance, that Laurie thinks this guy looks like somebody else? Unless we've already *seen* that prior somebody else and arrive at the same, simultaneous conclusion as Laurie, we're not going to recognize the connection she has just drawn.

How do we know she has been in love before and, even worse, had her heart broken as a result? Is this something she has already mentioned in an earlier conversation? Have we been exposed to a flashback of that prior relationship?

How do we even know it was in Nebraska? Is a Nebraska reference even crucial to the plot? You'd be surprised at just how much minutia wanders its way into a script, never to be brought to any mention out loud and yet curiously deemed important enough for the writer to throw into the directions.

How then, *would* you communicate Laurie's state of angst if you couldn't use a nice little "thought-bubble" above her head like a cartoon or, as in Woody Allen's *Annie Hall*, subtitles?

One approach is the voice-over. In this framework, whatever the character is "thinking" is heard out loud in a sort of hollow, resonant level to distinguish it from just being part of a ventriloquist act. Obviously, its uses are limited. For example, if all your characters were thinking out loud at the same time, no one could hear the conversations going on underneath. Voice-overs are also perceived by directors and producers as a way to mask weak writing and poor dialog skills. If you have to resort to explaining all the subtext via this device of first-person narration, there's probably something wrong with the script.

Another alternative available to you is the mini-flashback or dream sequence. Specifically, a character sees something or someone across the room and momentarily "blinks-out" to an earlier place and time. Used in excess, however, this can really be annoying.

Option three is the mutter. In this instance, your character suddenly says something under his or her breath to no one in particular. Actually, that's not quite true. They *are* saying it to someone. They're saying it strictly for the benefit of the audience because it's the only way the writer could think to expeditiously get the information into play. ("Oh no, it's Arthur. I hope he doesn't come this way. He's probably still mad at me about last Christmas at my sister's even though I think he must have known none of it was my fault ...") Contrivance with a capital "C."

Is Laurie at the party with a friend? Take a look at how dialog can convey what's on your character's mind:

ANNIE: Let it go, girlfriend.

LAURIE: What?

ANNIE: Him. Mr. Hunk you can't take your eyes off of.

LAURIE: So sue me. Can I help it if he reminds me of Nick...

ANNIE: Oh puh-leeze! Not *him* again!

LAURIE: Oh come on! Don't you think just a little?

ANNIE: It's better than not thinking at all.

LAURIE: Maybe this guy will be different. I wonder what his name is... ?

ANNIE: Different name, same game. Trust me, sugar. You're lookin' at a dead-end no matter how you play it.

Dialog observations amongst other characters in the scene can also be used to relate "internal" information. For instance:

BRAD: What's with your roomie? She looks lost in space.

ANNIE: Neh, she's looked that way ever since she moved in.

BRAD: Ever ask why?

ANNIE: I don't have to. She tells me about him eighty thousand times a week.

BRAD: Him?

ANNIE: Nick. Corn King of the Heartbreakers.

Finally, there's the direct approach. Laurie not only notices Jack but boldly walks up to him and says, "You know, you remind me of someone I knew in Nebraska who broke my heart."

At least now he knows what she's thinking. And so do we.

Rule to remember: If there isn't a way for the camera to see it or hear it, leave it out of the script!

Your Assignment

How many places in your own script have you included non-filmable directions or information? Yellow highlight each place where this occurs. For every scene where you have supplied written detail for thoughts or backstory that are not subsequently related through visuals or conversation, ask yourself the following questions:

1. What specifically needs to be conveyed to the audience in this scene?

2. What things can be implied about the characters' feelings or personalities through means other than direct dialog?

3. What doesn't need to be in the script at all?

Selling Scripts in Cyberspace

The Internet is dramatically changing the way that producers — and, accordingly, agents — are doing business. From independent production companies to major studios, the electronic bandwagon is being hopped on from all directions. Says Terence Michael of Michael/Finney Productions, "Although we respect agents and admit that the overall quality of the material they send us is higher, the percentage of scripts we read and acquire from the Internet or direct e-mail has now overshadowed those from the agencies. We can log on anytime and search for exactly what we want."

How can you as a new screenwriter tap into this valuable resource ... and should you?

Jerrol LeBaron, creator/owner of Writers Script Network, has become an expert on how to get exposure for writers of screenplays and shorts. Growing up in a construction background, but with entrepreneurial spirit, Jerrol purchased his first business at age twenty-three. Later on, he dabbled in acting and writing and it was this experience that inspired him to create Writers Script Network. His opinions on how technology is making Hollywood more accessible to beginners are included herein with his gracious permission.

Can the Internet be an effective tool for screenwriters? Five years ago, the answer would have been an emphatic "no". To many of the "old school" industry professionals, the answer is still "no". The good news, though, is that Hollywood is being firmly nudged to embrace what has become an inescapable facet of modern technology: cyber promotion.

Up until the Internet, screenwriters had a particularly tough time of getting recognized. Between the Writers Guild and Copyright Office, there are approximately 90,000 works for stage, television and film that are registered annually in the U.S. Although a good percentage of these are screenplays, only a few hundred will ever make it to the silver screen each year. Why? Because Tinseltown is a tightly closed community, operating on the popular catch-phrase, "You're only as good as your last film." As a result, many well known artists share the same frustration as their lesser-known rivals in finding just the right project. Directors and producers as well share the labor-intensive plight of having to read hundreds of treatments and scripts in the quest for discovering one that will be a good vehicle for their careers.

Further complicating the access issue from the writer's standpoint has been the prohibitive nature of getting a new screenplay, sans agent, into a particular talent's hands. Short of moving to L.A. and parking on someone's doorstep, aspiring screenwriters have endured the dismal reality of spending months — even years — on a project, only to have it rejected or, worse, never read at all.

With digital equipment and the Internet, however, the odds in favor of linking authors, actors, and film companies have increased dramatically. For one thing, the entertainment industry is gearing itself to start showing full-length features on the Internet twenty-four hours a day. There are now scores of companies, such as Ifilm.com where you can view thirty-second to fifteen-minute shorts. Such groups are aggressively soliciting produced material that can go on line immediately, not only providing writers with credits but invaluable experience and sometimes even money! As an entry-level opportunity, the demand currently exceeds the supply.

Another positive development is the proliferation of marketing opportunities via personal computers. More and more producers and studios world-wide are now utilizing cyber-space for their future film projects. As the months go by, we will see a growing trend of directors and producers who have the wherewithal to produce micro-budget films and garner three to ten picture deals looking to this resource for original material.

As an example, I recently had a working but unknown actor named Richard Cody visit my website (http://www.WritersScriptNetwork.com) in search of a character-driven script that could be produced for roughly $100,000. Shortly after providing him access to the site and sending out notices to writers I know, a creative executive for Disney made contact with him. The next thing I knew, Richard had an interview. Through our cooperative efforts, previously inaccessible doors were suddenly opening up to him. He now has a budget of one to three million and has found three suitable projects to pursue.

Taking advantage of this burgeoning Internet marketplace requires a fair share of research and groundwork. Because it's still a relatively new field in terms of pitching scripts, all of the "rules" are still in the embryonic stage. The plus for writers in this, of course, is that the long-standing Catch-22 regarding credits and representation can't really be applied. The sky, as they say, is the limit.

Whether your objective is to write shorts or features, it's important to know their respective idiosyncrasies and formats. In either case, the lower the budget, the higher your chances of seeing it sold and produced. This means fewer characters, minimal special effects, and concentrating all of the events in the fewest number of locations (i.e., one house, a park, a cemetery, etc.). Playwrights might find it especially easy to adapt some of their material for this new venue, given the already existent economy of production.

Planning to post your synopsis or script on a web site for review? There are several which specialize in making scripts available to industry professionals (www.storybay.com, and www.thesource.com.au, which originates in Australia. Many of these organizations will require a release form and/or WGA registration. A few warnings: 1. Don't sign release forms that use the word *identical*; 2. Don't post your entire script if the site isn't password protected and doesn't track records of who is viewing your work; and 3. Always protect your work, whether it's a two-minute short or a two-hour feature. Protecting your work is relatively easy, inexpensive, and can even be done quickly online.

This is the way the market is going. Take advantage of it!

John Johnson, Executive Director and Founder of the American Screenwriters Association, voices a similar view that the old way of doing business is undergoing a substantive facelift:

The marketing of script ideas through the Internet is in its infancy, much like the concept of being able to purchase airline tickets online was in the early 1990s. But as technology advances and people become more comfortable with using the Internet to market scripts, the frequency and constructive use of such sites will increase dramatically. Right now this type of marketing is not as effective as it can be because the web sites offering these services are so new. Screenwriters have to learn about the existence of these sites, and get past the problems of confidentiality and insecurity of someone "stealing their script." I do envision that one day marketing one's script through the Internet will provide a valuable entry into Hollywood and will be as substantial as (but will never completely replace the personal aspect of) personal pitching. In its truest form, placing your script on a web site is a pitch. The real question is, will producers, agents and industry professionals adopt this technological marketing of scripts as the norm? Personally, I think they'd be crazy not to, but the world changes slowly and Hollywood is no exception. The plus side for industry professionals is that they can now log onto a secure web site at their convenience and view the scripts they are interested in by quickly reviewing the loglines and/or synopsis. Realistically however, Hollywood is and always will be a "personal" business. Decisions are made because of who you know, how good your work is and good ol' fashioned networking to get your script into the right hands at the right time.

A Wealth of Screenwriting Websites

Break out those electronic bookmarks! You truly don't need to live in Hollywood or New York to take advantage of all the script placement services, directories, professional associations, or online classes that are available from the convenience of your own computer.

American Screenwriters Association (ASA)

http://www.asascreenwriters.com

ASA was founded in 1996 in Cincinnati in response to the void which Executive Director John Johnson perceived between emerging screenwriters and the industry. ASA now boasts 650 plus members in eight countries, conducts two international competitions, is implementing an exciting pilot project with Time Warner Cable, and recently acquired responsibility for the longest running screenwriting conference in America, *Selling to Hollywood*. Taking control of this premier screenwriting conference will continue to elevate ASA's visibility, not just through the marketing of the conference in trade publications, websites and direct mailings, but also in the delivery of successful programs taught by some of Hollywood's top experts.

Writers Script Network

http://www.writersscriptnetwork.com

Writers Script Network is a password-protected site which allows writers to post their loglines, synopses, and full scripts for agent, director, and producer review. A feature has also been added which allows writers to post loglines for shorts.

Zoetrope

http://www.zoetrope.com

This site is the brainchild of Francis Ford Coppola and offers both beginning and professional screenwriters the chance to post their scripts free of charge for evaluation and feedback by other participants. Access to the site is password-protected, and members must read and review a designated number of new scripts before receiving the results of their own submissions. Those which receive significantly high marks are then forwarded to Coppola staff for production consideration.

Movie Bytes

http://www.moviebytes.com

Who's Buying What? For $30 a year, you'll have the answer at the flick of a keystroke, plus be privy to first-time success stories. Yours could become one of them!

HollywoodLitSales

http://www.hollywoodlitsales.com

HollywoodLitSales not only opens the door to new material, but regularly updates its database of American and foreign producers seeking projects that can be shot for less than ten million dollars. It also has one of the most comprehensive resource links I've found to agents, production companies, film festivals, and monthly/annual script competitions. Online seminars and topical articles by entertainment professionals help to keep new writers abreast of what Hollywood is looking for and how best to deliver it.

Write Movies

http://www.writemovies.com

A variety of competitions are launched each year through this site, providing contestants a chance to showcase their best work in screenplays, books, short stories, journalism, and plays. French and German versions of the same website are also available.

Script P.I.M.P.

http://www.scriptpimp.com

This "Pipeline Into Motion Pictures" is an Internet matchmaking service between new scripts and producers. In addition to providing full-coverage critiques of your submitted material, the staff at Script P.I.M.P. is committed to walking it through the Hollywood process and into the hands of industry execs looking for specific types of films. Prior registration with the U.S. Copyright Office or

Writers Guild of America is required, along with a standard release form (available at the site). If you can spring for the $100 screenplay fee, what you'll receive in return is an objective analysis of what works and what doesn't in terms of marketability. What you won't receive, of course, is any guarantee of a sale once the script is put in circulation. A better way to go, particularly if you have done well in contests, had previous critiques done and/or simply like your film exactly the way it is, is to pay a $40 fee to get your script into the system. Scripts can be submitted electronically or by snail mail.

Hollywood-101

http://www.hollywood-101.com

Frederick Levy, Vice President of Development and Production at Marty Katz Productions, is the creative force behind this informative and entertaining site regarding what it takes to write for today's movies. It's also a solid inducement to purchase Levy's best-selling text, "Hollywood 101: The Film Industry" or sign up for his ongoing film classes at UCLA Extension.

Backstage

http://www.backstage.com

Although the primary focus of this website is theatre, one of its best features is the callboard for writers and directors. There you will find notices posted by television and independent production companies looking for specific types of scripts and/or screenwriters to develop concept pieces. Little or no pay seems to be the general trend, but keep in mind that the opportunity to work one-on-one with indie directors and producers is yet another way to build credits and valuable experience.

The Source (Australia)

http://www.thesource.com.au

This site down under has its own Spec Script Library, analysis and representation services, a "Scripts Wanted" feature, and is the sponsor of the annual Big Australian International Screenwriting Contest. It also provides screenwriting tips each week which are e-mailed for free to anyone who'd like them.

New York Screenwriter

http://www.nyscreenwriter.com

NY Screenwriter is available as a print magazine, too, and features interviews with today's hottest writers and producers, in addition to articles and books to help further one's career.

StoryBay

http://www.storybay.com

A contest and coverage site for writers who want to put their work in circulation, as well as network with fellow authors.

Screenwriters Utopia

http://www.screenwritersutopia.com

Screenwriters Utopia is replete with industry interviews, articles, script reviews, and books to add to your library on the craft of screenwriting.

Script Sales

http://www.scriptsales.com

This site has a tremendous number of industry links to commend it, but my favorite feature is the one which lists all of the major production companies and the actors/actresses who run their own.

FilmMakers

http://www.FilmMakers.com

A site chock full of information on independent film companies, film festivals, upcoming contests, and interviews with new and established directors.

Success by Degree:
What College-Bound Film Students Need to Know

The world of cinema combines all of the narrative arts, thus its attraction as a medium of unparalleled communication possibilities. Learning the rudiments in a progressive collegiate or internship environment is just the beginning of the new screenwriter's career journey. The following interview was collaboratively composed by Dr. John Schultheiss, Chair of the Department of Cinema and Television Arts, and Dr. Bob Gustafson, Director of the Entertainment Industry Institute, College of Arts, Media, and Communication, California State University, Northridge.

Q: Suppose a student asked you whether he or she should pursue a degree in film or get a degree in a discipline which will pay the bills while they're trying to break into the market?

A: It is emphatically recommended that students *not* go into a discipline just to pay the bills while trying to break into the film industry; students should go where their passion is! Once a person is "out of the loop," it is almost impossible to get back in. We consistently advise students, even after they have graduated, that if they have not obtained a job in the entertainment industry (specifically the film industry) —they should get an internship. [Even if they have graduated] — enroll in extended learning, pay for your credits, get an internship, and get back "into the loop," where you will meet people.

Q: In other words, good networking?

A: Jobs come from people! They do not come from institutions, nor do they really come from resumes. And, this may appear bizarre, jobs do not really come from skills! The film industry is not a science, as in having a degree in medicine where skills would lead to a job. The film industry offers no comparison to that situation. In the film industry, people get jobs from other people — who do you know, where did they see your work ethic actually being auditioned? The answer is an internship.

Q: What does the film program at CSUN offer in that regard?

A: The curriculum of the Department of Cinema and Television Arts offers the full complement of courses — everything from film theory to film and television production and multimedia. But a most valuable element of the curriculum is our internship program. In fact, we have more internship opportunities than we have students! Students can be most selective and obtain the best internship offerings available anywhere in the world, especially since Los Angeles is the center of mass entertainment. The primary door for jobs for students into the film industry is internships, and this is our major contribution to and vehicle for the students.

Q: **Are there any figures available in terms of the percentage of your film majors who end up actually working in the industry?**

A: The "film production" option contains the greatest number of our majors. The overall percentage of students who actually get jobs in various aspects of the mass media is seventy-three percent. But the film production majors do not always end up in positions in film. Many end up in television. The reason for this is that there is so much more television production. Compare the hundreds of television programs (including soap operas, sitcoms, cable shows, documentaries, music videos) that are produced to the number of feature films created in any given year.

Q: **What can aspiring film students do to distinguish themselves while still in high school that will assist in their getting accepted into a university film program?**

A: An important element is having a demo reel — a compilation of what the student has actually produced: three to five minutes of created material. The availability of digital equipment (cameras and editing tools) makes this a possibility and a necessity.

Q: **Filmmaking technology has improved tremendously over the decades. But has the quality of storytelling kept pace?**

A: It has not kept pace. The parallel is to the situation of the late 1920s, with the advent of sound — the emphasis on "all talking, all singing, all dancing" — just because the technology made it possible. Today there are films that

157

basically have no story, are very heavy on special effects (like *Jurassic Park*), which appeal to those audiences who want to respond on that level. It is speculated that this is a transitional phase; people will get tired of this, and will want to return to storytelling. But right now, this is paying off at the box-office, because people seem to be impressed with these techniques.

Q: What would you say are the three best films from which a young screenwriter could learn technique?

A: The essence of this question is so inherently subjective as to be practically meaningless to a young person. To refer a young student to *Casablanca*, *To Be Or Not To Be*, or *Double Indemnity* (from the studio era), or *Amadeus, Memento,* or *The Deep End* (from the contemporary era) is to invite incomprehension. A more pragmatic exercise: purchase a copy of the script, watch the film on videotape or DVD at home, and see how the script changed from the printed page to finished screen version — and get used to the idea that you are a part of a collective art.

Q: What is the most challenging aspect of filmmaking that students struggle with?

A: To understand the reality versus the publicity. The publicity is that the business is glamorous, everybody is having fun, everybody gets rich, and that they lead full, exotic, active lives — when, in fact, there is no such thing as glamour unless you are with the public. There is no glamour at work. It is all work, and it is all collaborative. Nobody can do anything alone. The writers think they are in charge. The directors think they are in charge. The actors think they are in charge. The money people think they are in charge. The studios think they are in charge. The theatres think they are in charge. All of this is correct. Everybody is in charge — all at the same time. So what the students need to know is that they will never be in charge. You always have a series of bosses, and the bosses have bosses. The public is the ultimate boss because they put thumbs up or down on an individual project. So students need to abandon the idea of a "solo artist." If they are interested in a solo art career, they should go into the fine arts. In terms of the film or entertainment business, it never happens that an individual can do what they want to do all the time.

Q: What's your best advice for young people who want to write for the movies and television?

A: Be aware of the following reality: Most people who write for films and television do not do it full-time. The number of full-time writers who can actually employ themselves is a tiny percentage of persons in the Writers Guild. The advice for those who want to write for film and television is to have a second career in entertainment simultaneously — not an outside career, like the actor who is a waiter in a restaurant. But like a writer who also works in production, who also works in the film business, in distribution, or something like that. The writer needs to have an agent. The writer needs to know people. The writer needs to be seen. To be part of the family is really how it works. The person needs to become a part of the film and television industries. Let your colleagues know that you are also a writer, that you have a lot of really good ideas, and are willing and able to show them to them. The chances of being a full-time writer are very slim.

Q: Finally, the age-old question: What is Hollywood looking for?

A: The same thing it was always looking for: people who can communicate very well — written, spoken, and listening. This includes social skills. Can the person get along in a team effort? This is a collective art. The number of people involved in any project is enormous. What Hollywood is looking for is somebody with communication skills. These are obtained by taking classes that promote writing, reading, comprehension, interpersonal communication. Hollywood is also interested in people who possess an excellent work ethic — people who are self-motivated, who have a sense of urgency, who don't have to be told things. They do them automatically. These are people who always, on their own, seem to be in a hurry. These are people who are motivated without anybody supervising — and love it! Hollywood is also looking for people who are not critical. It is not interested in those who blame Hollywood for

America's vulgar culture. Hollywood actually may be the cause of this, but this is not an attitude to communicate. Hollywood is looking for people who want to join a family, a family of people who work extremely hard. (Most projects fail, most television shows do not make it, most movies lose money.) Hollywood is looking for people who love entertainment, who love movies, who love television — and who would really probably enjoy doing it if they were not paid at all. They are just doing what they love. They love being creative, they love being busy, they love doing really difficult things very well. There is no production that is easy. Everything is hard. Everything is complicated. Everything is a compromise. So, they are looking for people who are motivated, who are good communicators, with good social skills, who are, of course, computer literate (in terms of word processing). The primary skill the studios are looking for, believe it or not, is typing. Can the person actually type? In summary, Hollywood is looking for a positive attitude, a great work ethic, a sense of urgency, excellent communication, and social skills.

Topics to Think About and Talk About

1. What other elements of film production do you think would be beneficial to learn to further your goal of becoming a screenwriter? (100 words or less)

2. What activities are you currently engaged in, or have the opportunity in the near future to be engaged in, that will further your career in film? If you have none, how will that effect your further educational plans? (100 words or less)

3. Describe what first got you interested in film. Since then, describe what has happened in your life to maintain your interest. How important is furthering your education to you in achieving your goal?

Chapter 12

How Do You Keep Someone from Stealing Your Movie Idea?

After you've invested all this time writing the next box-office blockbuster, the last thing you need is for someone else to come along and steal it out from under you. While this chapter may not be as fun as the previous ones, it nevertheless looks at important ways you can keep your idea safe.

The Legalities of Screenwriting

Film companies are particularly sensitive to the subject of idea theft, given the number of lawsuits they handle which revolve around authors claiming that the script they submitted and got rejected was later turned into a hit. It's for this reason that writers need to register their work at the outset in order to establish the date of origination, and filmmakers are likewise behooved to have every submission accompanied by a standard release form. Such documentation acknowledges the existence of similar concepts and that the author is precluded from suing the company in the event that a film of comparable plot by a different writer is subsequently produced.

Before you panic and interpret this protocol as giving them permission to steal your best ideas, there are two things you need to remember:

1. With so many projects already cooking on all burners, Hollywood would much rather buy a perfect script which is already written than to steal an idea and assign it to someone else to write from scratch.

2. There are only so many plots which exist in the world; the reason it seems like there are many more is because of the multitude of "voices" and life experiences which shape specifically how those tales are told. While there is a risk in any business of having a great idea copied, no two writers will relate it in exactly the same way. It is the uniqueness of voice and heart that gets a script sold.

A Sample Standard Agreement

The following standard agreement was graciously provided by Bannon/Oleshansky, a full service production and management company, the partners of which have spent much of their careers identifying, packaging, negotiating and/or advising others in the option and development of film projects, publishing, merchandising, television series, and the creation of several cable/digital niche channels.

In addition, Bannon/Oleshansky is currently consulting for SPACEHAB (Nasdaq: SPAB), the first company to commercially develop, own, and operate habitable modules that provide laboratory facilities and logistics resupply aboard NASA's Space Shuttles, with regards to the creation of SPACEHAB's new space media unit, and SPACEHAB's commercial space habitat, Enterprise™, module to be attached to the International Space Station. Of more earthly concern to the rest of you, of course, is that they are also receptive to new clients with completed projects, whether they currently exist as screenplays, published books, or theatrical works. They can be contacted at:

Bannon/Oleshansky

1313 9th Street, Suite 11

Santa Monica, California 90401

or by email at: bannonoleshansky@aol.com.

RELEASE AGREEMENT

As of the _____ Day of _____, 2001

Gentlemen:

I, _____ (Print Name), desire to submit to you for your consideration, the following described material, ideas and/or creative work ("said material(s)") to Bannon/Oleshansky:

_____

_____

_____

WGA REGISTRATION NO. _____

or Copyright Registration No._____

or Neither _____ (check one).

As an inducement to you to examine said material, I represent, warrant and agree, as follows:

1. I acknowledge that because of your position in the entertainment industry you receive numerous unsolicited submissions of ideas, formats, stories, suggestions and the like and that many such submissions received by you are similar to or identical to those developed by you or your employees or otherwise available to you. I agree that I will not be entitled to any compensation because of the use by you of any such similar or identical material.

2. I further understand that you would refuse to accept and evaluate said material in the absence of my acceptance of each and all of the provisions of this agreement. I shall retain all rights to submit this or similar material to persons other than you. I acknowledge that no fiduciary or confidential relationship now exists between you and me, and I further acknowledge that no such relationships are established between you and me by reason of this agreement or by reason of my submission to you of said material.

3. I request that you read and evaluate said material with a view to deciding whether you will undertake to option, acquire, and/or represent it.

4. I represent and warrant that I am (check one):

❏ AUTHOR/RIGHTS HOLDER of said material, having acquired said material as the employer-for-hire of all writers thereof; that I am the present and sole owner of all right, title, and interest in and to said material; that I have the exclusive, unconditional right and authority to submit and/or convey said material to you upon the terms and conditions set forth herein; that no third party is entitled to any payment or other consideration as a condition of the exploitation of said material.

❏ INDIVIDUAL submitting said material to BO as the basis for a feature film, made for television movie, or television series. I acknowledge that, often people have similar ideas. If more than one person submits a similar project or concept, said material with earlier postmark will prevail, and no obligation will be due to the other submission(s).

5. I agree to indemnify you from and against any and all claims, expenses, losses, or liabilities (including, without limitation, reasonable attorneys' fees and punitive damages) that may be asserted against you or incurred by you at any time in connection with said material, or any use thereof, including without limitation those arising from any breach of the warranties and promises given by me herein.

6. You may use without any obligation or payment to me any of said material which is not protectable as literary property under the laws of plagiarism, or which a third person would be free to use if the material had not been submitted to him or had not been the subject of any agreement with him, or which is in the public domain. Any of said material, which, in accordance with the preceding sentence, you are entitled to use without obligation to me, is hereinafter referred to as "unprotected material." If all or any part of said material does not fall in the category of unprotected material it is hereinafter referred to as "protected material."

7. You agree that if you use or cause to be used any protected material provided it has not been obtained from, or independently created by, another source, you will pay or cause to be paid to me an amount which is comparable to the compensation customarily paid for similar material.

8. I agree to give you written notice by registered mail of any claim arising in connection with said material or arising in connection with this agreement, within 60 calendar days after I acquire knowledge of such claim, or of your breach or failure to perform the provisions of this agreement, or if it be sooner, within 60 calendar days after I acquire knowledge of facts sufficient to put me on notice of any such claim, or breach or failure to perform; my failure to so give you written notice will be deemed an irrevocable waiver of any rights I might otherwise have with respect to such claim, breach, or failure to perform. You shall have 60 calendar days after receipt of said notice to attempt to cure any alleged breach or failure to perform prior to the time that I may file a Demand for Arbitration.

9. In the event of any dispute concerning said material or concerning any claim of any kind or nature arising in connection with said material or arising in connection with this agreement, such dispute will be submitted to binding arbitration. Each party hereby waives any and all rights and benefits, which he or it may otherwise have or be entitled to under the laws of the State of California to litigate any such dispute in court, it being the intention of the parties to arbitrate all such disputes. Either party may commence arbitration proceedings by giving the other party written notice

thereof by registered mail and proceeding thereafter in accordance with the rules and procedures of the American Arbitration Association. The arbitration shall be conducted in the County of Los Angeles, State of California and the then prevailing rules of the American Arbitration Association. The arbitrators' award shall be final and binding and a judgment upon the award may be enforced by any court of competent jurisdiction. I waive all rights of injunctive or other equitable relief (including rescission) against you, in connection with this agreement.

10. I shall not have the right to use (nor authorize the use of) your name, in any manner or means whatsoever.

11. I have retained at least one copy of said material, and understand BO will make best efforts to return material to me, only if I enclosed a S.A.S.E. for return of the material. However, I release you from any and all liability for loss or other damage to the copies of said material submitted to you hereunder.

12. Either party to this agreement may assign or license its or their rights hereunder, but such assignment or license shall not relieve such party of its or their obligations hereunder. This agreement shall inure to the benefit of the parties hereto and their heirs, successors, representatives, assigns and licensees, and any such heir, successor, representative, assign or licensee shall be deemed a third party beneficiary under this agreement.

13. I hereby acknowledge and agree that there are no prior or contemporaneous oral agreements in effect between you and me pertaining to said material, or pertaining to any material (including, but not limited to, agreements pertaining to the submission by me of any ideas, formats, plots, characters, or the like). I further agree that no other obligations exist or shall exist or be deemed to exist unless and until a formal written agreement has been prepared and entered into by both you and me, and then your and my rights and obligations shall be only such as are expressed in said formal written agreement.

14. I understand that whenever the word "you" or "your" is used above, it refers to (1) you, (2) any company affiliated with you by way of common stock ownership or otherwise, (3) your subsidiaries, (4) subsidiaries of such affiliated companies, (5) any firm, person, or corporation to whom you are leasing production facilities, (6) clients of any subsidiary or affiliated company of yours, and (7) the officers, agents, servants, employees, stockholders, clients, successors, and assigns of you, and of all such person, corporations referred to in (1) through (6) hereof. If said material is submitted by more than one person, the word "I" shall be deemed changed to "we," and this agreement will be binding jointly and severally upon all the persons so submitting said material.

15. Should any provision or part of any provision be void or unenforceable, such provision or part thereof shall be deemed omitted, and this agreement with such provision or part thereof omitted shall remain in full force and effect.

16. This agreement shall be governed by the laws of the State of California applicable to agreements executed and to be fully performed therein.

17. I have read and understand this agreement and no oral representations of any kind have been made to me and this agreement states our entire understanding with reference to the subject matter hereof. Any modification or waiver of any of the provisions of this agreement must be in writing and signed by both of us.

Very truly yours,

_____

Signature(s)   Date

SUBMISSION CHECKLIST:

❑ SIGNED RELEASE AGREEMENT
❑ TYPED SCREENPLAY
❑ SCRIPT SIZE S.A.S.E. (optional)

Print Full Name(s) _____

Street Address _____

City _____ State ____ Zip _____

Project title _____

Best place/time to contact me:

Office Phone _____

Home Phone _____

E-mail Address _____

Type(s) of Material Submitted:

Copyright Protection

U.S. Copyright Office

http://lcweb.loc.gov/copyright

Once upon a time if writers wanted to call upon Uncle Sam to help them protect their creative projects from unscrupulous idea thieves, they had to send away to Washington D.C. for an information package and copious forms. Not only did it take a long time to receive these materials by mail, but it took even longer to actually get manuscripts processed through the system. The bad news is that it still takes a long time to receive a copyright certificate; on the brighter side, however, the Copyright Office can now save time at the front-end of the submission procedure by having all of the requisite forms accessible on-line, along with the most frequently asked questions regarding what copyright means. In a nutshell, the $30 filing fee will protect your work for your lifetime plus seventy years thereafter.

Click Industries

http://www.clickandcopyright.com

To appeal to the terminally lazy, Click Industries, a Minnesota-based corporation is appearing on a number of scriptwriting sites as an alternative to dealing directly with the U.S. Copyright Office. Both an archival and fee/application processing service, ClickandCopyright is essentially a middleman between writers and government. For $30 plus, they will file your manuscript for you and send a confirmation of that filing as proof of registration. Suffice it to say, it still takes an interminable amount of time to receive the actual copyright certificate from Washington. Until they can figure out how to shorten the duration, this may not be the best way to go.

Writers' Guild of America

http://www.wga.org

Registration with WGA is available to both members and non-members, and covers all stages of script development for radio, television, and feature films. In the event that legal action is ever initiated against a registered work, it is helpful to have had the

167

submission date duly logged with the Guild as evidence of its origination. It should be noted that many screenwriting contests now require WGA registration as a prerequisite to participate. This registration is valid for five years and may be renewed for an additional five years. Cost to members is $10; nonmembers pay $20.

First Use

http:/www.firstuse.com

In a hurry to protect your new script as well as get it quickly into public circulation? First Use is an innovative, international registration service which allows writers to catalog their work at any stage of development from synopsis to final product. This method of direct, online filing is certain to gain in popularity, particularly since it can be performed at the cost of only $10 (less for volume submissions), provides a verifiable paper-trail of progress, and remains in effect for ten years. Best of all, this type of registration is instantaneous, as opposed to the U.S. Copyright Office, which can take between six weeks and six months for processing!

Protect Rite

http://www.protectrite.com

Protect Rite is another online registration service which was established to protect intellectual properties. Treatments, drafts, and completed scripts created with any word-processing program can be submitted electronically to this site and placed in ten-year storage at the cost of $18.95. Just as with First Use, participants are e-mailed confirmation receipts establishing the submission date of their material.

Write Safe

http://www.writesafe.com

The WriteSafe Group is newest on the registration scene, having just launched in 1999. While it is similar in scope to other electronic filing services and at a comparable price ($10 for initial filing/$15 for every two subsequent pieces), it also offers an optional publishing component whereby your work can be viewed by others. This may or may not be a practicality, depending on your needs. Although the electronic date stamp can prove when the work was first registered, the likelihood of a potential producer actually surfing the site for a hot new project is probably remote. On the other hand, the likelihood of someone else getting inspired and writing a different-but-suspiciously-similar adaptation of the same idea is pretty high.

For more information on copyright, trademarks, and whether it's OK to put Elvis in your latest flick, the following site provides a host of timely articles, as well as a question and answer component:

http://www.Hollywoodnetwork.com/law. Likewise, the Writers' Guild of America (http://www.wga.org) includes a free mentor section in which your screenwriting rights questions can be posted and answered by industry professionals.

A Word About Websites

Once upon a time, it was widely believed that if a company had business cards and professional-looking letterhead, they were obviously legitimate. After all, why would they have gone to the time and expense of investing in such lovely stationery if they were just a fly-by-night operation?

Suffice it to say that investment in paper PR products is a small price for an unscrupulous person to pay. After all, the amounts that can be brought in by preying on the gullibility of the public will not only be an easy return on their print-shop payment but quite a bit of long-term profit as well.

I've been asked to mention this as a warning by nearly every professional who contributed his or her expertise to the making of this book. In this techno-slick world we live in these days, Internet websites have become a powerful medium by which to attract new business ... and new victims. Not a day goes by that we don't read in the paper about sting operations which reveal the identity of individuals pretending to be something or someone they're not in order to gain the trust of those with whom they correspond. The most prevalent, of course, are those which promise romance, masking the darker intentions of sexual predators, con artists, and those behind bars seeking some easy cash, sympathy, and a new

169

place to call "home" when they get out.

While the lonely hearts category takes a lion's share of victims of all ages, the biggest bait for today's teenagers resides in the category of "I Can Make You a Star." It's a con that consistently works well because of the one thing that scam artists have in common with their prospective marks: They remember what it was like to be young themselves and full of dreams to be fashion models, rock stars, actors, and yes, even rich and famous screenwriters.

Their websites are nothing less than professional, often utilizing eye-popping colors, interactive demos, and "testimonials" alluding to a close and personal relationship with Britney Spears, Jennifer Lopez, Matt Damon, etc. You, too, they hint, can join the in-crowd elite and be the envy of all your friends. The catch, of course, is that it means you'll have to part with some money up front ("good faith" is usually the excuse given) and/or act quickly because only a select few are being "invited" to participate in this opportunity to have their work — or themselves — discovered by talent scouts.

If an offer sounds too perfect to be true — well, there's a good reason for that. Success in anything rarely comes overnight but is, instead, the end result of years of hard work and persistence. Tempting as it may be to enter every contest and answer every cattle call for new scripts, learn to be discriminating about what you're getting into.

If it's an agency or production company, do your homework in finding out what — if anything — they have actually gotten produced. If it's a contest, who is sponsoring it and how many years has it been running? You'll also want to check out the www.moviebytes.com "report card" on screenwriting competitions, as well as post inquiries at screenwriter chatrooms. This is an industry where word travels fast; if others have been burned by an Internet scam, they're quick to get out the warning to their peers.

Last but not least, never sign a contract unless you have a thorough understanding of what the whole thing means.

Option Agreements

Let's say you've just read a couldn't-put-it-down book or come home from a theatre performance that knocked your socks off.

"This would make a great movie," you tell yourself, "and I'm the person who wants to write it!" How, then, do you go about making that a reality?

In order to adapt an existing work to the medium of film, you must first acquire the rights to it from the author or the publisher. Which one it is depends on the particulars of the original contract and which rights the author or author's representative negotiated to retain. A phone call or letter is usually all you need to contact the publisher's subsidiary rights division and inquire who owns the copyright and whether film rights are available to third party interests.

Obviously if the book du jour is a best seller, acquiring the film rights to it could be an expensive proposition. (Odds are that someone else has already grabbed them up long before you got there.) An alternative, then, is to look to works that are: 1. older and out of print, 2. mid-list books that the publishers aren't heavily promoting, or 3. e-book authors. In the case of scenarios 1 and 2, the fact that no one has done anything movie-wise with them to date means that you're not going to have a lot of competition in negotiating to adapt them to a screenplay. Scenario 3 is a much newer source of hot material, owing to the fact that, for the majority of cases, only the electronic rights have been granted and for a specified duration (usually one to two years). Because a number of e-book authors are not represented by agents and are dealing with their editors directly, the enticement of having an e-book adapted to a screenplay means more publicity for the website for having published the novel first. If both you and the author believe in the project and are willing to go forth on good faith, the deal can be sealed with as little as a dollar and a minimum of paperwork.

Screenplay to Big Screen

For an explanation of how option agreements work in the film industry, I'm pleased to include the advice of entertainment attorney Bruce David Eisen.

Eisen, who negotiated actor/director/producer/talent agreements in his previous position as Senior Vice President of Trimark's Legal/Business Affairs Division, is now Executive Vice President of CinemaNow, Inc. (http://www.cinemanow.com), an interactive enterprise linking indie filmwatchers to indie filmmakers.

The purpose of an option agreement, like all other agreements, is to memorialize, in written form, the agreement reached between two or more parties. In this case, the agreement that is being memorialized is the grant of a certain "right," the right to acquire a property in the future at a pre-determined price. This right is called the "option." The pre-determined price is typically called the "Purchase Price."

A simple example would be if I am trying to sell my car. I put my car on the market for say, $5,000. You come along and want to buy the car but don't have $5,000. Right now all that you have is $500 but you know that you'll get the rest of the money within thirty days. So you ask me to not sell my car to anyone for thirty days and you promise to buy it from me thirty days from now for $5,000. I tell you that I don't really want to wait and I'm going to sell it to whoever gives me $5,000 first. Since you really want the car, you offer me $500 today to not sell the car to anyone for thirty days and allow you to buy it from me at anytime within the next thirty days. I say OK but if you don't buy it by the end of the thirty day period, I can sell it to someone else *and* I keep the $500 that you agreed to give me. You agree.

I have just granted you the right (or the "option") to buy my car at a set price, $5,000 in this example, at any time during the next thirty days.

This sort of transaction is very common in the motion picture industry when it comes to buying scripts and other written material. Writers will often grant producers the right to buy the writer's script at any time within a set period, referred to as the "Option Period" (often twelve months but it could be eighteen, twenty-four, or any other period) for a set amount of money (the "Purchase Price"). In most cases, the producer will pay the writer ten percent of the purchase price up front as the "Option Payment." That is the amount of money that the producer pays to keep the script off the market and to give them the right to buy it later. The $500 in the car example is the Option Payment in that scenario.

Producers like to do business this way because it reduces their risk. During the Option Period the producer has the right to "set-up" the movie. That is, arrange for the financing of the movie and/or hire actors and/or hire a director and/or most anything else they want to do other than actually make the movie. This way if the producer can't get the film financed, etc., they have not lost all the money that it would take them to buy the script. Instead, all that they have lost is the Option Payment.

A writer would usually rather sell the script outright rather than option it (since the writer is guaranteed getting the full Purchase Price instead of just the Option Payment), but in most circumstances the writer doesn't have the clout to demand such an arrangement. The writer might be able to get the producer to pay the Purchase Price up-front, but typically the producer would pay a lower Purchase Price up-front than if they had optioned the material first. The reason for this is, again, the producer's desire to reduce his risk. If the producer doesn't know that the film will get financed or made, he wants to keep the amount of his money at risk as low as possible.

There are a few key provisions that must be in any option agreement. The first is the Option Payment. That is, how much is the producer paying the writer for the option? This can be anything from one dollar to hundreds, thousands, or even millions of dollars. The typical amount is ten percent of the total Purchase Price. Another question is whether or not the Option Payment is applicable against the Purchase Price. That is, if the Purchase Price is $1,000 and the Option Payment is $100, when the producer exercises the option, does the producer owe the writer an additional $1,000 (not applicable) or only an additional $900 (the Option Payment is applicable against the Purchase Price). It goes both ways and is a matter of negotiation.

Which brings us to the second key provision, the Purchase Price. The Purchase Price is the amount that the Producer must pay the writer to acquire the script. This must be specified. It cannot state that it will be an amount

173

that the parties agree to later. The reason is that an option is basically a promise by the writer to sell the script to the producer at a later date for a specified amount of money. If the amount of money is not specified, what is the promise worth? Using our car example, would you pay me $100 for me to promise to sell you my car without knowing how much I would sell it to you for? What if I decided that I wanted $1 million for my beat-up 1975 Dodge? Not a very good deal for you. You just wasted $100.

The option agreement must also specify the time that the producer has in which to exercise the option. That is, how long will the writer keep it off the market? Any amount of time is possible but one year is typical. Oftentimes the producer will have the right to extend the option for an additional amount of time by paying an additional option payment. Oftentimes the Option Payment for the first part of the term is applicable against the Purchase Price (that is, the Purchase Price is reduced by the amount of the Option Payment that the writer has already received) but the second Purchase Price is not reduced by the Option Payment for the second period.

Another aspect that the option must specify is what rights is the producer getting if he exercises the option? You wouldn't pay me $100 for me to promise to sell you something in the future without knowing what it was I was going to sell you. If you thought you were getting the right to buy my 1999 Honda Accord for $5,000 you would be very upset to find out that I thought you wanted to buy my 1999 Honda motorcycle. Therefore, the option agreement must specify exactly what rights to the script that the producer is getting. Is it all rights to the script? Is it the right to make one motion picture? What about a television program? Live stage? Internet rights? It all must be specified. All rights is typical, but it is certainly possible for the writer to hold back (that is, not sell and keep for himself) certain rights. If a book is being optioned, it is common for the writer to hold back the book publishing rights as well as the book sequel rights.

Lastly, it is necessary that the option agreement be in writing and signed by the writer. A verbal agreement by the writer to option the script is not legally binding. Under U.S. federal copyright law, any exclusive transfer of a right under copyright must be in writing and signed by the party granting the rights. That said, it need not be a formal document written by a lawyer but it must be in writing and signed.

One other aspect that should be mentioned is exclusivity. From the producer's point of view, the option should state that the producer is getting the exclusive rights. For obvious reasons, the producer certainly doesn't want to have someone else acquiring the same rights that he is getting.

In negotiating an option agreement, the writer needs to think about the likelihood of someone else wanting to buy the script, book, etc. If it is a "hot" property with several or many people interested in acquiring it, then the writer might not want to option the property but rather, sell it outright. And, if that is not possible, then the writer might be able to negotiate either a higher Purchase Price and/or an Option Payment that is greater than the typical ten percent of the Purchase Price and/or an Option Period that is shorter than the typical twelve months. Conversely, if the writer has a property that has been on the market for a while with no interest but from a single producer, then it might make sense for the writer to option the property to that producer for an Option Price of one dollar to give the producer a chance to see if he can setup a movie based upon the property.

The Pros and Cons of Collaboration

Who says that you need to be in the same room — or, for that matter, even in the same city — in order to collaborate creatively? For over ten years now, my experience with "out-of-sight" partners has been living proof of how technology and nonstop imaginations can bring artists together as never before. While it boggles people's minds to hear that I currently work with professional musicians in New Mexico and South Carolina, a medieval times expert in Pennsylvania, and an independent film director in Maine, the fact remains that we probably turn out more ideas across multiple state

175

lines than fledgling collaborators who work across a hallway — or desk — from each other.

While success can certainly be tied to compatible visions and mutual wavelengths, there's much to be said for defining such a partnership before it ever gets underway. If you've ever toyed with the idea of co-authoring a teleplay or matching a blockbuster script to your best friend's orchestral score, the following considerations may shed some light on whether you choose to fly solo or work as a team.

Who's the Boss?

In most endeavors, there are those who lead and those who follow. In collaboration projects, however, this rule doesn't always work. In fact, it can be injurious to the health of the friendship if there's any kind of grapple for power to be the boss. I think what works in my association with these various pros is that we each think our counterparts have all the talent and, accordingly, tend to operate in a perpetual state of awe. The respect we have for each other's area of expertise puts us on equal footing in contributing to a project's development.

In the case of collaborating on a novel, for example, one partner may have a better handle on narrative while the other's forte is snappy dialog. There are even some partnerships where one person does all of the historical research and the other does the actual writing, yet both share fifty/fifty credits on the finished product. With screenwriting, the division of labor could actually be contingent on physical location; i.e., the one who lives in Los Angeles or New York is responsible for pitching the script in person. Is your partner better at writing synopses and treatments? Do you have the better voice or charismatic personality on the phone for setting up crucial meetings? Capitalize on your respective strengths. And don't get in each other's way!

Do You Need a Written Contract?

The presence of a legal agreement doesn't necessarily guarantee a smooth-running partnership any more than the hiring of an agent solidifies one's place in the literary world. In collaborations of my own, I've always trusted the gut-level instinct of "Would I believe in this person as a friend even if we weren't working together?" Unfortunately, in our lawsuit-driven society, intuition isn't enough to hold up in court in the event that: 1. you and your partner come to a parting of the ways, 2. you experience "creative differences" halfway through the project's completion, or 3. one of you dies and your mourners suddenly have an attack of greed.

As starry-eyed as many people are when approaching the benefits of collaborating (there's a correlation here to marriage vows, I think), it's only prudent to consider what your legal options will be if you ever come to loggerheads. Having such understandings in writing will avoid an ugly scene should the partnership/friendship unravel prior to champagne on Oscar night.

For the legally impaired, there's a comprehensive guidebook by Writer's Digest entitled *How to Write with a Collaborator* (publication date 1988). Not only does this text include a host of sample contract agreements in the appendix, but addresses issues such as personal chemistry, soliciting experts for non-fiction works, and defining respective responsibilities. (There's even an appendix on ghostwriting!)

Entertainment Publishers (http://www.entertainmentpublisher.com) also offers a wide range of fill-in-the-blanks contracts in their software release entitled, "Automated Contracts for the Film and Television Industry." This package enables users to view the contracts on screen, make modifications to fit their individual circumstances, and then print them out directly for signature.

What's the Message?

It's important if you're going to create something that you're both in agreement on what that something is. Sounds obvious, of course, but I can recall one of my earlier theatrical collaboration disasters when a composer and I were not only on different planes but probably different planets. While the musician had the creative skills and professionalism to turn out a first-rate score for the high school/college market, we hit an immediate impasse at his interpretation of the script's intent. The musical, *First Ladies*, was based on the premise of four former presidential wives stepping out of their portraits to offer advice and counsel to an incoming First

177

Lady. Such diversity was reflected through the "ghosts" of Martha Washington, Dolly Madison, Rachel Jackson, and Mary Lincoln. "The concept's passable," the musician remarked with a definitive yawn, "but I'd rather do something with Eleanor, Mamie, Nancy, and Roslyn."

"I'll get back to you," I replied. I didn't.

A similar incident occurred when two of my students decided to join forces on a made-for-TV film which would be set against the dramatic backdrop of the Pacific Northwest and involve park rangers. After two weeks of intense writing, it became clear that one of them was writing a love story while the other one had her sights set on a sensational murder mystery. They came running to me to mediate, each convinced that her own way of telling the story was better. "She wants to kill off Bradley in the first scene," the romantic argued. "That's 'cause her 'Bradley' character is an idiot," her partner countered, apparently not realizing that Bradley was pegged to be the heroine's heartthrob and, thus, meant to last for more than three pages.

Getting It There

In the olden days of snail-mail, the major disadvantage to collaboration efforts across state lines was that you couldn't just hand your partner a page of text and say, "So what do you think?" Nor was it always practical to tie up the phone lines on long-distance, painstakingly reading the revised material over and over. Fortunately, with the proliferation of fax usage and e-mail, those problems have been reduced to nil, affording us the chance to shoot ideas back and forth as rapidly as we can type them.

Chat rooms, as well, provide an opportunity for brainstorming sessions that could not otherwise be facilitated until such time as we're all rich and famous and can jet around the country. Technology is also a lifesaver when the scriptwriter lives in one part of the US and the director is on location somewhere else. At the blink of a keystroke, script changes can be e-mailed to the set, thus averting expensive delays for both cast and crew.

Where Did the Time Go?

If you're going to work together, it's critical that you and your partner(s) not only march to the same drummer but also at the same lively pace. Several people who responded to my initial advertising for a collaborator took as long as ten months to send a sample of their work. The message that kind of time frame conveyed to me was that either it had taken them that long to pull together their best material or that they were extraordinarily lazy about finding a postage stamp. Promising as some of the pieces were (when they finally arrived), my decision to ultimately pass on them stemmed from my past experience of getting frustrated with delays that aren't of my own making. If, for instance, it takes someone two weeks to write a single scene and it takes their partner over three months to respond with the subsequent scene, it will either take years for them to finish anything cohesive ... or no time at all to end the friendship.

If and when you *do* find someone with whom to write a film, approach the project just as you'd approach an assignment at work; specifically, by determining intermediate deadlines for completion of each component. While it's certainly true that some people work better under pressure and like to wait until zero hour to turn anything in, it's not a practice that lends itself to working as a team.

Sharing the Fame (and Money)

Just like loaning money, it's always good practice to get agreements in writing before anything is ever started. By delineating who's in charge of what, what the percentages will be, and how the property will be marketed, you will save major headaches (and potential lawsuits) down the road. It's also wise to include a clause pertaining to the property's ownership should one of the partners get run over by a bus (it does happen, you know) or if one of you decides to subsequently adapt the sold/unsold script to a novel or Broadway musical and the other is lukewarm to the idea.

By laying a solid foundation of understanding, a good collaboration should bring to it the best of all talents, a shared expectation of the result, and — last but not least — someone with whom to celebrate when the first check comes in!

Your Assignment

1. If you and a friend are thinking of collaborating on a screenplay, make a list of the respective talents that each of you can bring to the project.

2. How long do you think it will take to create something together?

3. How will you resolve any differences of opinion?

Listen to the Mockingbird:
An Interview with Director/Producer
Laurie Durrett, Mockingbird Productions

From the first time she trod the boards at age ten, Ms. Laurie Durrett knew that acting and directing were in her blood. Today, she is literally running the entire show as the driving force behind the cameras at Mockingbird Productions in her native Texas. She took time from her busy schedule to share what it took to put her imagination and talent into full gear and where she'd like the next road to take her. If you're thinking of applying for an internship at your local news or cable station, you may find yourself in a similar happy ending!

Q: We share something in common in that the first "stage" of our respective careers actually *was* on a stage. Did your early experiences in theatre influence how you run your own film production company now?

A: My early experiences had *everything* to do with how I conduct my business! Besides acting in school and professional productions, I was always the one given the responsibility of organizing the tournaments and awards ceremonies every year, as well as the one in charge of getting the groups together for our monthly theatre outings. I was extremely shy throughout school, but theatre made me learn how to relate to people and improved my communications and organizational skills tremendously. It also helped me in getting a theatre scholarship to a small college in East Texas, Lon Morris, plus a scholarship to the American Academy of Dramatic Arts in L.A. and a scholarship in theatre to White University in Europe.

Q: So what was it that moved you from being in front of an audience as an actress to behind a camera as a producer?

A: The inciting incident that sparked my interest came while I was working at a small television station in Beaumont, Texas where I hosted a morning talk show. One day our production coordinator quit and they couldn't find a replacement before my next show, so I told them I would book the talent and arrange the schedule. It was like old home week in high school! The job came very easily. They didn't hire anyone and let me do the position, which I really liked because I could book who I wanted for talent and crew. It also gave me a job to go to after I graduated; it was much easier than acting ... and it paid more. Starting my own company was a no-brainer. I was so tired of working on productions that were about as inspiring as watching paint dry, so a friend of mine came to me with a script that she had written. The project involved creating a commercial informing the public how to yield to emergency vehicles. (Believe it or not, a lot of people don't have a clue.) The scripts were great so I went to a couple of investors and convinced them to go for it. It was sooo exciting to be working on something that was all mine and to be proud of it at that! A double whammy!

Q: Speaking of scripts, do you write all your own now?

A: Sadly, I don't. I was teased as a child on my poor writing skills so that's one hurdle I haven't jumped yet. I do, however, work very closely with all of my writers. That's one thing that totally amazes me: how a director can take a script, never meet with the writer, and create his own vision. I love to get the writer's vision. After all, two heads are much better than one. Whether I'm shooting a corporate gig or film, I always take their vision and just elaborate on it in order to bring it to life. Obviously if the writer is not available (or has died), then that's a different story.

Q: A number of your credits have been industrial and corporate films. Is this a viable route for young people who want to get their feet wet on a local level?

A: If you would like to get into the corporate world of writing, I would advise getting hired as a production assistant with a production company and telling them that it is one of your goals to write scripts. Learn all you can about the business and start writing short scripts as examples for the boss. One day after work, stop in and have a short chat with them and show them your portfolio. Let them see what you can do. I can't name how many projects have come my way because I just happened to be in the office when a project came across the decision maker's desk and they said, "Who could we get for this one?' I would always speak up and say, "Let me have a stab at it!" (I beg a little also!) That was how I got my first directing gig. You have to speak up. Also, if you take on a corporate project, find out everything you can about that company ... and I do mean *everything*. Nothing is more embarrassing than having your first creative pow-wow and not realizing that the CEO is sitting in the room with you. Corporate projects are a wonderful source of income, especially if you don't live in L.A. or New York. Plus there's nothing more exciting than showing your video at a sales convention with thousands of people cheering it along.

Q: **How has the Internet impacted the number of doors that are open to new screenwriters and filmmakers?**

A: Well, I can't say enough about how wonderful the Internet has been for Mockingbird Productions. The technology is a success in every aspect, from advertising to millions who would have otherwise never have had the opportunity to view your work to making the deal right there in your e-mail.

Q: **So tell us about *The Fast Lane* and how it came about.**

A: *The Fast Lane* will be the first full-length feature for Mockingbird. I was in a masters directing workshop in L.A. when I met a doctor who was participating in the same class. During a break we started a conversation and found out we were both from Houston. He was taking the workshop because he had written over twenty-five screenplays and wanted to learn more about the industry and to possibly produce one of his scripts. I was taking the workshop because I make a point of taking one workshop a year just to improve my skills. We both hit it off and had a meeting when we returned to Texas. He let me read the script, which was wonderful and created a trailer as a calling card for other investors. I won't go into details about the script but we're expecting to go into full production this fall. It's a wonderful family film with a great message on just learning how to be yourself. It's my *"Fried Green Tomatoes"* film.

Q: *"Fried Green Tomatoes"?*

A: Yes, I'm a total *"Fried Green Tomatoes"* kind of girl. Ten years from now I would love to be a *small* production house that turns out quality class A films. The two scripts I have right now are in that category. I'm very excited about them, and it takes a lot to get me excited about any script. I'm currently in negotiations with a writer from Oklahoma who has written a beautiful novel that he wants to transpose into a screenplay and I would produce and direct.

Q: How did he find you?

A: In a nutshell, he opened the Texas production manual, turned to the directing section, closed his eyes and put his finger on a page. My name was the page he picked. (Go figure.) The working title is *Potato Charlie*. It deals with the dust bowl era and spans sixty years. It's a beautiful novel with wonderful characters that I would be honored to direct. He also has the money for the feature.

Q: So you're receptive to hearing from newcomers?

A: I am always, always looking for great scripts. I love humanistic stories. Stories of great compassion and human spirit. I really love true stories. *October Sky* ... *Apollo 13* ... *To Kill A Mockingbird* (Where do you think I got the name of my company?). These kind of story lines are the ones you remember for the rest of your life.

Q: Having been there and done that, what would you tell someone who wanted to write for the big (or small) screen?

A: Write from the heart! It's sappy but true. If you're passionate about something, grab all of the information you can ... eat, sleep, and drink the subject. How can you write a script on what it's like to live in Mississippi in 1960 being black if you haven't lived it, experienced it, or know someone who can tell you every intimate detail of what their life was like? The public is not stupid. And at times they can be very unforgiving. Don't insult their intelligence. Write the truth. Last but not least, this is a very ego-driven business. Remember, though, that everyone puts their pants on the same way, one leg at a time. It's the best business in the world!

For more information on Laurie's past work and future projects of Mockingbird Productions, pay a visit to www.directorsnet.com.

Topics to Think About and Talk About

1. In 100 words or less, explain whether you think a screenplay is better if it is based on personal experience or is entirely a work of fiction, and why.

2. In 100 words or less, describe how you think a screenwriter views a subject differently than a director.

3. Describe in 100 words or less how (or if) you think your life experiences limit your ability to be an effective and successful screenwriter?

It's All About Rewrites!

The difference between good writers and great writers is that the great writers never stop learning new ways to improve upon what they already thought was perfect. In this chapter, you'll learn how to become your own best editor, as well as how to borrow real-life plots from the past.

How to Use Feedback

As humans, we never get tired of hearing how wonderful we are. Praise is the carrot that encourages us to keep moving forward, getting better and better as we go.

Yet what about those times when there's a "but" attached?

"I really like your story but — "

"This idea is really clever but — "

"The premise of your screenplay caught my interest but — "

No matter how the rest of that sentence gets filled in, the message is the same: I love you. You're perfect. Now change.

I once had an editor, in fact, who — upon receipt of my latest 400 page novel — remarked, "The new book is great but I'm having a problem with pages five through 392." What exactly, I wondered, did she think was the "great" part — just thirteen pages of it?

I offer this in warning to anyone who plans to put their creative efforts into public view: The world is full of critics and not all of them are going to be applauding. You probably knew that already, of course. Whether it's family or friends or teachers at school, I'm sure you've encountered a fair share of criticism that you disagreed with. The bad news is that it's not going to change after you graduate. The good news is that, when it comes to your writing, there are only three voices you need to listen to:

The voice of experience.

The voice of opportunity.

The voice inside your own head.

Suppose one of your friends read your screenplay and thought it was great. You'd be pleased, right? You then turn in that same project to the instructor in your filmmaking class who tells you that your dialog needs some more work and that your resolution is too contrived. Which voice are you going to listen to? Supportive and enthusiastic as our friends can be, they're not always the best judges of our work. On the other hand, someone who comes from a long background of evaluating the kinds of scripts you want to write is going to have a pretty good handle on what works and what doesn't. Because you are under this person's tutelage to learn the craft yourself, you need to remember that they're not criticizing you with the intent of *ruining* the story but, rather, making it better.

Here's another scenario: You've managed to land yourself a pitch session with an independent producer who likes your latest story and wants to make it his next movie. "The script is quite good," he says, "but I'm having a problem with pages five through eighty. If you can change it to Roswell, add a spaceship chase across the desert, and make the squadron commander a female, I think we have a deal."

In other words: "I love your script. Now make it something else."

Essentially, you have two options here. (A third option, of course, would be to argue, but I can already guarantee that you'd lose. Forget option three.) The first choice is to listen to this ding-dong's advice and rewrite the script per his specifications. Why? Because this person is in a position of power which, accordingly, can open a door of opportunity for you. Just like the instructor in screenwriting class who told you that your dialog needed more work, a producer isn't going to purposely sabotage his next project unless (à la *The Producers*), he's just looking to rake in a lot of money from investors and go for a tax write-off when it bombs. Your second choice is to walk away and try to sell your script to someone who will appreciate every single comma of it and won't want you to change anything.

Maybe that will happen. Maybe it won't.

I recall how ecstatic I was back in 1980 when I received a check for the sale of my very first play, a medieval comedy entitled *The Knight of the Honest Heart*. In the course of preparing the work for publication, the letter said, it was requested that I delete four specific lines of dialog.

My excitement quickly spiraled into anger. "They already sent me a check for it," I told my husband. "That means they should keep my script exactly the way it is!"

He pointed out that my acceptance of the check was conditional. "If you feel that strongly about keeping the lines in, they'll probably want their money back."

Fortunately, I saw the wisdom of his advice and complied. To tell you the truth, I don't even remember what those four lines were, much less why I ever felt so impassioned that the success of the play hinged on them being there. I do know, however, that the show's debut could have been significantly delayed if I had held fast to balking with the editor. The happy ending to the story is that I went on to sell scripts to this same publishing house for the next twenty years. I must have been doing something right; specifically, delivering exactly what they wanted and being open to constructive criticism.

Last, but definitely not least, is the fine art of listening to the feedback of your own heart. After all, who knows the story and its characters better than you do? Many an example can be found in the history of writers who simply couldn't sell their brainchild to any of the traditional markets, figured out how to publish or produce it themselves, and made millions! If, in spite of countless rejections and reams of advice, your heart is still telling you to stick with it, you'd be wise to listen. Inevitably, it may not be the script that opens the doors to Hollywood for you, but the passion and commitment with which it was originally written, will shine through and distinguish you from those who simply wrote to follow existing trends.

Your Assignment

Identify at least three individuals in your life whose advice and counsel you value regarding your writing expertise. What kind of qualifications in terms of education and experience do they bring to the table to evaluate what you're doing? Do you often incorporate their recommendations into your projects? If so, how do you feel those suggestions have made your work potentially more commercial?

In for a Trim

As writers, we are sometimes prone to bond with the literary fruits of our labor to the point of obsession. We convince ourselves that the act of sending even a single syllable to the cutting room floor will do irreparable damage to the manuscript as a whole.

In reality, however, most of us are way too yakky for our own good and could benefit from learning the fine art of downsizing. The result? The lucky words that get to stay will carry a lot more weight without slowing down the pace.

Let's see how this works in practice:

Throughout this book, you've had the chance to read what working professionals and entrepreneurs are saying about the movie industry. Following each interview, you and your peers have had a trio of questions to answer and/or debate, clarifying your own views on what to expect from a career as a screenwriter. I'd like you to go back now and pick one of those questions which called for a fifty to 100 word reply. It doesn't matter which one you choose, as long as you feel your answer to it was especially well crafted.

Count how many words you used in your reply. Whatever number it turns out to be, divide it in half. That number is _____. Without compromising the integrity of your original response, rewrite your answer now but do not exceed the new word limit.

A torturous exercise? Absolutely! The happier you were with your first version, the harder it is to fathom cutting it in half! Curiously enough, though, this is one of the best ways to teach yourself how to edit your own material and eliminate the superfluous.

This method also has valuable application to other types of creative or journalistic writing you may find yourself doing in the future. Let's say, for instance, that you decide to supplement your regular income by writing magazine articles. As you'll discover, every publication plays by its own set of rules, especially in the area of word length. Imagine that you've just written a 1,500-word piece about snowboarding. The editors love it ... except for the fact that the maximum length freelance item they'll accept is 1,200. Do you really want to let 300 words stand in the way of a paycheck and the chance to see your name in print? It's amazing what you can learn to let go of when the chance for gain is high.

So do you think it's easier to edit your work or someone else's? Because of the emotional attachment that comes from spending a lot of time and thought on an essay, a short story, or a script, most writers find it more difficult to trim down their own work than to take a red pen to their peers' creations. This next exercise will show you what I mean.

Go back and select another one of your fifty to 100 word responses that you really liked. Make two copies of it. You'll be keeping one for yourself and giving the second one to someone else in your group. Likewise, you'll be receiving a copy of his or her essay to edit. It doesn't matter which one you do first; the only rule is to trim both of them by ten percent without altering the meaning, then compare your self-edits against the recommendations your peer made for the same material.

What this exercise will reveal about the very nature of editing is something that generally takes a beginning writer a long time to learn. Certainly it took a long time to figure it out for myself! Specifically, what someone else thinks can be easily sacrificed for the good of the cause could turn out to be what you thought was the most vital issue in the entire piece!

In their quest to create something "perfect," a number of students I've mentored have literally edited their work to death before they ever got it off the drawing board. Trying to second-guess what someone else will want is as bad as incorporating *everyone's* suggestions to the point that the original intent is completely lost. You're never going to know what someone will like or dislike until you get the first draft out there and invite a reaction.

Painful as the editing process can be, the funny thing to keep in mind is that words are *meant to* be recycled. It won't hurt their feelings, especially when they know they're probably going to end up in something else before the week is even over!

The final editing assignment involves your current screenplay. Whether or not you've just started writing it or already have 120 pages that you can't wait to sell, the purpose of this lesson is to make whatever you've done the very tightest it can be.

If your script is still in the beginning stages, I want you to take the first ten pages of it ... and trim it down to five. Yes, yes, I know that you're really happy with those ten pages and feel that it gets your story off to a Wow!-Pow!-Zing! start. Maybe it does. But maybe it could be a lot better. Do you have nine pages of exposition before the fireball explosion that sets the whole story in motion? What, for instance, would happen, if the explosion got moved up to page three? Or even page one? What's vital is to get the plot underway as early as possible.

OK, for those of you who have already finished your entire script, I'm going to guess that it's around 120 pages. A lot of screenwriting books like to recite this number as "desirable," because it's a nice average and, given the one page equals one minute rule you've learned, represents a tidy, two-hour film. The truth, though, is that when it comes to numbers that directors and producers like to read, 120 is considered high. The number they really like is 100. Why? Because the first thing they flip to when they receive a new script is the back page to see how long this thing is. Anything that's 120 or higher is going to get a harsher scrutiny than a more compact 95-100 page script.

You also need to remember that it's much easier to pad a scene out later if your potential buyer wants more layers added than it is to scale down and possibly have to eliminate entire scenes and characters. If you get in the habit at the outset of writing lean scripts, your chances of getting them read in the first place will go up immeasurably.

With that in mind, I want you to take your 120 page project and determine how to shave twenty minutes off it.

If your completed script is already at the 100 page mark, good for you! You get to sit this lesson out.

Or, better yet, go start writing your *next* film!

Dr. Livingston, I Presume?

Screenwriters have long enjoyed — and reaped the profits from — redefining/interpreting history through the magic of cinema. Whether it's a science fiction/time-travel in which contemporary characters strive to alter known events or sweeping epics in which the resident locals have no clue what's coming next, the only two requirements are: 1. be sure of the accuracy of your facts and

2. make your historical characters' worries and concerns *relevant* to a modern audience.

In the classes I teach, I often use the television example of *Dr. Quinn, Medicine Woman* to illustrate the latter concept. On the surface, it wouldn't seem that any of us would have much in common with a bunch of townfolk living in 1870s Colorado. Mending fences, keeping an eye out for Army deserters, and deciding what kind of pie to take to the barn dance generally don't figure that high in our workaday priorities.

What made the show successful, however, was the regular dose of present-day topics (job discrimination, single motherhood, alcoholism, peer pressure, racism, romance, cancer, births, deaths, and natural disasters) against the backdrop of the frontier historical setting. There was also the occasional drop-in visit by personages whom we knew to have actually existed in western history at that time (i.e., Custer, Walt Whitman, etc.), thus lending a contrived and yet charming authenticity to everyone else who was just the product of a writer's keyboard!

Question of the day: If your story takes place in the past, what "modern" issues or feelings will your audience be able to easily relate to?

Although you can't re-write the outcome of what are already documented events, you can nevertheless manipulate the significance of those events in your characters' personal lives. There are several ways to do this:

1. Living in a vacuum: The rest of the world is going on but he/she is too absorbed in personal battles to really notice.

2. The game of what-if: The antagonist is plotting to bring something about which could drastically alter the balance; i.e., a scheme to sell California and Arizona to Mexico. The lovers' deeds, of course, manage to thwart such mayhem. Likewise, it can be implied that the protagonist was instrumental in implementing positive actions which did indeed end up in the history books.

3. Going about business: In this scenario, the lead characters are participating in a real event (the Gold Rush, immigration, the Battle of Bull Run) but are not directly influencing its outcome.

4. Let me give you some advice: Last but not least, the protagonist(s) offer casual advice to historical figures which, ultimately, the latter appear to have heeded. Unlike time-travel novels in which the hero has intimate knowledge of the future and attempts to impart it, the lead character in the purely historical or retro genre is simply speaking from the heart and unwittingly directing the life choices of local luminaries. A good example? *Forrest Gump.*

Unless you provide some sort of back-story/explanation as to why your characters defy the values and expectations of their contemporaries, however, you run the risk of imposing your own modern thoughts on period personae. This is especially glaring among romance writers, for instance, who like to craft "sensitive" thirteenth-century warriors who sit around sipping latt'es and discussing their feelings, or Civil War southern belles who want to burn their crinolines and go save the rain forest from global warming.

In order to write credible historical pieces (unless you're purposely writing a spoof), you need to put yourself in their shoes, boots, or sandals and understand that they just don't possess the same frame of reference by which to solve their problems or buck the stodgy conventions of the day.

Will you be relying on sources such as family letters, autobiographies, or books about these people that other authors have already published? Always make sure you have acquired the necessary permission *in writing* to use these materials in the development of your own screenplay.

I also feel compelled to warn you against taking an event in which there was a finite, well-documented number of participants and using your creative license to people it with a few more. This would be akin, for instance, to doing a movie about Neil Armstrong's first walk on the moon and arbitrarily throwing in a couple of extra astronauts on the same trip. We know they weren't there. We saw the pictures. We read the newspaper. Why is this writer trying to hoodwink us? Maybe the *rest* of the story is lying to us as well ...

With events involving large masses and/or migrations of humanity, you can get away with that kind of "extra casting." In a smaller group, though, it's much harder to hide a figment of your imagination, especially if that figment is supposed to be playing a lead role in how history itself came out.

Never Give Up:
An Interview with Richard Parkin

Mr. Richard Parkin is a twenty-four-year-old U.K. filmmaker who, as of this writing, was off to a remote Scottish island for five weeks to produce a factual series for youth TV. ("Rather like *Survivor* with a bit of *Big Brother* for good measure. If *I* survive, I'm sure I'll be able to take on anything!") He wrote his first professionally produced play, *Friday the Halloweenth,* at the age of sixteen. Richard studied film, TV, theatre, and literature at university and began working in TV as a camera operator soon after graduating. Current credits include: *Watching U* (horror-drama series-writer); *Karisma* (youth drama series-storylining and Bible writing); *Daylight Robbery 2* (major TV drama series-camera); *Young, Gifted and Broke* (arts showcase-camera/director); *Cruel Summer* (reality TV show for young people-assistant producer). Richard has also worked as a Drama Development Director for an independent production company, developing drama and writing treatments/proposals.

Q: When did the "film bug" first bite?

A: Ever since I can remember I have wanted to be involved in drama. I have always loved the power of films — the magic they possess to transport us into other worlds, to make us laugh, cry or scream in terror. As a child, I grew up watching hours and hours of TV (sorry Mum and Dad!) and dreamed of becoming an actor. As I got older, I became more and more interested with everything that was involved in making films and TV. As I hit my teen years I became very self-conscious and decided that I could never really make it as an actor. This self-doubt and my ever-growing interest in things behind the scenes moved me towards the dream job of directing and writing movies.

Q: What kinds of local opportunities were at hand for you to learn your craft?

A: I grew up in Manchester, England — a city rich in dramatic arts. I was lucky to have parents who encouraged me and were happy to take me to see plays and films from an early age. Whilst I found a lot of easily available theatre resources, there were not as many in film and TV. Theatre, by its very nature, is easier to produce — all you need is a space and some actors! With film and TV you need space, actors and a camera of some sort. As a result of this, I would write plays for amateur theatre companies and eventually had one professionally produced at Manchester's Contact Theatre. All the while, I would do everything I could to learn about filmmaking. I would buy books or visit the local library, watch TV shows which went behind-the scenes of movies. I even subscribed to American magazines such as *American Cinematographer* and *Cinefex* which helped my understanding of what was involved in making films and TV.

Finally, I went to university to study film, TV, literature and theatre. This was really important for me as it gave me the opportunity to put everything I had learned into practice. Here I was able to use cameras, lights and editing equipment. I was able to make films — good or bad — and learn from each experience. I also learned more about writing. Before university I had just written without really thinking too much about the process. Now I began learning about the importance of narrative structure, character, and dialog.

Some people are lucky enough to have resources readily available to them. Their parents may have friends who are filmmakers, writers, actors etc. Others — like myself — were not so lucky. This does not mean that you cannot learn about your art. Read books and magazines, watch films and TV, surf the web — there are thousands of really useful sites which offer advice. Take the trouble to root out the information and you will soon reap the rewards!

Q: **I'm sure you had plenty of people giving you advice once you announced your intentions to break into film. Anything you'd like to share?**

A: I once asked writer-director Bruce Robinson what guidance he could offer me. The exchange was brief and went a little like this ...

ME: Hello! I'm hoping to work in the film industry one day. Is there any advice you could offer me?

BRUCE: Yeah, don't do it.

ME: (*tentatively*) Oh. Anything else?

BRUCE: No. Don't do it. Simple as that.

Oddly enough, I decided to ignore this advice.

Q: With all the "homework" you did watching movies, which one(s) influenced your passion for the medium?

A: One film more than any other made me want to work in films and TV. I fell in love with it the first time I saw it and it has remained my favorite to this day. Whilst at university, I was derided by my film studies class who could not believe I ranked this film equal to (if not above) the likes of *Citizen Kane* or *Battleship Potemkin*.

Q: Enough with the suspense already! What's the film?

A: *E.T. — The Extraterrestrial.* All right, I know what you're thinking — but don't! It is a great film and should not simply be dismissed as a kids' movie. Scratch the surface and you find there's a whole lot more to this film than you thought. A broken home missing its father, a single mother trying to keep her family together. There is a lonely child in need of friendship, governmental secrecy, a race against time as well as a wonderful celebration of imagination and childhood. The film is perfectly directed by Steven Spielberg — cinema's greatest storyteller — beautifully shot by Allen Daviau and given an immense emotional depth through John Williams' wonderfully moving score. And yes — I still cry like a girl at the end of the movie (but don't tell anyone!).

Q: Suppose someone tells you, "I've just written the next blockbuster!"

A: So you've just finished a script and you think it's pretty good. What next? Well, to be honest, there are various options available to you. I would first advise that you get a friend to read the script, someone whose opinion you value and who preferably knows a little about films or theatre. I usually give a script to some close friends who will offer me honest and constructive advice and thoughts about the script. This will often lead me to revise my draft or re-think certain elements of the structure. A number of my friends are also actors, so I will use them from time-to-time, asking them to line-read the script so I can hear the dialog spoken by professionals. Again, this may suggest new changes and you shouldn't be afraid to make them. Scriptwriting is a constantly evolving process and changing your work here and there is part of the job.

So now you have a script that is ready to be read by professionals. You could send the script to an independent production company or to a broadcaster or studio to read. However, before doing this, do a bit of research. Find out about the companies you are sending your work to and make sure they have a good reputation. Most do, but sadly, there are some companies who will reject your script, steal the idea, and make the story without your involvement. You could apply for copyright on your work and this can only help you if things get tricky later on. Don't be fooled — if you get into legal proceedings with a major Hollywood studio, you will lose, but having some sort of copyright on your work is a limited and useful starting point to protect your work.

Companies get thousands and thousands of scripts through their mailboxes every day. It's a challenge and you're up against a lot of other writers, but hopefully, your script will be optioned, developed, or bought by the studio. If not, *don't give up*! So many different factors are involved in deciding which scripts to produce — economic factors, current or predicted audience trends, the personal taste of the script reader, etc.

Q: What about filming the project yourself?

A: I have done this in the past, using actor friends, and shooting the project of a broadcast quality camera (such as a Sony VX1000 or Canon XL1). This process will teach you a great deal about writing and the way in which the script is transferred onto screen. Some writers have been very successful in doing this. Kevin Smith wrote the screenplay for *Clerks* and then set about raising enough money to film his idea. The result was a masterpiece of low budget filmmaking and set Mr. Smith on the road to Hollywood success. However, you might not be as lucky and you may find — like me — that the finished film or video is only ever seen by friends and family. You should still consider sending the scripts to people who can invest proper financing and expertise into your work. It may mean that your work changes a little or is made differently to how you imagined it, but it also means that you will be paid and a wider audience will see your work.

Q: Are contests a good way for newcomers to get noticed?

A: There are a lot of them about and a number offer cash prize incentives. Be warned, though; some of these contests are disreputable and may simply steal your ideas. This is not true of all, but I know from several friends in both the UK and America that many such contests are highly questionable. Check them out first and if you're not sure, don't enter.

Another option you might consider is to get an agent. Sounds easy doesn't it? Think again! Getting a good agent at an established firm is actually quite difficult and you might find that you have to submit several scripts before they take you under their wing. If you have broadcaster/studio interest in your work, then this will make the process easier. I have never had an agent, but some friends do and whilst they moan about the percentage the agent takes from writers' pay, they admit that they would not necessarily have as much work if it weren't for their agents. Do some research — ask other writers advice, see whom they would recommend as good agents. Get hold of Rob Long's book *Conversations with My Agent* — it's a great read, funny, and very true!

Q: So what's been keeping you busy lately?

A: My most recent work was writing a Series Bible for a new long-running youth-drama series in the UK. A friend had devised the idea and written a two-page treatment which he sent to a major broadcaster. Interested in the idea, the broadcaster gave him development funds to write a sixty-page Bible that would outline all the characters, dramatic environments and an outline of the first fifty-two half-hour episodes. The only catch — they wanted it completed within one month!

I came on board to write the Bible, developing storylines and characters and turning this information into a concise, tantalizing "selling document." We spent a week researching the subject, another devising and developing storylines and character arcs, and a final fortnight writing the Bible — all the while ensuring that the ideas were interesting to the target audience of twelve- to twenty-five-year-olds. This Bible has now been returned to the broadcaster who will decide whether or not to "green-light" the project. If it gets commissioned I will be joining the show as part of a team of young writers who will write the first fifty-two episode series. Fingers crossed!

Q: What have you learned from this process?

A: Overall this experience was a great challenge and a fantastic learning experience. Whilst I was not writing dialog, I was still using all my (limited!) screenwriting skills in developing well-rounded characters and storylines. I learned a great deal about drama and how to construct a format that will attract the interest of a studio or broadcaster. It was also a lot of fun to be involved at the beginning of the creative process and have input into the creation of a new dramatic world.

Q: What words of wisdom do you have for other young people who want to be writers?

A: The best advice I could offer anyone wanting to work in TV, theatre or films would be this: *don't give up — ever*! If you love what you do and you want to do it above everything else, then you *will* do it. I know how difficult it can be sometimes. I sat through six months of depressing unemployment, watching my friends get jobs in TV and films. I came very close to giving up. Eventually I was offered unpaid work in TV, which led to paid work and the employment I have had since.

Q: So what kept you going during all the rejection?

A: Well, I always knew that even if I wasn't making films or writing scripts as a profession, I would always do it as a hobby. Because I loved doing it so much I would always do it. Sure, no one might see or read my work, but I would still be making films on a home video camera or writing screenplays for my friends to read. If you love it — do it. No one can stop you. No matter what you are told, however, William Goldman's advice still rings true and always will do: "No one knows anything!"

Q: Looking back on it all ... ?

A: One of the most painful aspects I experienced when professionally writing my first drama was the constant criticism from those producing the script. You really do have to be resilient, as producers will always point out what is wrong with your work, rather than praise what is right. I was on my thirteenth draft of a drama (yes — thirteenth!) and I was feeling very worn down and tired of the whole process. I went into a script meeting with the producers who spent the following hour highlighting the aspects of the script they didn't like. I left feeling totally crushed and wanting to give up on the idea completely. The key is *not to give up*. Just take it that your script is good and that any criticisms have been suggested so that you can make your script better!

Sometimes you will hear suggestions that you don't agree with. My advice is to take time to consider all ideas and then decide whether or not to follow them. Some young writers are very protective of their work and will not change a word. Others (myself included) will be so happy to be professionally writing, that they may make any change asked of them — even if they think it is a bad idea. Find a balance between these two approaches. I found that after consideration, some ideas suggested to me were quite useful. Your producers probably have a few years more experience than you — so listen to what they have to say and learn from their expertise. However, do not be afraid to stand up for elements of your work you feel passionately about. Explain why you disagree with some suggestions and see if a compromise can be found.

It can be an uphill struggle at times, but be strong — it's worth it in the end!

Topics to Think About and Talk About

1. In 100 words or less, describe your reaction to having your screenplay rejected, or if you have not yet submitted a screenplay, describe how you think you will react if it is rejected.

2. Identify your favorite television program, and in fifty words or less, analyze why it is your favorite.

3. List five prominent people (living or dead) whose lives would make a compelling film. For each, describe five events in chronological order that make their lives compelling.

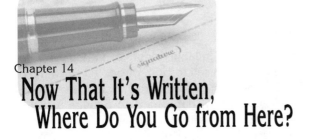

Chapter 14

Now That It's Written,
Where Do You Go from Here?

Like many writers, I used to believe that winning the lottery was more likely than ever landing a film contract. Even if one of my novels was optioned, I thought, the likelihood of it ever being produced seemed remote, even if I moved to LA and "hovered." While luck and persistence were certainly factors in my current association with two separate filmmakers, the timing has never been better nor the market more approachable for aspiring screenwriters to dust off their scripts and take a look at independent producers.

Getting to Hollywood via the Indies

By definition, "indies" (as they're called) are companies that raise their own capital in order to produce selected film projects. Driven by passion more than paycheck, many first-time directors and photographers have honed their craft on independent productions, savoring the excitement of coloring outside traditional lines in order to tell a story their own way. In contrast, the Hollywood studio system assigns creative decisions to executives and company managers who subsequently dictate the style and policies for a hired director.

Where studios have the luxury of titanic budgets, huge crews, and custom-made sets, indies function on ten to 500 grand per picture, employ fewer than twenty technicians, and can comfortably fit into private homes and businesses that would cramp large-scale operations. And although many major stars might decline a role in an indie, just as many more are amenable to taking a pay-cut for the freedom to push their talent in new directions and, accordingly, widen their options. Says Carol Patton, publisher of *Imagine* magazine, "The number of viewers and believers in the indie is growing as people tire of Hollywood predictable blockbusters and formula pictures."

Getting Started

The first thing you need is a salable script, a gameplan, and lots of tenacity. If you're aiming to sell to Hollywood, you also need an agent. The Catch-22 of agents, unfortunately, is that they want writers with the level of experience that's hard to acquire without representation. While it's not impossible to scale this wall, indies offer a more accessible, user-friendly path.

Just because indies are sometimes regarded as a stepping stone to bigger things, however, doesn't mean the quality of work should be that of a novice. Know the craft and format inside-out before you ever pick up the phone or put a stamp on an inquiry letter. Write constantly. Watch films of all kinds. Read scripts. Write the kind of movie that you yourself enjoy on a Saturday night.

What Kind of Scripts Are Selling?

The truth about selling to either market is that neither one knows what they want until they see it ... whereupon large studios will proceed to furiously imitate it until the next hot idea comes along. Indies take a more eclectic view, regarding each project as a chance to expand creative dimensions.

The worst mistake any author can make is to assume that whatever genre of storytelling is currently selling will continue to sell. If a script is unique, it actually has a better chance of getting picked up than one that simply mimics ephemeral trends. Speaking of trends, a lot of emphasis in screenwriting courses and textbooks is placed on plot and structure, yet some of today's most popular movies rely heavily on the utilization of big-budget special effects, with actual "plot" falling by the wayside. How do you reconcile those differences in crafting a marketable script? I put that question to John Johnson, Executive Director and Founder of the American Screenwriters Association:

> I recently read an interview where someone suggested a new movie genre: Special Effects. Heresy, I hope not! Don't misunderstand me, I like special effects, but only when they advance the film and make it interesting to watch, not when the whole film is special effects with no plot or likable characters. *The Matrix,* for instance, was good not just because of the special effects but also because

202

running underneath was a plot and some interesting characters. Or consider *U-571* where the underwater scenes of submarines dodging one another and on-coming torpedoes helped bring the audience into the picture and relate to the characters. On the other hand, *Battlefield Earth* had tremendous explosions and other special effects, but that didn't save the movie because the dialog, plot, and characters were so weak.

As stated in an earlier chapter, it's much easier to add in glitz later than to build your entire premise around special effects, outrageous sets built from scratch, and hordes of extras that will be pricey and, accordingly, limit the number of markets to which a first-time writer can sell. The strength of the film must rest entirely on a good story and compelling characters to tell it. Everything else is gravy.

Finding a Buyer

The proliferation of indies throughout the world means that writers can conceivably find film opportunities right in their own backyard! For instance, each state has a film commission, serving the dual purpose of assisting Hollywood productions on location and maintaining a database of local actors, "tekkies," investors, and writers. Not only does this network benefit producers in search of regional talent, but promotes the word that you — the writer — are available to develop and revise scripts. Whether an indie invites your participation depends on the existence/absence of a writer-director team, as well as the feasibility, resources, and expense of filming your particular story.

Four additional routes are available for locating potential directors: monthly trade magazines (i.e., *Filmmakers Magazine, American Cinematographer, Independent, Imagine*), screenwriting competitions (*Disney, Nicholl Fellowships, Writers's Digest*), film festivals (*Sundance, Filmfest DC*), and online resources. Through many of the Internet sites, in fact, you'll not only learn who is looking for what but actually post treatments and full scripts for potential buyers to review.

Don't Call Us: We'll Call You

Let's say that one of your cover letters lands you a pitch session, an invitation to tell a prospective director what your script is about. The biggest difference between pitching to indies and studios is that the latter is almost always done by professional agents. Indies typically aren't governed by such formality, nor are writers left hanging indefinitely as committees debate a script's marketability. Indie writers can expect to play a more active role in a film's development than they would at a studio, where revisions are often penned by someone on staff.

It also isn't necessary for indie material to have been "audience-tested"; i.e., a published novel or play. While studios gravitate to established works that represent lower risk, indies are fearless about pushing limits and thrusting lesser-known projects into the limelight. To use a restaurant analogy, studios are serving up burgers and fries; indies are offering vegetable pakoras and tandoori.

The same protocol governing employment interviews applies equally well to the nature of pitch sessions:

1. Be on time.
2. Be prepared.
3. Be enthusiastic.
4. Be succinct.
5. Be focused.
6. Be natural (don't rely on notes).
7. Be open to feedback.
8. Be quiet when they're talking.
9. Be polite.
10. Believe.

Show Me the Money

Any opportunity to prove your screenwriting mettle is always worth pursuing. Who's to say that a modest film won't suddenly take the public by storm and become an Oscar contender? On the other hand, if it withers into obscurity at the box office, you won't be scarred for life; you simply learn from your cinematic mistakes and move on.

While indies are clearly not as liberal with their cash flow as the big guys, there are nonetheless tidy sums and perks to be earned from working with them. For example, the adaptation of my Scottish time travel, *The Spellbox*, includes my airfare and lodging when the crew goes on location to the Highlands, not far from where my husband and I were married!

Always make sure that you have negotiated a reasonable salary long before the cameras ever roll and get that agreement in writing, no matter how casual the relationship between consenting parties. Be wary, for instance, of arrangements that cite "deferred pay" which, in many cases, translates to "probably not in this lifetime."

So how "reasonable" is reasonable in terms of your time and your script's value? If you're a dues-paying member of the Writers Guild, there are already established minimums in place (found at the WGA website) which govern what writers must be paid for virtually any type of screenwriting. Nor surprisingly, a number of indies specify that potential screenwriters not belong to WGA. Why? Because it does not obligate them to pay WGA minimums but rather to set their own price for services.

With a studio, the compensation and perks are based on industry standards and an agent's chutzpah. Likewise, an established reputation as an already "hot" author is an influence on the number of zeroes on a check. With an indie, however, the package is based on a compromise of what the producer can realistically afford and what the writer can willingly sacrifice for the euphoria of getting his or her story to the screen.

Writer's Market offers a nice thumbnail guide each year on the going rates for various writing services, screenplays among them. If you are unsure of what to charge, the listings under audiovisual and electronic communications will give you a good starting point to negotiate. Another option is to base your fee on a percentage of the full budget, with half of that fee payable upon commencement of the contract and the second half due upon delivery of an acceptable script.

Don't rule out chatrooms, either! If you're truly stymied on how much you should be getting for a first-time script, toss the question out to your fellow screenwriters. Those who have been there and done that are always more than happy to offer advice and make recommendations on how to seal a rewarding deal. Whichever route you take, never forget the one thing that indies and studios have in common despite their significant differences: The script is the backbone, the essence, the very reason that cameras roll, directors direct, stars are born, and magic unfolds everyday on the screens of theatres nationwide.

Without the writer, audiences would be left sitting in the dark.

Where the Indies Are

Film Threat

http://www.filmthreat.com

This site, plus a weekly newsletter covers independent and underground films. If you're researching potential directors, it's a good pulse point to discern their respective interests and budgets.

Centropolis Interactive's iF Magazine

http://www.ifmagazine.com

A weekly e-zine similar to Film Magazine in scope and content.

IMAGINE Magazine

http://www.imaginenews.com

P.O. Box 382322

Cambridge, MA 02138

IMAGINE is both a hard-copy monthly newspaper and a website which is primarily targeted to Northeast screenwriters and filmmakers. Its articles, however, aptly apply to anyone interested in the independent production company route for their scripts.

Independent Film Channel

http://www.ifctv.com

A site connected to the Independent Film Channel, a cable network placing high emphasis on indies, documentaries, shorts, animation, and unedited, commercial-free coverage of all major film festivals around the world.

Indie Films
http://www.indiefilms.com

This is a Hollywood based network which matches up independent producers with investors, grants, and film distributors.

Hollywood Creative Directory
http://www.hcdonline.com

The print versions of HCD's resource directories can get a little pricey, particularly since the turnover in listings could necessitate buying the latest edition each time it comes out. A noteworthy feature, however, is that HCD's website provides a free job board for the entertainment industry and telephone numbers for those listed in its creative, agents', and managers' directories.

A Sampler of Canadian Indies

Don't rule out independent production companies outside the U.S., either! By and large, I've found some of the foreign markets to be very receptive to American talents, not to mention the doors this can open in terms of cultural exchange and new friends. A number of these also generate newsletters and links to additional production companies for you to query.

Artatak Films (www.inforamp.net/~bondfast/index.htm)

Blink Pictures Inc. (www.blinkpictures.com)

Crescent Entertainment (www.crescent.ca)

Eastside Film Company (www.eastsidefilm.com)

General Coffee Company Film Productions (www.generalcoffee.com)

Jerian Pictures Inc. (www.jerianpictures.com)

Postman Productions (www.postmanproductions.com)

Primitive Features (www.primitive.net)

Rainmaker Entertainment Group (www.rainmaker.com)

Real World Films Inc. (www.realworldfilms.com)

Silverfilm (www.silverfilm.com)

Sphinx Productions (www.sphinxproductions.com)

Sullivan Entertainment (www.sullivan-ent.com)

How to Win Screenwriting Contests

On any given day, a screenwriting contest is probably being held somewhere. Should you pay fees to enter? Who are the judges? Will you get a critique whether you win or lose? Where do you go from here with your winning (or losing) script? Such are the questions which plague writers planning to put their screenplays up against total strangers in a competitive forum.

The enticement to participate, of course, is the fact that these scripts are actually being asked for, as opposed to the customary pitching route of writing copious letters, making telephone calls, and knocking on doors to see if someone, anyone might like to read your material. The even better news is that, with certain exceptions (usually tied to direct association with the sponsor or regional/membership restrictions), they are open to all and are extremely well publicized on the Internet and in trade magazines.

The prizes awarded are as diverse as the material being sought and range in significance from a nice chunk of change and/or an option agreement (Hurrah!) to a cheap certificate and complimentary plastic comb (Oh). Somewhere in between are scriptwriting software packages, agent representation, expense-paid seminars, mantle-worthy awards, screenwriting books, and consultations in person or in print by industry experts. I think the delightful irony here is that although your lack of experience/credits could preclude you from getting a Disney exec to even read an unsolicited letter, your participation in a Disney-sponsored script contest will assure that your material is reviewed, judged, and maybe even selected!

There is also a lot of latitude in terms of entry fees, most of which go toward administrative processing costs, reimbursing the judges for readings/critiques, and paying for the prizes. While your personal budget picture is obviously the determining factor in how many contests you choose to enter, those which will yield some measure of professional feedback on your work are generally well worth the cost of admission. (And don't forget that you can deduct those fees on your income taxes as writing expenditures, along with membership dues, subscriptions, and supplies.)

What can you do to increase your chances of winning?

1. Follow the instructions!

2. Enter early as opposed to waiting until zero-hour. The same psychology of theatrical auditions curiously applies to the order in which scripts are read; those viewed first tend to set a precedent for those that follow. Toward the end, the judges are more rushed and impatient to get through the stacks. Suffice it to say, a lot of scripts begin to look exactly the same at that point.

3. Fill out the requisite releases and contest forms legibly and in black ink.

4. Include the appropriate contest fees in the same envelope with the entry forms and the script. (You'd be surprised how many people forget to do this.) Your check should be paper-clipped to the entry form, not submitted loose where it could accidentally be tossed out with the envelope.

5. In the event that you move or change your phone number during the competition period, it would be prudent to let the contest officials know that via mail. If their letter of congratulations comes back returned or they call only to hear the message that your number has been disconnected, do not count on them investing a lot of time to find out what happened to you.

Sam Quo Vadis, whose script "The New Faerehaven Witch Trials" was selected for Telluride IndieFest 2000, adds the following advice: "With literally tens of thousands of screenplays being written each year, the challenge of getting one's script read has exceeded the challenge of writing a solid, marketable story. Placing well in a contest is almost on a par with a personal recommendation. It lends a writer an aura of legitimacy. For me, it means that influential people in the industry are much more receptive to reading my work and, in some cases, will even seek me out. It's also a great affirmation. Every writer encounters those who doubt his or her ability to succeed in an industry where the vast majority fail. In that environment every success becomes a vindication. One of the nicest accomplishments is to see the doubters slowly become believers!"

Ready, Set ... Write!

Nearly every screenwriting site listed has an announcement section for upcoming competitions. My own favorite in terms of user-friendly features is the contest section found at http://www.moviebytes.com, where you can find the rules and advance information on contests held monthly, yearly, internationally, and even those which charge no fees to enter. The brief sampling below will give you an idea of what's in the works for aspiring contestants:

Nicholl Fellowships in Screenwriting
http://www.oscars.org/nicholl/index.html

The Nicholl, an international contest held annually, is open to any writer who has not optioned or sold a treatment, teleplay or screenplay for more than $5,000. Up to five $25,000 fellowships are offered each year to promising authors.

Austin Heart of Screenplay Competition
http://www.austinfilmfestival.org

This contest invites entries in both the Children/Family and Adult/Mature categories. Cash prizes and passes to the Austin Film Festival are awarded to the lucky winners.

Chesterfield Film Company Writer's Film Project
http://www.chesterfield-co.com

Up to five winners (in any genre) are eligible for $20,000 stipends for one-year fellowships based in Los Angeles to learn more about the craft of screenwriting.

Walt Disney Studios Fellowship Program
http://www.members.tripod.com/disfel

The people responsible for that famous mouse also hold a screenwriting competition every spring. Like the Chesterfield, the prize is a residency program in LA for eight lucky writers, with round-trip airfare and one month's accommodations provided for those who live outside Southern California.

Writer's Digest Writing Competition

http://www.writersdigest.com

The television and movie script division of this annual contest is still fairly new, but already attracting a high number of applicants. Unlike other contests in which the entire script must be submitted, WD calls for only the first fifteen pages plus a one-page synopsis. Cash awards, books, and WD subscriptions are in the offing, with the Grand Prize being an expense-paid trip to New York City to schmooze with publishing industry execs.

Moondance International Film Festival

http://www.moondancefilmfestival.com

The objective of this international contest is to promote and encourage women screenwriters and filmmakers. Screenplays, animation, stage plays and short stories are all eligible for review. Helpful tip: Moondance judges encourage non-violence as a solution to conflict, and place high emphasis on character-driven, intelligent, and non-stereotypical roles for females.

Film Festivals

Cannes. Sundance. Telluride. Even the names sound glamorous, a veritable playground of actors, directors, producers, and screenwriters who assemble annually to view each other's latest projects and air-kiss over glasses of champagne. Well, sometimes. Most of the time, it's all about networking and locking down financing, marketing, and distributors.

While the majority of festival activities are geared toward those who have films that have already been completed, a number of screenwriters attend them as well, primarily as a schmoozing opportunity to determine which filmmakers might be the best target for an inquiry letter and script review. Even a small-scale, hometown film festival can yield global results. Keep in mind that, like yourself, new filmmakers are aggressive about getting themselves known; they want to meet people who can make that happen. And the way it happens is with a hot script that can show off their best work.

Norwegian film director Tonje Nordgaard of Iceberg Productions shares that the festival circuit by itself isn't enough to gain a foothold: "It is important to remember that film competitions might be just as important in your search for awards as film festivals. There are so many festivals out there, and they cost so much to attend that it is useful to research the festivals to hit the ones interested in what your movie is about. Never think of film festivals as the only way to be noticed, though, and don't get discouraged if your film doesn't get selected. Think creatively about ways to bring your movie out, and ways to make money from it. After all, you are trying to make a living out of your passion of making film!

"Awards alone will not bring you to your goals. You always have to keep hustling. Try to sell your movie, go to TV channels (even small, local ones), make copies and sell it to relatives, friends and through the Internet. The dream of making a living out of filmmaking takes more than awards from one of the many film festivals. It helps, but it is no guarantee, just one of the many tools in your toolbox. Make sure you have enough tools."

Agents

There's a lot of similarity between courting a prospective film agent for your work and testing the waters of a new relationship. Specifically: 1. Do you have enough in common to sustain a long-term association, 2. were you introduced by someone who knows both of you, and 3. how much should you reveal at the start if you want to ensure a satisfying pursuit?

Suffice it to say, many new writers approach Hollywood reps in much the same fashion as those who have been out of romantic circulation for awhile: nervously, desperately, and placing far more weight on the outcome than on the process of defining what exactly it is they want from the experience. Time and again, I've counseled writers who have been so thrilled that someone — *anyone* — has finally agreed to pay attention to them, they end up sabotaging themselves and/or tolerating all manner of shoddy behavior.

Herein are some tips for not only ensuring call-backs from the right people but heeding warning signs about the wrong ones. (If they work for your love life, too, so much the better!)

Common Ground

If you were seeking a potential date for a dance, would you flip open a telephone book and call the first name your pencil-point dropped on? Of course not! Yet how many writers use a similar technique with the rationale, "Don't they all work pretty much the same way?" The fact of the matter is that agents — good agents — specialize in representing certain types of projects and genres. The time and effort invested in establishing contacts has paid off for them in terms of reputation; production companies recognize that scripts that have crossed these agents' desks and been forwarded for review are the cream of the crop.

So how do you know which one is the best match for you?

Track Record:

Would you pursue someone who wasn't gainfully employed or was purposely evasive about what he or she did for a living? On the same note, would you feel secure with someone who had either: 1. never sustained any long-term relationships, 2. blamed all failures on the other party, or 3. couldn't remember any names because none of them stayed long enough?

Availability:

Is your target agent genuinely interested in meeting someone new at this time or is their plate already full? Congenial as they may be at a party and ask you to give them a call sometime, the truth is that very few of them actually hope you will. Another clue is whether the agency has an actual address or just a post office box. If they only want to meet you at bus station lunch-counters, you might want to think twice about deeper involvement.

High Maintenance:

Will the agent expect you to foot the bill for all postage, photocopying, phone calls, and adult beverages? Likewise, will he or she expect you to pay out large sums of money in order for him or her to tell you how wonderful you and your films are?

Exits and Exclusivity:

How difficult/expensive will it be to extricate yourself from an unpleasant arrangement (i.e., agents who demand a commitment of two years whether they sell anything or not)? You should also be wary of those who demand that you not see anyone else, even

213

though they have yet to declare their own intentions toward you or even return your phone calls.

Expectations:

Most agents will expect you to keep working after the honeymoon period is over. New screenwriters, on the other hand, have the rosy view that their days of struggle are finally gone now that their future is in someone else's hands. "One shot wonders" — alas! — are rarely enough to pay the rent for either of you. If you want an agent to stay committed to the partnership, how committed are you to keep supplying exciting manuscripts on a regular basis?

A Cautionary Note

Watch out for make-over artists. How many times have you been besotted with someone who possessed a never-ending list of improvements you should make to yourself — different hair, different clothes, different hobbies — the end result being that the custom-tailored persona got dumped anyway for someone uncannily similar to whoever he or she was originally.

Agents can be just as critical. While constructive advice certainly has its place, the last thing you need is someone who tries to reshape your style to fit the limitations of their own sales ability. I briefly was involved with such an agent in the book publishing business who tried to turn every mainstream plot into a formulaic romance. Why? Because the romance market was the only one in which she felt comfortable.

Always keep in mind that although an agent may possess the map to get you to your destination, the car still belongs to you.

Referrals

Back in the adventurous '70s, I often found myself coaxed into blind dates by well intentioned friends. I justified this practice by the wistful thinking that: 1. the odds of being fixed up with a loser were remote, and 2. my friends knew me pretty well. The reality, of course, was that Mr. Right never materialized from any of these encounters, nor are any of these friends still in the picture.

The film business, fortunately, is a little brighter in terms of matchmaking, owing to the openness with which established agents will consider new writers recommended by associates who have indisputable judgment. This is obviously a different level of networking than that found among friends who will set you up with virtually anyone who has a pulse. The reason is that there is more at stake in the professional arena than around the water-cooler; to unwittingly vouch for an author who has neither the product, the discipline, nor the attitude to be of value to the agent translates to only one thing — a diminishment of trust. Even if the next "find" should be pure gold, it only takes one dud to generate skepticism ever after.

On the plus side is the possibility that a third-party introduction can ignite a chemistry that might not have been discovered if they'd been left to their own devices. Who better than someone who knows the likes, dislikes, and objectives of both sides to bring them together in the middle?

What you can't do if you opt to engage a go-between, however, is to: 1. assume an outcome of success-by-association or 2. blame the intermediary for any subsequent rejection. The go-between is only a catalyst to get your project in the door; where it goes from there rests entirely on its quality, timeliness, and marketability.

But Enough About Me ...

To revisit the courtship analogy, a query letter is like a first date; sometimes in the zeal to make a good impression, a person will either: 1. exaggerate the facts or 2. just plain yak too much. The danger of embellishment, of course, is that sooner or later you'll probably be faced with having to actually produce the Porsche, medical credentials, or celebrity best-friend you so brilliantly fabricated to enhance your appeal. Likewise, the pitfall of divulging every single detail of your life within the first hour of conversation is not only an inducement for the listener's eyes to glaze over but also a kiss of death to creating any sense of mystique which might have guaranteed a return engagement.

Among the most common correspondence mistakes new authors make in approaching an agent for the first time are the following:

Dear Ethel:

"Ethel" is how you can address her after Ethel, a total stranger, specifically encourages you to. Up until then, she is "Ms. So-and-So." In spite of society's growing trend to put everyone on a first-name basis, you need to remember that a number of agents consider themselves deity-like in stature and, thus, command a certain level of awe and respect. (Oh yes, and it also helps if you spell their names correctly.)

And so then there's this scene the next day at the grocery store that's actually supposed to be a flashback of when ... :

Brevity needs to be your operative word in pitching a plot. Much as you may want to share every scintillating detail of your story — including all the names of the heroine's cats — a query letter is not the place to do it. The purpose of the query letter is to provide a tantalizing taste of what's to come and make the reader — the agent — absolutely salivate to get the rest. Oftentimes authors forget the sheer volume of unsolicited material that crosses agents' desks every day; the sight of a neatly typed and concise summary of a film's merits and the author's qualifications to write it will always be a far more welcome sight than an introductory letter that is nearly as long as the movie itself. Word to the wise: if you can't sum up your film and your background in less than a page, you're talking too much.

This script will definitely be the next "Gone with the Wind":

As fervently as any author dreams of global success, premature proclamations and comparisons are more of a turn-off than an enticement. As proud as you may be of your finished product, this isn't the time to assume the role of a critic or psychic and imply in any way that the agent would be a fool to pass up this blockbuster opportunity. Nor would it be prudent to reveal that you have already purchased a new outfit to wear on Letterman or that you're available for a cameo. These are the kind of letters that make agents roll on the floor in fits of side-splitting laughter.

Finish What You've Started

If your first screenplay exists only in the embryonic stage, an agent will not be interested. For first-timers, agents want to know that the script has actually been completed. They also want to know the page-count and target market. Even if your script is finished, however, do not send any portion of it unless you have been specifically asked to do so. When that request does arrive, send only what the agent has specified. Don't make the assumption that if a treatment and ten pages are good, the whole thing would be even better. If they ask for ten, send ten. No more. No less.

The Waiting Game

Last but not least in the quest to find the right match is the amount of time you're likely to spend sitting by a telephone or mailbox. In romance, it's the frustration of someone saying they'll call and your naivete in believing it will really happen. In show biz, it's the expectation that the recipient will see how wonderful you are and not want you to get away; the trouble is that they may take up to eighteen months to come around to that conclusion before writing back to see if you're still alive.

The decision of how long to give someone is entirely up to you. Obviously playing the field and having lots of creative irons in the fire helps minimize the impatience of wanting "The One" to step forward with a solid commitment that will make you both happy. In the meantime, the variety of feedback garnered from multiple sources (i.e., contests and Internet film sites) is a valuable lesson in reaffirming that writing, after all, is entirely subjective and affects different people in different ways. The confidence you'll accordingly glean about yourself and your talent will serve to make you that much more attractive to the right agent who, even at this moment, is probably looking for you.

Your Assignment

It's never too early to start doing your homework regarding agencies. Start a file box or notebook with a separate entry for each of the companies listed below. Whenever you find yourself with some free time to make a phone call, look up a website, or write an inquiry letter, you will want to learn: 1. what are the agency's submission policies, 2. to whom should new submissions be sent (name and correct title), and 3. what types of films does this agency represent? (Note: This is only a partial listing. Many more can be found at resource sites such as Writers Guild of America.)

Above the Line Agency
9200 Sunset Blvd., #804
West Hollywood, CA 90069
(310) 859-6115

ACME Talent & Literary Agency
4727 Wilshire Blvd., #333
Los Angeles,CA 90010
(323) 954-2263

Agency for the Performing Arts
9200 Sunset Blvd., #900
Los Angeles, CA 90069
(310) 273-0744

The Agency
1800 Avenue of the Stars, #1114
Los Angeles, CA 90067
(310) 551-3000

Aimee Entertainment Assoc.
15840 Ventura Blvd., Ste. 215
Encino, CA 91436
(818) 783-9115

The Artists Agency
1180 S. Beverly Drive, Ste. 301
Los Angeles, CA 90035
(310) 277-7779

The Bennett Agency
1129 State Street, Ste. 9
Santa Barbara, CA 93101
(310) 471-2251

Bruce Brown Agency
1033 Gayley Ave., Ste. 207
Los Angeles, CA 90024
(310) 208-1835

William Carroll Agency
139 N. San Fernando Rd., Ste. A
Burbank, CA 91502
(818) 848-9948

Coralie Jr. Theatrical Agency
4789 Vineland Ave., Ste. 100
N. Hollywood, CA 91602
(818) 766-9501

Creative Artist Agency
9830 Wilshire Blvd.
Beverly Hills, CA 90212
(310) 288-4545

Endeavor Agency, The
9701 Wilshire Blvd., 10th Floor
Beverly Hills, CA 90212
(310) 248-2000

Favored Artists Agency
8489 West 3rd Street, #2
Los Angeles, CA 90048
(310) 247-1040 Fax: (323) 801-2124

Film Artists Associates
13563 ¹/₂ Ventura Blvd., 2nd Floor
Sherman Oaks, CA 91423
(818) 386-9669

The Gage Group, Inc.
14724 Ventura Blvd., Ste. 505
Sherman Oaks, CA 91403
(818) 905-3800

The Gersh Agency, Inc. (L.A.)
232 North Canon Drive
Beverly Hills, CA 90210
(310) 274-6611

Michelle Gordon & Assoc.
260 S. Beverly Dr., #308
Beverly Hills, CA 90212
(310) 246-9930

Henderson-Hogan Agency
247 S. Beverly Dr., Ste. 102
Beverly Hills, CA 90212
(310) 274-7815

Ifa Talent Agency
8730 Sunset Blvd., Ste. 490
Los Angeles, CA 90069
(310) 659-5522

Leslie Kallen Agency
15760 Ventura Blvd., Ste 700
Encino, CA 91436
(818) 906-2785
(Queries responded to if company is interested)

Jon Klane Agency
120 El Camino Dr., #112
Beverly Hills, CA 90212
(310) 278-0178

The Candace Lake Agency
9200 Sunset Blvd., #820
West Hollywood, CA 90069
(310) 247-2115

Lenhoff & Lenhoff
9200 W. Sunset Blvd., #830
West Hollywood, CA 90069
(310) 550-3900

Media Artists Group
6404 Wilshire Blvd.
Los Angeles, CA 90048
(323) 658-5050

The Orange Grove Group, Inc.
12178 Ventura Blvd., #205
Studio City, CA 91604
(818) 762-7498

The Daniel Ostroff Agency
9200 West Sunset Blvd., #402
Los Angeles, CA 90069
(310) 278-2020

Paradigm
10100 Santa Monica Blvd., Ste. 2500
Los Angeles, CA 90067
(310) 277-4400

The Lynn Pleshette Literary Agency
2700 N. Beachwood Dr.
Los Angeles, CA 90068
(323) 465-0428

Diverse Talent Group
1875 Century Park East, Ste. 2250
Los Angeles, CA 90067
(310) 271-1414

The Irv Schechter Company
9300 Wilshire Blvd., Ste. 400
Beverly Hills, CA 90212
(310) 278-8070

Shapiro-Lichtman, Inc.
8827 Beverly Blvd.
Los Angeles, CA 90048
(310) 859-8877

United Talent Agency
9560 Wilshire Blvd., 5th floor
Beverly Hills, CA 90212
(310) 273-6700

Ann Waugh Talent Agency
4741 Laurel Canyon Blvd., Ste. 200
N. Hollywood, CA 91607
(818) 980-0141

William Morris Agency
151 El Camino Drive
Beverly Hills, CA 90212
(310) 859-4000

Writers & Artists Agency
8383 Wilshire Blvd., Suite 550
Beverly Hills, CA 90211
(323) 866-0900

Hollywood, Here I Come!

There are lots of different routes to go to get your script — and you — in circulation. Regardless of which ones appeal to you the most, however, you need to accept that fame and fortune probably aren't going to occur overnight. Granted, there are lots of talented people who sometimes appear to have sprung forth into the public eye in less than twenty-four hours, but if you were to examine their lives closely, you'd likely discover that they themselves have been a work-in-progress for some time (largely learning by trial, error, and luck) and that if their scripts had been earning frequent flyer miles during that process, they could probably travel free for the rest of their lives.

Pecking Order

So how fast does something actually get read by a studio exec once you put it in the mail? Frederick Levy, Vice President of Development and Production at Marty Katz (*Reindeer Games*) Productions, has provided his own "pecking order" of reading priorities:

1. Spec scripts. An agent goes out wide with a spec. Each producer will receive one territory, a studio or buyer. If you snooze, you lose. First thing the next morning, the agent is expecting my call saying I want to take the script into the studio. Some days multiple specs go out, which doesn't leave much time for other reading.

2. New drafts of active development projects. A great rewrite could mean spending the next several months actually making a film. New drafts of active projects are highly anticipated and usually will be read upon receipt.

3. Samples for open assignments. When I'm looking for a writer to rewrite a script, the process of reading samples can become quite time-consuming. However, once I narrow down my favorites, I can proceed to hear writers' takes and actually get them working on the project, pushing the results of their work into category two, above.

4. Projects which I think I can set up. Our deal is at Miramax and Dimension Films. These companies are looking for

specific types of material (see www.hollywood-101.com to find out what we (i.e., they) are currently looking for). Hence, I keep an eye open to any such projects that come along, whether by agent or unsolicited query, that might fit our current needs.

5. Projects which sound interesting to me. Yes, I do actually read scripts, whether by agent or query, that just interest me on a personal level. Unfortunately, the priority for such material is low. This may explain why I never seem to have time to just read for fun.

6. Scripts by friends and referral. Sure, I'm happy to do favors and read scripts for friends, but as you can see, there's just not a lot of time."

Note: Levy is author of the best-selling *Hollywood 101: The Film Industry* (2000) published by Renaissance Books. If you want to add to your knowledge of how to survive in Tinseltown, as well as land a job in the industry, this is a must-buy for your personal library!

Making Ends Meet

Much has been written about the serendipity of being in the right place at the right time to pitch a script to an actor/director/producer who just happened to be desperately in need of fresh material. While such happy occurrences are more the stuff of fiction than reality, there are nevertheless plenty of jobs in Los Angeles and New York which can put you in convenient proximity to the film industry's movers and shakers. These are, coincidentally, many of the same jobs that aspiring stars hold down whilst waiting for their big break; i.e., parking cars, serving food, driving taxis, tending bar, making deliveries, etc. Job listings can be found in the classified sections of the major metropolitan newspapers.

You may also want to start brushing up on the "star sightings" found in Hollywood gossip columns as a basis for narrowing down target restaurants to approach for a job. For instance, you're more likely to encounter the glitterati at Spago's as opposed to the International House of Pancakes.

While the paycheck isn't necessarily stellar, such positions offer you a flexibility of schedule, are relatively mindless in scope, and provide you with the warm and fuzzy support from your peers in the kitchen or at the garage who are all trying to do pretty much the same thing you're doing. They also put you in the nice position of overhearing good gossip, given the propensity of executives to talk fairly freely around those whom they put in the same class as "servants." If you're particularly skilled at whatever menial job is providing you sustenance until your big break, the scenario could even transpire of having a star or studio exec specifically request your table or your car.

What these jobs don't give you, however, is permission to intrude on their privacy (unless invited to do so) and/or use the job as an inappropriate forum to pitch your work (i.e, "Here's the Cobb salad you ordered, Mr. Pitt, and by the way would you like to read this copy of my screenplay?"). Not only will this alienate the person you're trying to impress but, more than likely, also get you fired.

Suffice it to say, of course, your clientele won't be limited to the rich and famous; while you're holding your breath and hoping Steven Spielberg will be the next one to hail your cab, you'll have to schlep all of those total nobodies around town in the meantime. The plus side? Think of all the characters you'll meet that you could incorporate in a future plot!

There are also plenty of jobs within the industry that attract future screenwriters as well: clerical jobs, accounting jobs, technical jobs, personal assistant jobs, freelance readers. I even know of one enterprising scriptwriter who worked for a whole summer at Disneyland in the hope of rubbing elbows with Michael Eisner and casually giving him a script. He never managed to meet any of the Disney bigwigs while he was there, but he did lose twelve pounds from sweltering in a Goofy costume.

By the way, there's generally a high turnover in lower-level staff at production studios, especially those positions which are filled by college-age applicants. They, too, are looking for a big break and will either find one, thus vacating the position to the next Hollywood-hopeful, or burn out from impatience and decide that driving a cab is a steadier source of income.

Another popular entry-level avenue is available to those who have specialized skills: costume design, construction, animal handling, stuntwork. Yes, it puts you "on location" with the stars, but carries with it the two drawbacks that it will either "niche" yourself into being perceived as only able to do one thing well (for instance, falling off buildings onto your head) or leave you so exhausted that you're too tired to work on that screenplay when you drag yourself home after a long day's work!

Listings for these "insider" types of positions can be found in the classified sections of metro newspapers and industry trades, as well as at studio websites. Rather than list them all in this text, I'd recommend that you go to your web browser and do a search on either "film companies" or "movie studios." This will generate a list that not only includes all of the major production companies but independents as well. The Human Resources Departments at these sites will post all of their available positions, appropriate contact people, filing deadlines, and how to apply (i.e., standardized application, resume, telephone call, or applying in person).

Whether you choose to interview for an insider job or a menial one, I do need to caution you against "the kiss of death line." Specifically, do not volunteer to them that you are an aspiring scriptwriter. Why? Because it suggests that you are only using this job as a springboard to getting discovered (even if, in fact, that's exactly what you are doing). Training someone new — even for a relatively mundane job — still takes time. Faced with the choice of hiring you, the aspiring screenwriter, or someone to whom washing cars is an unparalleled joy and lifelong ambition, which one do you think will get picked? Obviously if, after securing the requisite menial job to pay your rent, the word leaks out that you are penning your first flick, you can humbly acknowledge that yes, it's true.

Last but not least are what I call "well-paying-but-relatively-mindless" occupations. These are: 1. jobs in which you're allowed to spend a lot of time by yourself (time to write, of course!) and 2. temp jobs that free you to leave at a moment's notice if a hot opportunity comes up. To paraphrase the late novelist Marion Zimmer Bradley, you need a job that will adequately take care of the bills yet not sorely tax your creativity and energy to still pursue your goals.

Writing for Joy:
An Interview with Linda Seger

Author, lecturer and screenwriting consultant Ms. Linda Seger knows what it takes to make a good story great. The same principles can also be applied to real life to ensure that the dream of a lifetime doesn't take over as your worst nightmare.

Q: So what did you want to be when you were growing up?

A: From the age of ten, I wanted to be a writer. My first dream was to write Nancy Drew mysteries and detective stories.

Q: You 'n me both.

A: I wrote short stories. I wrote poems. I wrote my first novel when I was thirteen.

Q: Pretty impressive! Did you ever get it published?

A: No, never! It was about four sisters and was a direct rip-off of *Little Women*! I worked on it for three months every day after school. When I finished, I wrapped a blue ribbon around it and showed it to my best friend. She said she cried because one of the daughters in it died, which I presume meant it was really good.

Q: So how long was this tome?

A: It was twenty-six pages, handwritten, but to me it was still a real novel!

Q: So what came next?

A: I always saw myself as writing *dramas* but then I got into drama. In college, I began to direct plays and then I began teaching drama after graduate school. I've noticed that many of the people who are successful writers as adults began writing by the time they were teenagers. Maybe they didn't specifically know what kind of writing to do but they knew they liked doing it.

Q: When did you narrow the field yourself?

A: When my first book came out at the end of 1987, I found my real calling was writing non-fiction. For all writers, at some point, you need to know what kind of writing you like to do.

When we're younger, we don't really know.

Q: Do you think we put limitations on ourselves as we get older?

A: When you're young, you really have to write for the joy of it. You need to write because you want to and need to. As a teenager, you shouldn't be thinking about money but rather about learning your art and learning to do it well.

Q: How did you get into the script consulting biz?

A: I did my college dissertation on why a script works or doesn't work and developed a method for analyzing its various components. Many people who were analyzing scripts were throwing solutions at the script rather than really analyzing the problems or helping improve the writer. When I began applying my method to a script, many writers would say to me, "I've been struggling with this for five years and, in one hour, you pinpointed exactly what the problem was and what to do about it."

Q: What kind of fees did you charge?

A: At first I worked for free just to get known. Then I put an ad in the paper and started to get regular clients.

Q: Enough to pay the rent?

A: Eventually. But before that, I had about fourteen years of instability.

Q: Fourteen? How did you hang in there?

A: Mostly because I just kept thinking that it was going to change! What all of this affirms, though, is that every writer I've known has gone through a difficult time and managed to survive it. With screenwriters, you often hear that they wrote five scripts before anything was sold or optioned. Maybe it wasn't until their eighth or tenth or maybe even their fifteenth before they got a big break. Most people, I think, would have given up by then.

Q: My theory is that the ones who make it are simply the ones who outlast all the competition.

A: Exactly! One of the best known screenwriters in television movies is Cynthia Whitcombe. I think it was her tenth script that finally made it for her. By the time that happened, she was probably the cheapest, most experienced writer that anyone could hire! She is now — and has been for at least the past fifteen, maybe even twenty years — one of the top television movie writers and mini-series writers.

Q: In the twenty years that you've been a consultant, movies have certainly improved technologically. Do you think the story content has kept pace?

A: The structure has definitely gotten better. When I first started, I'd say that eighty-five percent of the scripts I worked on didn't have much structure; for instance, the first turning point was on page seventy! Nowadays, I'd say that eighty-five percent of the scripts seem to be fairly well structured and sometimes fairly well crafted. Now writers need to learn to be more original. Craft isn't enough. You need art.

Q: Is that because they're relying on special effects to carry the momentum?

A: Certainly there are many films that rely too much on special effects, but too many scripts aren't interesting or they look exactly like other films. They're derivative, rather than original. Sometimes the story they want to tell is just too difficult for them to tell because it's only their first or second script. Sometimes, of course, you write a difficult script because it's a good learning script. However, it's important that teenagers and writers writing their first screenplay are not concerned about marketing and being commercial. That comes later.

Q: But isn't the whole idea to sell the finished product?

A: Eventually, yes. But when you're young and new at this, what you need to do is write what you really care about and not just try to follow a commercial trend. Writing is also a combination of being creative and solving creative problems. Part of writing is evaluating your work, but if you do that too early in the process, you can stop the creative flow. Write what you love until the flow gets going and you're really *excited* about what you're doing and discovering how much remains to be learned. It's also important that you always surround yourself with people who can *nurture* your writing. That means you have to have teachers and you have to have friends who will be enthused and happy about what you're doing and encourage you to keep doing it even when you're not selling anything.

Q: One of the books you penned was *When Women Call the Shots*. What are some of the advances you've seen for females in an industry which is predominantly run by men?

A: Actually I've seen very *few* advances with either women writers or women directors. During the first twenty-five years of the twentieth century, there were *plenty* of women directors and then they pretty much disappeared for fifty years.

Q: How come?

A: Primarily it's because the studio system took over and the studio system was a business that was run by men and for men. If you look at other kinds of writing, for instance — novels, non-fiction, poetry — it's fairly equal between men and women. Not for screenwriting, however. Generally only about fifteen percent of all screenwriters are women and that doesn't change that much from year to year. You don't see women writing any of the "big" movies like *Pearl Harbor*. However, there has been progress with women becoming development executives at studios and production companies. There's also a tendency for women to be slightly more open to hiring other women. So we might see more opportunities for women as more women move into hiring positions. Interestingly enough, film editing is one of the few areas where you can go back to the very beginning of film and find women editors; it's probably the one field where they didn't drop out.

Q: So what kind of shelf-life can new writers expect to have, given the curse of ageism?

A: It seems that it's slightly longer in television — maybe forty-ish to fifty. In movies, it tends to be around thirty-five. Television has been just a little better for women, partly because of the demographics and programming slanted toward females. Ageism is a terrible problem, though. I know a lot of fabulous writers, for example, who will "get the meeting" and after the meeting, absolutely nothing happens. It's unfair because they're some of the best writers in the industry. As a result of this, a lot of them are now turning back to theatre rather than writing screenplays for film.

Q: So it sounds as if the strategy for a pitch session is to send in a front person who is twenty-something.

A: It happens! A lot of older writers are pairing up with younger partners who do the pitching while they stay behind the scenes and do all the work. In my own line of work — the business of script consulting — it hasn't hit as hard, primarily because the people who come to me are aware that experience *does* count. It also helps that I started this business from the ground up and set my own rules!

Q: So what are your thoughts on the new rash of "reality programming?"

A: Reality programming has opened up some new doors for women directors and women producers but not for women writers as much.

Q: What's the best advice anyone ever gave you about getting into this business?

A: Actually *no* one ever gave me good advice. Bad advice, yes! Plenty of it! What helped was when I finally got some clarification on where I wanted to be and how many steps it was going to take to get from here to there. People just don't realize how much there is to being successful in this business beyond getting the education and building your craft. There's a lot of social skills and diplomatic skills and strategy skills that go into it; if you're fortunate, maybe there'll be someone to teach them to you or, if they see you making mistakes, will take the time to be helpful and tell you what you're doing wrong. But there is a great deal you just have to learn on your own. You will make mistakes. Some of those mistakes cannot be undone. So it's important to be prepared for the break when it comes to you, to seek advice if you need it, and to trust your intuition.

Q: So what do you tell people who have dreams of Oscar gold?

A: When opportunities come, you need to follow them and, particularly early in your career, you should never put money first. The very worst thing someone can do on their first or second script is worry about how much they're going to make from it. You want to try to make something happen, whether it means you sell a script or have it optioned, or even write a script for free for the experience.

Q: And once that happens?

A: Never put the brakes on! Maybe you'll only move forward by baby steps or maybe it'll happen by leaps and bounds. Whatever way it happens, though, you need to be ready for it. There's a quote I really like by Ray Bradbury who once said, "Pray that your success does not come too soon." There are certainly many people who have had success dumped in their laps that they didn't have to earn and they blew it by losing their value system and their appreciation for hard work. It's also easy to let your ego get out of hand in this industry and forget why you got into it to begin with, which was because, once upon a time, you had the need and the desire and the love to write.

If you're lucky, it's a gift and a love you'll never lose. And it's a gift you can share with the world.

Linda has consulted on over 2,000 projects and eighty produced films and has mesmerized students and clients on every continent (except Antarctica!). Check your local bookstore for her current titles: *Making a Good Script Great; Creating Unforgettable Characters; The Art of Adaptation; From Script to Screen: The Collaborative Art of Filmmaking; When Women Call the Shots: The Developing Power of Women in Television and Film;* and *Making a Good Writer Great: A Creativity Workbook for Screenwriters.*

Topics to Think About and Talk About

1. What three personal characteristics do you possess that will enhance your ability to sell a screenplay? Explain in fifty words or less.

2. In 100 words or less, describe what aspect of screenwriting you consider to be the most fun.

3. What qualities in an individual do you think are necessary in order for you to have that person read and comment on your work? Compare your answer to the answer in Question #1.

Conclusion:
Getting It Out of Your System:
What Your First Screenplay Can Teach You About Yourself

For over thirty years, my beloved Aunt Liz has been apologizing for her waffles. The words and routine are predictably the same every Sunday brunch. "Don't look at the first one," she says, hurriedly plucking it away before anyone can comment.

Uncle Bob, just as constant in his own way, offers the endearing rejoinder, "It's probably just fine."

"The next one will be better," she retorts. "It always is."

And so it goes. Not just with waffles but with the phenomenon of first scripts as well.

First *any*things, for that matter. Marriage. Children. Macramé plant hangers. The reality is that everything always looks easy in a how-to book until you actually try to follow any of the steps. Frustration then begets procrastination which, in turn, fuels the fear that whatever it is probably won't work (or sell) anyway.

Such is the thought process of wannabe authors who desperately long to get published or produced but just can't seem to focus on finishing what they've started. Or worse, never commit themselves at all.

The genesis of this chapter was sparked by one of my WRU screenwriting students who clearly *isn't* afraid of the "C" word. As he aptly observed from the outset, "I just want to do this to see if I really *can*."

The significance of his — and your — first script experience shouldn't be underestimated. Herein are four stories why. Though primarily shared in the context of crafting a novel, what the writers have gleaned from their "first time" holds just as true for the glamorous lure of the silver screen or the bright lights of Broadway.

I Can't Believe I Said That

Maggie already had several sales under her publishing belt when she asked if I'd mind reading one of her books and rendering an opinion. The fact that this particular novel already had a readership, of course, speaks to the subjective nature of writing; whether I liked it or not had absolutely no bearing on its marketability. Nonetheless, as I later commented on some of the story's weaker elements, I was surprised to hear Maggie voice the same criticisms.

"I wrote it over ten years ago," she said, "back before I had any clue what I was doing!"

The moral: Like fine wine, writers should get better with age. No one, after all, expects the first batch of creativity to be without a fair dose of flaw. After you've finished cringing from reading what the younger you once thought was totally brilliant, take a moment to praise yourself for recognizing how far you've come.

Hold All My Calls Unless It's Letterman

Like a proud father, Bob was busily dispensing virtual cigars. His baby — weighing in at a hefty 111,000 words of political intrigue and conspiracy theories — had just rolled out of the printer only two days before. Bob was already predicting a stellar future and a phone call from Oliver Stone to do lunch.

"Do you think this suit would look good for Letterman," he asked, "or should I go with something more conservative?"

The manuscript, mind you, hadn't even been circulated yet.

It was hard to fault Bob for his giddiness. We've all been there, catapulted into euphoria at the joy of having finished something monumental, even more exalted by the realization that total strangers will actually pay money to read it or see it at the neighborhood cineplex.

The very first agent he sent it to felt that the story had promise and "Oscar" potential. "It just needs a few tweaks by a book doctor to get it 'ready'," she said.

Not surprisingly, she just happened to know someone who could whip Bob's plot into salable shape ... and provide her a nice kickback for the referral. Convinced that his entire future was riding on the success of this — his first completed tome — he proceeded to shell out the requisite fees to ensure his future place on the best seller list.

Nearly two years and $10,000 later, Bob's book has yet to meet the agent's obscure definition of "ready." Disillusioned by the entire venture, his first try also turned out to be his last.

The moral: Beware of anyone who promises to make your project a star for "X" amount of money. Nor is it wise to pounce on the first acceptance that comes along; too often in the happy distraction of just having finished the darn thing, it's easy for one's judgment to be impaired.

Practice Makes Perfect

Of all the students I've mentored, there are few I'm quite as proud of as Lynn. I still recall her coming up to me after a lecture one summer evening and clutching a thick binder that contained her first attempt at "serious" fiction.

"I really want to do something with this," she declared. With absolutely no background in structure, characterization, or conflict, she had merrily plunged headlong into a macabre medical thriller, utilizing every cliché imaginable and casting mobster villains with language straight from Central Stereotype.

Still, her enthusiasm for the craft of writing was hard to ignore. As I often used to say back in my theatre days; it's easier to direct someone who has no talent but lots of heart than to work with an accomplished actor who feels that he already knows everything.

Without any preconceived notions of what it takes to be an author, Lynn was not only receptive to what I had to teach her but open to suggestions from her peers as well. Week after week, she'd excitedly return to the group with a sheaf full of rewrites. With each subsequent draft, her writing began to improve.

She also began drafting her next book. Even from the first chapter, it was evident how much she'd absorbed from the ongoing process of critique.

"My third one will be even better," she predicts, having learned something that many fledgling writers simply don't stay in the game long enough to realize or appreciate; specifically, that the journey can be as much fun as the destination.

The moral: You need to write (and complete) a first book/play/film if for no other reason than to get all the bugs out and discover just how much you don't know.

Can You Say "Catharsis"?

I always promised my best friend Susan that someday she'd see the title, *When It Rains*, in print. Its inclusion in this book, however, could well be the extent of it: The novel to which it's attached is now starting its sixteenth year of dust in the hall closet. It's not that I never sent it out. Quite the contrary. I sent it to *every*one. Fortunately, they all had the good sense to reject it and save me the embarrassment of having to later run out and buy every single copy ever published.

The problem wasn't the writing itself. Several editors, in fact, were generous in their praise of the snappy dialog and scene descriptions. Some even suggested that it would make a pretty funny play (which, oddly enough, it already *had* been before I decided that a novel would bring in more money). What they had a hard time swallowing, however, was the "unlikely premise." To add insult to injury, one of them even opined that the two female leads were "one-dimensional."

Considering that the whole book was based on my friendship with Susan, you can imagine my reaction. It wasn't until long afterward I finally figured out that the reason I had penned this quirky account to begin with had absolutely nothing to do with getting it published. I also realized that the only audience who could ever really admire its depth and hilarity were the two who had already lived the real version.

The premise was born of our respective experience — twelve years apart — with the same man. I had known of Susan long before we ever met, owing to my divorced boyfriend's constant references to his "rotten ex-wife." Lo and behold, by the time he dumped me for someone else, who should happen to cross my path but — yes, you guessed — the rotten ex-wife. To my even greater amazement, we could very well have been sisters for as much as we discovered we had in common. The resulting amusement level that sprang from speculating how our mutual Lothario would react to this unexpected development was enough fodder, I thought, for a full-length tale.

I mention all of this for three reasons. The first is the off-chance that somewhere a movie mogul is reading this and thinking, "Wow! What a cool plot! It's exactly what I'm looking for." The second is to reinforce that it's not every "first whatever's" destiny to be sold, as fervently as this may be our expectation when we begin. Suffice it to say, sometimes the only purpose of writing something from scratch is simply to test our mettle to write everything else that will follow. Third, is the fact that "catharsis" isn't synonymous with "commercial."

The moral: Truth may indeed be stranger than fiction but that doesn't mean it's print worthy. While the experience itself can't be dispatched as easily as one of Aunt Lizanne's bad waffles, our narrative of it can, clearing the decks for something much better.

* * * * *

I hope you've enjoyed this book and that the tools and resources I've provided will help you in achieving your own dream of a writing career. When that happens, I'd like to hear about it, as well as any comments on which chapters helped you the most in defining your story and your style.

If you take away only one thing from this text, may it be the following definition of success: It's not just about propping open the door of opportunity and allowing others to follow your lead, but having the judgment and maturity to recognize those times when it's of higher value to let someone else go first.

About the Author

Former actress and theatre director Christina Hamlett is the published author of seventeen books, ninety-eight plays and musicals for young people, and over 250 magazine and newspaper columns on the performing arts, humor, travel, health, and how-to's for writers. She is also lead screenwriter for an independent film company, and teaches an innovative online screenwriting course through WriteRead University (www.writereaduniversity.com).

A degree in Communications from California State University, Sacramento, led to various stints in public relations, radio and cable television, as well as mentoring new writers in the genres of mystery, suspense, and romance.

Recently married in Scotland, she and her husband are currently collaborating on several book and film projects. The work she remains the most proud of? Two anthologies of comedy scripts for high school students and the opportunity to ignite young minds to spread their wings and aim for the stars.

In addition to her staff writing for the American Screenwriters Association and Writers Script Network, she is the Screenwriting Associate Editor for *Writer on Line*, as well as a feature writer Independent Publisher and many other trade magazines newspapers located throughout the United Kingdom and Austr

Order Form

Meriwether Publishing Ltd.
PO Box 7710
Colorado Springs CO 80933-7710
Phone: 800-937-5297 Fax: 719-594-9916
Website: www.meriwether.com

Please send me the following books:

_____ **ScreenTEENwriters #BK-B253** $16.95
by Christina Hamlett
How young screenwriters can find success

_____ **Characters in Action #BK-B106** $14.95
by Marsh Cassady
Playwriting the easy way

_____ **Everything About Theatre! #BK-B200** $19.95
by Robert L. Lee
The guidebook of theatre fundamentals

_____ **The Theatre and You #BK-B115** $17.95
by Marsh Cassady
An introductory text on all aspects of theatre

_____ **Winning Monologs for Young Actors** $15.95
#BK-B127
by Peg Kehret
Honest-to-life monologs for young actors

_____ **Theatre Games for Young Performers** $16.95
#BK-B188
by Maria C. Novelly
Improvisations and exercises for developing acting skills

se and other fine Meriwether Publishing books are available at
local bookstore or direct from the publisher. Prices subject to
ge without notice. Check our website or call for current prices.

ion name: _____

_____

_____ State: _____

_____ Phone: _____

ng   closed
for   terCard / Discover # _____

$ Expiration
                         date: _____

quired for credit card orders)

Please add 3% sales tax.

75 for the first book and 50¢ for each additional book ordered.

a copy of your complete catalog of books and plays.

About the Author

Former actress and theatre director Christina Hamlett is the published author of seventeen books, ninety-eight plays and musicals for young people, and over 250 magazine and newspaper columns on the performing arts, humor, travel, health, and how-to's for writers. She is also lead screenwriter for an independent film company, and teaches an innovative online screenwriting course through WriteRead University (www.writereaduniversity.com).

A degree in Communications from California State University, Sacramento, led to various stints in public relations, radio and cable television, as well as mentoring new writers in the genres of mystery, suspense, and romance.

Recently married in Scotland, she and her husband are currently collaborating on several book and film projects. The work she remains the most proud of? Two anthologies of comedy scripts for high school students and the opportunity to ignite young minds to spread their wings and aim for the stars.

In addition to her staff writing for the American Screenwriters Association and Writers Script Network, she is the Screenwriting Associate Editor for *Writer on Line*, as well as a feature writer for *Independent Publisher* and many other trade magazines and newspapers located throughout the United Kingdom and Australia.

Order Form

Meriwether Publishing Ltd.
PO Box 7710
Colorado Springs CO 80933-7710
Phone: 800-937-5297 Fax: 719-594-9916
Website: www.meriwether.com

Please send me the following books:

_____	**ScreenTEENwriters #BK-B253** by Christina Hamlett *How young screenwriters can find success*	**$16.95**
_____	**Characters in Action #BK-B106** by Marsh Cassady *Playwriting the easy way*	**$14.95**
_____	**Everything About Theatre! #BK-B200** by Robert L. Lee *The guidebook of theatre fundamentals*	**$19.95**
_____	**The Theatre and You #BK-B115** by Marsh Cassady *An introductory text on all aspects of theatre*	**$17.95**
_____	**Winning Monologs for Young Actors** **#BK-B127** by Peg Kehret *Honest-to-life monologs for young actors*	**$15.95**
_____	**Theatre Games for Young Performers** **#BK-B188** by Maria C. Novelly *Improvisations and exercises for developing acting skills*	**$16.95**

These and other fine Meriwether Publishing books are available at your local bookstore or direct from the publisher. Prices subject to change without notice. Check our website or call for current prices.

Name: _____

Organization name: _____

Address: _____

City: _____ State: _____

Zip: _____ Phone: _____

❏ **Check enclosed**

❏ **Visa / MasterCard / Discover #** _____

Signature: _____ Expiration
date: _____
(required for credit card orders)

Colorado residents: Please add 3% sales tax.
Shipping: Include $2.75 for the first book and 50¢ for each additional book ordered.

❏ *Please send me a copy of your complete catalog of books and plays.*